PRAISE FOR *The Martian's*

"How did a young Hungarian immigrant and his daughter both become leading advisors to Presidents of the United States? This richly detailed memoir not only illuminates Marina von Neumann Whitman's groundbreaking life, but sheds long-awaited new light on her father, bringing us as close as we may ever get to the autobiography that John von Neumann never had the chance to write."

—GEORGE DYSON, author of *Darwin Among the Machines,*
Project Orion, and *Turing's Cathedral*

"A fast-paced, readable, and deeply educational account of how the daughter of a genius made her own brilliant way as a heavily involved top economist and an equally involved wife and mother."

—GEORGE P. SHULTZ, The Hoover Institution, formerly
U.S. Secretary of State (1982–1989)

"This is a deeply personal book; some parts painful to read as the author traces her journey through what most would judge a privileged life, but not so privileged, it seems, if you happen to be on the inside looking out."

—PAUL O'NEILL, formerly U.S. Secretary of the Treasury
(2001–2002)

"Marina Whitman draws you into her life with lively anecdotes. She engagingly describes coping with a famous father, the challenges of a young mother with a high-level job in the Nixon White House, and combining executive responsibilities at General Motors with a strong marriage and a successful academic career. A fast-paced enjoyable read!"

—ALICE M. RIVLIN, The Brookings Institution

"*The Martian's Daughter* is a riveting account of an extraordinary woman—an economist who over a half century has risen to the top of government, academia, and business. Her wry description of the barriers she met along the way reminds us of a social era quite different from today. Her astute narratives about prominent persons with whom she worked (Presidents, Cabinet Ministers, congressional and business leaders) make this memoir a real page-turner."

—CARLA HILLS, formerly U.S. Trade Representative (1989–1993) and Secretary of Housing and Urban Development (1975–1977)

"Marina Whitman had extraordinary parents who loved her, but also wanted her to choose certain paths. But Marina was extraordinary too and chose her own way. This book charts the progress for a woman who has done it all—with grace and ability. But under all the famous names, fascinating events, and newsworthy achievements emerges the story of a real human being who makes those tough choices and has intelligence and integrity as her watchwords. What a read!"

—LYNN MARTIN, formerly U.S. Secretary of Labor (1991–1993)

"Flipping through the pages of Marina von Neumann Whitman's life . . . feels like viewing several extraordinary movies in one sitting."

—TOM WALSH, *Detroit Free Press*

The Martian's Daughter

A Memoir

The Martian's Daughter

A Memoir

Marina von Neumann Whitman

The University of Michigan Press · Ann Arbor

First paperback edition 2013
Copyright © by the University of Michigan 2012
All rights reserved

Published in the United States of America by
The University of Michigan Press
Manufactured in the United States of America
♾ Printed on acid-free paper

2016   2015   2014   2013   5   4   3   2

A CIP catalog record for this book is available from the British Library.

Library of Congress Cataloging-in-Publication Data

Whitman, Marina von Neumann.
    The Martian's daughter : a memoir / Marina von Neumann Whitman.
        p.   cm.
    Includes bibliographical references and index.
    ISBN 978-0-472-11842-7 (cloth : alk. paper) — ISBN 978-0-472-02855-9 (e-book)
    1. Whitman, Marina von Neumann. 2. Economists—United States—Biography. 3. Jews—United States—Biography.   I. Title.
    HB119.W4W44   2012
    330.092—dc23
    [B]   2012005031

ISBN 978-0-472-03564-9 (pbk. : alk. paper)

For Will *&* Lindsey

The rising generation
On whom, as always, the hope of the world rests

Acknowledgments

This memoir would never have come into being were it not for unremitting pressure from my dear friend, Susan Skerker. When mere words were ineffective, Susan combined the nimble mind that had brought her to the executive level at one of the nation's leading automotive companies with her tireless typing skills to coax out of me the seventy-six pages of stream-of-consciousness memories from which this book was born. From there, it was the investigative prowess of three research assistants, James DeVaney, Christine Khalili-Borna, and Google, that filled in the vast gaps in my memory. The two human assistants were, at the time, students in the Master's in Public Policy Program in the Gerald R. Ford School at the University of Michigan. Christine was at the same time a candidate for the JD at the University of Michigan Law School, and the search skills honed at the *Michigan Law Review* enabled her to unearth references that I feared would remain forever undiscovered. Funding for research assistance was provided by the Gerald R. Ford School of Public Policy and the Stephen M. Ross School of Business at the University of Michigan; both schools have my thanks and appreciation.

The list of people who responded to the myriad questions with which I peppered them during the writing process is so long and varied that I am bound to have left some out; to them I apologize in advance. The ones that remain in my notes are, in alphabetical order, William Bowen, Robert Chitester, Gerald Corrigan, Ernest Courant, Paul Courant,

Edwin Deagle, Robert Durkee, Freeman Dyson, George Dyson, Paul Ericson, Géza Feketekute, Tibor Frank, Frank Giarratani, Marc Goodheart, Ann Halliday, Martin Liander, Micheline Maynard, Paul McCracken, Mustafa Mohatarem, William Pelfrey, Craig Perry, Karl Primm, Mary Procter, Deborah Purcell, Edward Rider, William Rhodes, Albert Sobey, Maryll Telegdy, Linda Weiner, Edward Wuntsch, and my brother, George Kuper.

Several expert friends gave me invaluable editorial advice that guided the numerous revisions this book went through before it took final shape. They are Nicholas Delbanco, Sylvia Nasar, Philip Pochoda, and, above all, Leonard Downie. My editor at the University of Michigan Press, Tom Dwyer; his capable assistant, Alexa Ducsay; and my own indefatigable administrative assistant, Sharon Disney, all provided invaluable skills in steering this book through the publication process. Finally, my beloved husband and life partner, Robert Whitman, not only helped me with recall and gently corrected many faulty memories but also, though legally blind, struggled through multiple versions of the manuscript, improving virtually every sentence and paragraph as he went. It is Bob who, above all, gives meaning to the title of my concluding chapter, "Having It All."

Contents

Foreword: A Mind of Her Own

"A Beautiful Mind"

For the past decade, my ninety-four-year-old father, who is a <u>Muslim</u> <u>from Central Asia</u>, had one question and one question only for me: "Is your book almost finished?" All conversations with him ended with an injunction to "Finish it soon!" For as far back as I can remember my father's ambitions for me dominated our relationship. Perhaps partly because he was an immigrant to this country, his hunger for his children's success was greater than theirs. My adolescent vision of the future involved marrying "a rich man who'll let me sit around and read all day." My father, I later learned, dreamed of my becoming a *New York Times* reporter.

When I did become, more or less by accident, a journalist many years later, Marina Whitman was already the chief economist at General Motors and one of the few women at the top of the economics profession. The book in your hands is an evenhanded, if often wry, account of what it took for a woman to succeed in a man's world one generation before feminism and the Pill helped to break the male monopoly on the best jobs. It is also a coming-of-age saga about a young woman who wanted it all in an era that insisted that women must choose between work and family. Most of all, it is a moving story about fathers and daughters and what they want from and for each other, in particular the tension between a father's desire to mold, protect, and live vicariously through his daughter and the daughter's equally strong determination to develop a mind and life of her own.

The Martian of the title refers to John von Neumann, Whitman's father and arguably the most important mathematical mind of the twentieth century. Pampered, precocious, and rich, fond of strong drinks, dirty jokes, and fast cars, von Neumann was one of the geniuses who joined the Jewish exodus from Hungary in the 1930s and, in 1933 at age twenty-nine, joined Albert Einstein at the newly founded Institute for Advanced Study in Princeton. For the next twenty-five years, von Neumann was involved in and responsible for some of the biggest mathematical and scientific breakthroughs of the century: game theory, the bomb, and the programmable computer.

Considered the smartest man alive and capable of concentrating on mathematical problems in the middle of raucous parties, von Neumann hardly fit the popular stereotype of the abstract thinker perfectly at home in the crystalline world of ideal forms but hopelessly lost in ordinary life. True, his wife claimed that he didn't know where ice cubes came from, and he often read weighty books in the bathroom, but he dressed like a banker, preferred the company of generals and politicians to that of academics, and displayed an exceptional talent for dealing with large bureaucracies and running large projects. Moreover, he was not afraid of making decisions or taking a stand. He chose A-bomb targets in Japan, advocated a preemptive attack on the Soviet Union, and was the most influential member of the Atomic Energy Commission. At the time, in the treacherous atmosphere of the McCarthy years, he avoided the political blunders that wrecked the careers of other science stars like Robert Oppenheimer and Edward Teller.

"It doesn't matter who my father was, it matters who I remember he was," Anne Sexton, the poet, once observed. Rather than recalling the public figure, Whitman focuses on the private man. For all his charm and generosity, however, he comes across on these pages as a man who never learned to feel comfortable in close proximity to other human beings and for whom intimate emotional terrain would always remain an alien environment. When Whitman's mother, the beautiful, hot-tempered, socially ambitious Mariette, left him for one of his graduate students, taking their two-year-old daughter with her, he was more puzzled than heartbroken. He remarried quickly, within a year of his divorce, impulsively choosing a woman he met on one of his visits back to Hungary and who he hardly knew. Klara Dan turned out to be unstable, as well as neurotic, and von Neumann spent the rest of his life mystified by her fluctuating moods and frustrated by his inability to placate her fears and jealousies.

One of the most intriguing aspects of Whitman's upbringing concerns the unusual child custody arrangement with his ex-wife that von Neumann insisted on. In what was either a modern experiment in child rearing or a bow to the traditions of the European elite, Whitman was to live with her mother until she turned thirteen. Then, having reached the age of reason and capable of benefiting from proximity to genius, she would live entirely with her father in Princeton until she went off to college. She would be Eliza Doolittle to his Professor Higgins.

Judging by the outcome, the experiment was a success. Whitman flourished intellectually and socially in Princeton. While her stepmother could be difficult, her father showered her with affection, advice, and more tangible tokens of his esteem such as furs and cars. Whitman responded by working hard at school and winning admission to Radcliffe. Once there, she proceeded to get straight As, including in a calculus course. Relieved that she had not besmirched the von Neumann reputation for mathematical prowess, she declared her formal education in that field over.

In her senior year, Whitman announced that she intended to marry a young English instructor immediately after graduation. Her mother, who had long feared that Whitman's brains and intimidating pedigree would discourage suitors, was delighted, but von Neumann was devastated. His frantic appeals, which Whitman quotes at length, are a testament to the depth of his misgivings, and fears that she was closing off any chance of a significant career or, for that matter, material comfort. She liked money too much to be content on the salary of an academic, he warned her.

By then von Neumann was dying. He was fifty-three, confined to a wheelchair, the great head riddled with cancer, the lightning-fast brain barely able to calculate the sum of two single digits. When Whitman visited him in the hospital, she was overcome with grief and guilt. Another girl might have canceled the wedding. Whitman would not. However much she had absorbed her father's values, she had a mind of her own, and enough backbone to stick to her guns.

It was a good thing. In 1956, when Americans were marrying young, having babies, and moving to the suburbs, von Neumann could not possibly have foreseen the seismic changes that would make it possible, less than twenty years later, for President Nixon to appoint a female economic adviser, or for the country's number 1 company on the Fortune 500 to appoint a woman to a highly visible position on the management team. Mostly, though, he simply underestimated the emotional intelligence that let his daughter fulfill her own dreams as well as his.

Sylvia Nasar
Tarrytown, New York
July 8, 2011

Prologue

In September of 1956, I was sitting in the anteroom of an elegant hospital suite at Walter Reed Army Hospital in Bethesda, Maryland, in a VIP wing reserved for the president and other high-ranking individuals, both civilian and military. I was trying to distract myself by watching Elvis Presley's gyrations on a small, fuzzy black-and-white TV set. But not even Elvis could calm my apprehension as I waited to be called into the hospital room where my father, the mathematician John von Neumann, lay dying of a cancer that had by then spread throughout his body and into his brain.

My father had been given this suite partly out of respect for the central role he had played, first as a key member of the Los Alamos brain trust that produced the atomic bomb and later as a member of the Atomic Energy Commission and a senior adviser to several high-ranking military panels and committees, all deeply engaged in maintaining US nuclear superiority in the Cold War.

The more important consideration, though, was national security. Given the top secret nature of my father's involvements, absolute privacy was essential when, in the early stages of his hospitalization, various top-ranking members of the military-industrial establishment sat at his bedside to pick his brain before it was too late. Vince Ford, an Air Force colonel who had been closely involved in the supersecret development of an intercontinental ballistic missile (ICBM), along with General Bernard

Schriever and my father, was assigned as his full-time aide. Eight airmen, all with top secret clearance, rotated around the clock. Their job was both to attend to my father's everyday needs and, in the later stages of his illness, to assure that, affected by medication or the advancing cancer, he did not inadvertently blurt out military secrets.

I hadn't seen my father since the spring vacation of my senior year in college, the preceding April. My final exams and June graduation had been followed only a week later by my wedding at my mother's home on Long Island, which he had been too ill to attend. Right after I changed out of my wedding gown, my new husband and I had set out for the wilds of Maine, already a day or two late for the beginning of his summer job as the director of the junior division of a boys' camp. There we had lived in our own little honeymoon cabin in the woods and had quickly become Mama and Papa Woodchuck to his eight- to ten-year-old charges. Surrounded by the campers' energy during the day and the tranquility of the Maine woods at night, the world we had left behind seemed very far away.

Now I was returning to a particularly grim reality. I had been spending the past few months on an emotional high of academic triumph (I had graduated from Radcliffe at the top of my class) and newlywed bliss, while back in Washington my father and stepmother had been struggling every day with the disease that was destroying not only his body but, even more unbearably, his amazing mind.

To compound my guilt, I knew only too well that my father had been deeply upset and disappointed by my insistence on getting married so young. He feared that such an early commitment—particularly to an impecunious young English instructor at Princeton—would thwart my own opportunities for intellectual and professional development, miring me in the full-time domesticity that was expected of married women in the 1950s. In letter after letter—he often expressed in writing feelings he could not bring himself to talk about—my father had begged me, "[Don't] tie yourself down at such an early age" and thus "throw away any chance of fulfilling your own talents."

My father had already been hospitalized and unable to walk when I had last visited him, but his mind had still been in high gear. My stepmother had kept me posted during the summer regarding the inexorable advance of his illness, so I thought I was prepared. But I couldn't entirely conceal my shock when I entered the room and leaned down to kiss him. Tension and awkwardness choked my voice as I murmured, "Hello, Daddy." He looked small and shrunken in the bed. And though he still spoke in the clipped, analytical manner that had always defined him, his sentences were short and focused exclusively on his own condition. Terror of his own mortality had crowded out all other thoughts.

After only a few minutes, my father made what seemed to be a very peculiar and frightening request from a man who was widely regarded as one of the greatest—if not *the* greatest—mathematician of the twentieth century. He wanted me to give him two numbers, like seven and six or ten and three, and ask him to tell me their sum. For as long as I could remember, I had always known that my father's major source of self-regard, what he felt to be the very essence of his being, was his incredible mental capacity. In this late stage of his illness, he must have been aware that this capacity was deteriorating rapidly, and the panic that caused was worse than any physical pain. In demanding that I test him on these elementary sums, he was seeking reassurance that at least a small fragment of his intellectual powers remained.

I could only choke out a couple of these pairs of numbers and then, without even registering his answers, fled the room in tears. Months earlier we had talked, with a candor rare for the time, about the fact that, at a shockingly young age and in the midst of an extraordinarily productive life, he was going to die. But that was still a father-daughter discussion, with him in the dominant role. This sudden, humiliating role reversal compounded both his pain and mine. After that, my father spoke very little or not at all, although the doctors couldn't offer any physical reason for his retreat into silence. My own explanation was that the sheer horror of experiencing the deterioration of his mental powers at the age of fifty-three was too much for him to bear. Added to this pain, I feared, was my apparent betrayal of his dreams for his only child, his link to the future which was being denied to him.

My father had been shaped by, and then played a central role in, the defining events of the first half of the twentieth century. His youth was punctuated by global upheavals. Hungary had been on the defeated side in World War I and had been punished by the loss of two-thirds of its territory in the Treaty of Trianon in 1920. His family had fled in fear of their lives from a revolutionary communist government that seized power in Hungary and held it for 133 days in 1919. And he had made a prescient shift across the Atlantic, as a precocious young professor of mathematics, to Princeton from the University of Berlin just as the collapse of the impoverished and embittered German nation's democratic government paved the way for Hitler's rise.

Once settled in the United States, he became a key player in the Manhattan Project, which produced the atomic bomb and put an end to World War II, as well as in the development of the hydrogen bomb, whose shadow dominated the Cold War. His invention of game theory enabled innovative approaches to military strategy and gave birth to entirely new ways of analyzing and making predictions about such disparate phenomena as business competition, diplomatic negotiations, gambling strategies, and the evolution of cancer cells. And his description of the logical architecture that underpins the modern electronic computer provided an essential base for the development of successively smaller, cheaper, and more powerful machines, up to and including the infinite variety of smart electronics that, together with the Internet, have revolutionized every aspect of modern life and human interaction.

John von Neumann is often referred to as one of the "Martians," five Hungarian Jewish physicists born in turn-of-the-century Budapest, all of whom spent most of their scientific lives in the United States and made fundamental contributions to the Allied victory in World War II. Four of them—Leo Szilard, Eugene Wigner, von Neumann, and Edward Teller—were at the forefront of developing the atomic bomb; the fifth and oldest, Theodore von Karman, was a pioneer in supersonic flight. The story goes that some of the participants in the Manhattan Project, speculating on how there came to be so many brilliant Hungarians in their midst, concluded that these colleagues were really creatures from Mars who disguised their nonhuman origins by speaking Hungarian.

As this remarkable man's life was ending, I was just becoming an adult, starting out on a life path that would involve me closely in some of the defining events in the second half of the twentieth century. I was a pioneer in and early beneficiary of the feminist wave that swept the nation in the 1960s and 1970s, opening up new opportunities for women who dared to think that they could have it all. I ventured into economics, a field dominated by men, and climbed the academic ladder by focusing my teaching and research on the economic interdependence among nations long before *globalization* had become part of our everyday vocabulary.

I became the first woman on the President's Council of Economic Advisers when I was appointed by Richard Nixon, only to resign when I could no longer resist the mounting evidence that the president was implicated in covering up the Watergate scandal. I was elected as the first female member of the board of directors of some of the nation's most powerful companies just as they were starting to feel pressure to invite women into their boardrooms. And I was a senior executive of General Motors during the years 1979–92, struggling to awaken its top management to the threats that confronted it, as the Big Three's dominance of the US auto industry was being relentlessly overtaken by nimbler Japanese competitors and their inexorable decline toward disaster was under way.

To some extent, my involvement in all of these events was possible because I was in the right place at the right time. But my parents, and particularly my father, also played a crucial part. The example he set by his life, the environment in which he embedded my adolescence, his expectations of me, and my responses to those expectations were all critical in shaping my own life.

Were it not for his oft-repeated conviction that everyone—man or woman—had a moral obligation to make full use of her or his intellectual capacities, I might not have pushed myself to such a level of academic achievement or set my sights on a lifelong professional commitment at a time when society made it difficult for a woman to combine a career with family obligations. If I had not grown up in the cosmopolitan atmosphere of a family dinner table around which gathered some of the greatest minds of the twentieth century, I might have been less attuned to the economic and political relationships among nations that became the focus of my academic career. And without the example of my father's immersion in the affairs of government, I might not have felt the pull of Washington strongly enough to uproot my family and move there for three different government assignments in the space of three years.

Yet perhaps the most powerful motivator of all was my determination to escape from the shadow of this larger-than-life parent, my desire to prove him wrong in his fear that my early marriage would thwart his hopes and ambitions for my own future. I was determined to prove that his expectations for my intellectual and professional success and my own for marriage and children with the man I had fallen in love with while still a teenager need not be mutually exclusive. With every new achievement in my life, with every barrier broken, came an overwhelming urge to say to my father, "You see, I defied you by doing what I wanted, but I'm also doing what you wanted me to, after all."

The evidence of his mental disintegration that overwhelmed me in that hospital room brought home the finality of my father's untimely disappearance from the scene just at the beginning of the computer age that owed so much to him. It was also the moment that catapulted me into adulthood, into a life whose shape bore the strong imprint of my heritage and the expectations it carried with it.

· 1 ·

*T*he Golden Couple

My parents first met as small children. According to family lore, Mariette Kövesi rode into Johnny (in Hungarian, Jancsi) Neumann's life on a tricycle at the age of two and a half, as a guest at the fourth birthday party of one of his younger brothers. Unfortunately, there is no record of my father's reaction; he was just eight years old. The Neumann and Kövesi families (the hereditary nobility bestowed by the Austro-Hungarian emperor on my banker grandfather, Max Neumann, which allowed my father to add *von* to his surname, came later, in 1913) were friends and summertime neighbors, both members of the Jewish but highly assimilated Hungarian haute bourgeoisie, which flourished in Budapest in the years preceding World War I. These families, and others like them, were at the heart of the brief, shining moment when Budapest was not only co-capital, with Vienna, of the Austro-Hungarian Empire but also vied with its sister city for the title of intellectual capital of Europe.

Both my parents spent their childhoods in the privileged, warmly protected environment of highly educated, professionally successful, affluent, and close-knit families. Both families lived during most of the year in large, elegant apartments in the heart of the Pest—or more commercial—side of Budapest. The apartment my father grew up in occupied one floor of a building purchased by his grandfather, who used the first floor for his agricultural implements business and installed each of his daughters, their husbands, and their children on one

7

of the floors above. And both families spent summers in elegant "country" homes in the Buda hills overlooking the flat Pest area. The distance between the summer and winter residences was less than five miles, but each family made an annual hegira between them, with maids covering the city furniture with dustcloths and packing huge trunks and wardrobes for the trip.

My father's upbringing was singular, though, because his extraordinary precocity was recognized very early and his education was tailored to make sure that it was fully developed. His instruction at one of Budapest's three best-regarded secondary schools, the Lutheran Gymnasium, which also produced the Nobel Prize–winning physicist Eugene Wigner, was supplemented, beginning at age eleven, by private tutoring from prominent mathematicians at Budapest University. His first published paper was written jointly with one of those tutors when Johnny was seventeen. The paper, on a very abstruse theorem in geometry, already reflected a key characteristic of all his contributions to pure mathematics: his ability "to transform problems in all areas of mathematics into problems of [pure] logic."[1]

But my father's intellectual appetite was by no means narrowly confined to mathematics, and his passion for learning lasted all his life. He was multilingual at an early age; and until his final days, he could quote from memory Goethe in German, Voltaire in French, and Thucydides in Greek. His knowledge of Byzantine history, acquired entirely through recreational reading, equaled that of many academic specialists. My mother used to say, only half jokingly, that one of the reasons she divorced him was his penchant for spending hours reading one of the tomes of an enormous German encyclopedia in the bathroom. Because his banker father felt that he needed to bolster his study of mathematics with more practical training, Johnny completed a degree in chemical engineering at the Eidgennossische Technische Hochschule (ETH) in Zurich, at the same time that he received a PhD in mathematics from the University of Budapest, both at age twenty-two.

While my father was growing up in a family environment that involved structured discussions of philosophy, politics, banking, science, literature, music, and just about any subject on earth around the family dinner table—discussions in which Johnny and his two younger brothers, Michael and Nicholas, were encouraged to participate—my mother, Mariette Kövesi, was experiencing a very different sort of childhood. She was an only child, six years Johnny's junior (he was born in 1903, she in 1909). Her father was a highly regarded internist and professor of medicine at the University of Budapest, also with a wide range of intellectual interests, centered on music. But he was extremely busy, rather domineering, and reputed to be a chronic womanizer. He was also, for a considerable period of his adult life, addicted to drugs he first took for relief of postoperative pain; as a physician, he had easy access to supplies. My grandmother's response to boredom and neglect was to become a first-class hypochondriac; her immediate reaction to any family conflict was to take to her bed.

However difficult her parents' relationship with each other was during Mariette's girlhood, there was one matter on which they were in complete agreement: the importance of building a protective wall around their beloved, headstrong only child. She was not allowed to go to school until she reached high school age. Her father's fear of childhood infectious diseases, stemming from his experience as a physician in the days before vaccines or antibiotics, had been exacerbated by a near fatal bout of diphtheria Mariette had suffered as a small child. But Géza Kövesi also believed that classroom schooling would not allow enough time for other pursuits he regarded as important: languages, music, and above all sports. And Mariette did indeed become a first-class tennis player in her teens and, she proudly reminded her children, the first woman in Hungary to earn a diploma in dressage from the famed Spanish Riding School in Vienna, home of the Lipizzaner horses.

Mariette's academic isolation was by no means lonely or deprived of fun. She was at the center of a tightly knit group that included four other girls her own age from her parents' social circle. The bonds of friendship formed among the five members of this self-styled "cooking club" endured until their deaths, sundered by neither the Atlantic Ocean nor the Iron Curtain, which separated the ones who lived much of their adult lives in the United States from those who remained in Hungary. And they clearly had very good times together. As old women, they frequently regaled their relatives and one another with tales of the mischievous tricks they had played on their siblings and each other.

When she was in her teens, though, Mariette was moved to frustration and rebellion by the constraints her parents imposed on her social life. Even after she had entered Budapest University, majoring in economics, her parents insisted that she be driven to parties by the family chauffeur and that he wait for her to make sure she arrived home safely at the appointed time. Once, when she got home after curfew, her father met her at the head of the stairs with a sharp slap in the face, never mind that she was twenty years old and already engaged to be married.

This extreme protectiveness was all the more irksome because Mariette was very popular, a belle in her social circle. She was what the French call a *jolie laide,* actually quite homely when analyzed feature by feature but so witty, vivacious, and fashionable that the overall impression was that of a beauty. As her youthful charm matured into elegance, she retained this quality until the end of her days.

The privileged, family-centered lives enjoyed by both the Neumann and the Kövesi clans during Johnny and Mariette's childhood and youth were played out against the background of continuous turmoil in Central Europe. The upheavals began with Hungary's participation on the losing side of World War I, starting when Johnny was ten and Mariette four. There followed, in quick succession, the breakup of the Austro-Hungarian Empire, the 133 days of "Red Terror" brought on by Béla Kun's coup and declaration of the Soviet Hungarian Republic, and the successful countercoup of Vice Admiral Miklos Horthy, the last commander in chief of the Austro-Hungarian Navy.

Horthy's regime brought a degree of stability to the chaos-wracked nation, but a rising trend of nationalism and anti-Semitism was exacerbated by the 1920 Treaty of Trianon, under which Hungary lost some two-thirds of its territory to its neighbors Austria, Czechoslovakia, Romania, and Yugoslavia. Of particular importance to the parents of sixteen-year-old Johnny was the passage of the so-called Numerus Clausus, sharply restricting the access of ethnic Jews to higher education. Over the two decades that followed, Hungary engaged in a variety of arrangements and alliances aimed at regaining its lost territories, the ultimate effect of which was to push the nation increasingly in the direction of the Nazi-Fascist alliance.

The two families were outwardly relatively unaffected by the conflict that engulfed much of the world in 1914–18. The boys were too young for military service, and both families were able to maintain the accustomed patterns of their lives. Only when the communist coup of 1919 actually threatened the lives of well-to-do bourgeois families did the two households decide to flee the country. The von Neumanns sat out the 133 days of the Red Terror at a vacation home on the Adriatic coast, near Venice. They returned to Budapest to find their apartment and belongings unscathed as soon as the takeover ended.

Once back in Budapest, the families were clearly troubled by the growing anti-Semitism in their homeland; the Neumanns' pragmatic response was to send Johnny to the less restrictive environment of the German Weimar Republic for further education, even though anti-Semitism was also taking root there. The ultimate fate of Jews in both Hungary and Germany once Hitler had taken control was beyond their wildest imaginings, as it was for the millions of European Jews who paid with their lives for their inability to foresee the future in time to escape it.

Underneath the apparently unruffled exterior of their everyday lives, both Johnny's and Mariette's views of the world were strongly shaped by these years of turmoil. My father traced the origins of his hawkishness regarding the Soviet Union (he openly favored a preventive attack on that country immediately following World War II, when we had the atomic bomb and it didn't) to the traumatic impact of the 1919 communist coup. In hearings on his nomination to the Atomic Energy Commission in 1955, he was unequivocal: "My opinions have been violently opposed to Marxism ever since I remember, and quite in particular since I had about a three months taste of it in Hungary in 1919."[2] Both my parents retained throughout their lives a cynicism, a be-ready-for-the worst attitude toward world events, that contrasted sharply with my optimistic American worldview.

This difference was brought home to me in the summer of 1974 when, as the Nixon impeachment proceedings were under way, I was about to set off on a monthlong vacation in Europe with my husband and children. My mother was aghast that we would leave home at a time so fraught with uncertainty. My response was that, while I had no idea who would be president by the time I returned, I felt confident that my credit cards would continue to be accepted in Europe and that we would be greeted by the same grumpy but benign customs officials when we returned. It took the catastrophe of 9/11 to shake the American sense of security that separated my weltanschauung from that of my parents.

The relationship between my parents blossomed from childhood friendship into romance during the summers of 1927–29, when my father came home to Budapest on summer holidays from his position as a *privatdozent* (assistant professor) at the University of Berlin. Things accelerated rapidly from an unannounced engagement to marriage when my father was invited to spend a term lecturing at Princeton University from February to May of 1930 and wanted to take my mother with him as his wife.

By the time of their elaborate wedding on New Year's Day, 1930, Johnny had acquired international fame in mathematical circles on the basis of the thirty-two major papers he had published, at a rate approaching one a month.[3] Some of these papers were major contributions in different areas of pure mathematics, including logic and set theory. Others laid the foundation for his mathematical formalization of the new physics—the probabilistic approach of quantum mechanics that was replacing the determinism of classical Newtonian physics in explaining the behavior of atoms and subatomic particles. This latter work culminated in the publication in 1932 of his book *The Mathematical Foundations of Quantum Mechanics,* which is today still in print and regarded as a significant advance in modern physics.

Von Neumann's name is not always associated with the origins of quantum mechanics, but he is universally recognized as the father of game theory. A paper he published in 1928 set forth a proof of the minimax theorem, the basis of that theory, which he later developed in the pathbreaking *Theory of Games and Economic Behavior,* coauthored with economist Oskar Morgenstern. The crux of this proof was to show that, in any precisely defined conflict (which he called a "game") between two individuals where one's win is equal to the other's loss, there is a strategy that guarantees the smallest maximum loss or largest minimum gain for each player, regardless of what his opponent does.

While Johnny was building his brilliant academic career through an astonishing outpouring of significant contributions in a variety of fields, Mariette was a bright but not particularly serious student of economics at the University of Budapest, a pursuit she unhesitatingly abandoned in favor of marrying Johnny and venturing off with him into the New World. I can't help wondering if, along with her genuine affection for this brilliant, handsome young man whom she had known all her life, she wasn't motivated in part by the prospect of putting an ocean between herself and her overprotective parents. Johnny and Mariette were, in any case, a golden couple—both of them intelligent and witty, charming and gregarious, elegant and fun loving, and affluent enough to indulge their taste for luxury.

Mariette's family had demanded that Johnny convert to Catholicism before the wedding, as they themselves had done some years earlier, and he readily complied. Such conversions were common among the assimilated Jewish haute bourgeoisie of Budapest during the years of the anti-Semitic Horthy regime. For many in this group, whose ties to their ancestral religion ranged between loose and nonexistent, this attempt to cling to their assimilated status was a natural one, even though it was doomed to failure; the regime's definition of *Jewish* was clearly ethnic rather than religious.

These efforts to repudiate or conceal Jewish origins—echoing the response of the converted Jews to the vicious anti-Semitism of fifteenth-century Spain—followed my parents, and many other Central Europeans as well, to the United States. My father was entirely pragmatic about the matter; no one as well known as he was could hope to conceal his origins. In addition, many of his friends and colleagues were secular Jewish intellectuals like himself, their attachment to their ancestral roots consisting mainly of a large store of Jewish jokes, sometimes directed at the *goyim* (non-Jews) and sometimes at themselves. One of my father's best-known lines was, "It takes a Hungarian to go into a revolving door behind you and come out first." One of his friends recalled that they used to amuse themselves in boring lectures by holding up a finger for the other to see every time the speaker said something that labeled him a *nebbish*, a Yiddish term of condescension.

My mother's attitude was quite different, and she brought it with her across the ocean. Throughout my childhood and, even more, my adolescence, she impressed on me constantly the importance of concealing my Jewish ancestry, convincing me that it was some sort of shameful secret. The threat she felt was not to her life or her legal rights, but rather to her social acceptability, her fear of being regarded as an outsider. At a time when many clubs and other social organizations banned Jews, and private schools and Ivy League universities had unacknowledged but widely recognized quotas, this was not an idle concern. She bonded with America almost from the instant she set foot on its soil, and in her mind being 100 percent American did not include minority status.

Over the years, I have been constantly surprised and puzzled at how widespread this attitude was, not only among Central Europeans who emigrated to the United States before and after World War II but also among their American-born or American-raised offspring. Public figures such as former secretary of state Madeleine Albright and Senator George Allen have described their parents' efforts to conceal their Jewish origins from them, and questions about whether and when they actually knew the facts have become grist for the political and media mills.

I myself lied to my father's biographer, Norman Macrae, about my mother's ethnic origins—fortunately, I was neither a member of the president's cabinet nor running for public office. Although I felt craven at telling an outright lie that disavowed half of my ancestry, this feeling was outweighed by an intense need to avoid becoming alienated from my mother during what I foresaw might be the last year of her life. I knew she would never forgive me for outing the carefully hidden secret that had become such an important part of her self-identity.

My choice of what I saw as the lesser of two evils was confirmed by the Hungarian American author Kati Marton, whose book *The Great Escape* tells the story of my father and eight other Hungarian Jews who reached the pinnacle of success in their fields after emigrating to the United States. In the course of interviewing me for that book, she confided that, in terms of her relations with her own parents, she wished she had made the same decision I had. In her book *Enemies of the People,* Marton tells how she learned of her own Jewish ancestry, quite by accident, at the age of thirty. When her father learned that she had discovered his secret, she wrote, "It put a strain on our relationship for the next 25 years."[4]

At a 2006 family gathering of some forty-five descendants of a common ancestor brought together from all over Europe and the United States by an enterprising cousin for an all-day celebration in Budapest, I asked several American members of my children's generation what their experiences had been regarding the "Jewish question." Each of them responded that his or her parents had shrouded the issue in silence or mystery. Some of the families were devout Catholics; others were Protestants of varying denominations and degrees of religious commitment. All of the relatives I talked to—including myself and my daughter—had non-Jewish spouses. Among my generation, I appeared to be the only one who had chosen to tell my children about their Jewish background, emphasizing pride in that intellectual heritage rather than embarrassment or insecurity about their association with an oft-despised minority. And my daughter has made sure that her own children are just as knowledgeable about, and proud of, the Hungarian Jewish side of their ancestry as they are about my husband Bob's Mayflower American one.

Having put an ocean between themselves and the more overt anti-Semitism they had left behind, my parents arrived in Princeton filled with enthusiasm for life in the United States—fortunately, their multilingual upbringing had included the study of English—along with considerable naïveté regarding social customs and everyday behavior in the New World. This ignorance of the social mores of their new homeland led them to show up at Princeton dinner parties shockingly late and wildly overdressed, as had been the custom in their European circles. With one foot in their new world and one in the old, they spent roughly a third of each of the years 1930–32 in Princeton; a third in Berlin, with my father teaching an academic term in each place; and the third on vacation in Budapest, back in the arms of their families. This peripatetic existence was complicated by the fact that my mother's response to the weeklong ocean voyage—the only way of crossing the Atlantic at the time—was seasickness so severe that one ship's doctor feared that she might die of dehydration before they reached land.

While my father carried his busy and productive life as a member of the global mathematical elite to a new venue, my mother made the shift from protected young girl to mistress of a household in her own way. She expanded her belle of the ball persona to incorporate that of social hostess, holding evening open houses for my father's colleagues and students in their Princeton apartment. When it became clear to her that, in a country where chauffeurs were not a staple of academic life, a driver's license was essential, she took the advice of a friend who told her that the best way to acquire one was to offer the person in charge of the test drive a cigarette from a case containing a five-dollar bill—a substantial sum in 1931. The bribe worked, and my father apparently followed her example.

Accordingly, they both remained appallingly bad, albeit licensed, drivers until the end of their days. My father's car-totaling accidents were a more or less annual event, and when once asked why he habitually drove a very unacademic Cadillac, he replied "because no one will sell me a tank." Many decades later, in Washington, DC, my husband narrowly avoided having his own car struck by a vehicle that barreled at full speed through a stop sign. As it passed him, he recognized his mother-in-law at the wheel, with both of our young children as passengers. From that day forward, the children were strictly forbidden ever to ride alone with their grandmother until they were old enough to take the wheel themselves.

My father's professional life in the United States became full time in 1933, when he was appointed at the age of twenty-nine as one of the five original members of the faculty of the newly founded Institute for Advanced Study (IAS) in Princeton, along with three much older but also very distinguished mathematicians and, of course, Albert Einstein. The faculty of the institute did not—and still does not—have teaching obligations; the aim of its founding benefactors was to provide a pleasant, secure environment in which the world's leading mathematical minds could spend all their time thinking and writing (gradually, the institute expanded to incorporate a number of other academic disciplines as well) without the interference of other commitments.

Given what was happening in Germany, the institute appointment came just in time. In April 1933, the Nazi government passed laws mandating the firing of all civil servants (a category that included university professors) "descended from non-Aryan, especially Jewish, parents or grandparents."[5] Although my parents continued to visit their families in Hungary every year until 1939, they made their transits across Germany as quickly as train schedules allowed. My father began his tenure at the IAS in the fall of 1933; shortly thereafter, both he and my mother applied for US citizenship. Their lives as Americans had truly begun.

While Europe was, in my father's words, "relapsing into the dark ages,"[6] my parents were able to continue their gilded lives in their adopted country. The institute's professorial salary of ten thousand dollars per year was, during the Great Depression, more than adequate to support a lifestyle that included a series of luxurious rented homes on Library Place, Princeton's most elegant neighborhood, several servants, and my mother's Paris wardrobe. The von Neumanns soon became locally famous for their parties, at which resident and visiting geniuses imbibed large quantities of alcohol and generally let their hair down. My mother told a tale of one particularly exuberant evening at the end of which she and my father threw the dishes out the window rather than clean up.

These gatherings were not entirely frivolous, however. A growing number of scientists fleeing Hitler's expanding reach obtained temporary appointments at the institute, and the von Neumann parties, to which many of the world's most brilliant scientific minds gravitated, provided networking opportunities for these displaced scholars seeking permanent jobs.[7] The plight of many of his fellow European intellectuals underscored both my father's conviction about the scale of the disaster that was occurring in Europe—even though he didn't fully foresee the horrors of the "final solution"—and his goal of seeing his adopted country become the savior of civilization.

My father's assistance to Jewish intellectuals whose lives and livelihoods were threatened wasn't confined to helping them once they had reached the safety of the United States. Among his papers are a letter to Abraham Flexner, director of the institute at the time, pleading with him to intercede with the State Department (which was rife with anti-Semitism) to grant a visa to Kurt Gödel, a non-Jew who had nonetheless been deprived of his job by the Nazis, as well as letters to colleagues at various American universities, discussing the possibilities for jobs for refugee mathematicians and physicists. To save one of them, André Weil, von Neumann appealed directly to the French ambassador (representing the collaborationist Vichy government) to the United States. His mission was successful, and Weil ultimately spent many years on the faculty of the IAS. By helping in various ways to facilitate the ingathering of many of the world's finest minds, my father was making his own contribution both to the literal and economic survival of scientific colleagues and to the intellectual treasure that propelled the United States to the forefront of scientific discovery in the second half of the twentieth century.

My parents' social life was anchored in their relationships with my father's colleagues at the institute. These included Einstein, the only other European among the institute's original five professors. In those days Einstein was quite a social being, most unlike the recluse he became after his wife's death in 1936. My mother told of the excursion she took with the Einsteins while my father was out of town, to a concert in Newark, some forty miles from Princeton, when she was very pregnant with me. Apparently Einstein got bored with the music and nudged his wife, saying "Come on, Elsa, let's go." And leave they did, quite forgetting my mother, who had to take a milk train home. She awoke the next morning to find a large bouquet of roses from Einstein, along with a note of abject apology.

My own earliest memories of Einstein are of a much more reticent personality. By then his wife Elsa was dead and he had pretty much retreated from social encounters. He was visible mainly at a distance during the afternoon teas that took place daily in the institute's Fuld Hall, and his fame rested not only on his brilliance but also on his eccentricity, symbolized by his wild hair and the fact that he didn't wear socks. He had one close friend among his colleagues, Kurt Gödel, with whom he walked daily to and from the institute, deep in conversation as they went.

Gödel, an Austrian who spent long periods at the institute during the 1930s and moved to the United States permanently in 1939, had made his own major contribution to mathematics in his "incompleteness theorems." In them, he showed that no set of axioms (basic propositions) underlying a mathematical system could provide the basis for proving all the true statements within that system, that an attempt would always be stymied by a paradox of the sort inherent in the statement "I never tell the truth." He was also a close friend of my father's, even though his incompleteness theorems had demonstrated that von Neumann's own early effort to ground all mathematical statements in a set of fundamental axioms—the subject of his doctoral dissertation—was doomed to fail. Sadly, Gödel, who was subject to bouts of severe depression, became convinced toward the end of his life, long after Einstein and von Neumann were dead, that someone was trying to poison him. He refused to eat and died of starvation.

Despite her rising position in the Princeton social hierarchy when

Einstein left her behind in Newark, my mother was still very young, in her early twenties, and inexperienced in the ways of her newly adopted homeland. It is not surprising, therefore, that when she had doubts about Princeton's small-town hospital as a place in which to deliver her first-born, she should have turned for advice to the British-born wife of one of her husband's colleagues, Elizabeth Mary Dixon Richardson Veblen. Oswald Veblen, nephew of the famed social critic Thorstein Veblen and one of the leading lights of Princeton's mathematics department before he joined the IAS faculty, was my father's American mentor. He was responsible for Princeton offering my father a one-term per year lecture-ship in mathematical physics in 1930–32 and, when the IAS was founded, pushed strongly and ultimately successfully for his young protégé's appointment as one of the founding five professors there.

Mrs. Veblen, a rather formidable grande dame with solid British tweeds and a clipped English accent to match the formality of her name, was herself childless, but she recommended that my mother put herself in the care of her own obstetrician-gynecologist, an elegant and expensive Manhattan physician with his own private hospital on Madison Avenue. And so it was that, when she went into labor, my mother was driven to New York, sitting on a pile of towels, to give birth at The Harbor, the name that appears on my birth certificate. By the time my birthplace was discovered to have been operating as an abortion mill and was permanently closed down, my mother, divorced and remarried and living in Washington, DC, with her new husband, was no longer under Elizabeth Veblen's tutelage and well on her way to becoming a grande dame in her own right.

My own globetrotting in the wake of my peripatetic parents began early. I was born on March 6, 1935; my US passport, issued on April 8 of that year (I had to have my own because the processing of my parents' applications for US citizenship had not yet been completed), bears a photograph of a virtually bald, pug-nosed infant, pudgy hands clasped in the classical manner of newborns. Inside are the entry stamps of Hungary, Austria, Germany, and France, dated from 1935 to 1938. During those first three years of my life I crossed the Atlantic eight times, making the annual round trip in the first-class cabins of such luxury ocean liners as the *Queen Mary* and the *Normandie*. Both of these ships, the true queens of their day, came to unworthy ends. The *Queen Mary* became a tourist attraction in Long Beach, California, subjected to many changes of ownership and at least one bankruptcy. The *Normandie,* caught in New York Harbor when war broke out in Europe, was being converted into an American troopship when she caught fire, sank, and was ultimately scrapped.

Apparently my career as an enfant terrible also began early. According to my mother, when a ship's steward attempted to separate my one-year-old self from my parents to take me off to the ship's nursery, I bit him, hard. When I reappeared the next summer, a year older and with more teeth, he was heard to mutter, "Oh no, not her again."

During these years, the clouds were darkening, both over Europe and over my parents' marriage. As Hitler consolidated his position in Germany and then embarked on his planned European expansion with the annexation of Austria in 1938, my father's letters, particularly those to his close friend the Hungarian physicist Rudolf Ortvay, grew increasingly pessimistic. "I don't believe that the catastrophe will be avoidable,"[8] he wrote in 1938 and added, presciently, "That the U.S.A. will end up again intervening on the side of England (when an English victory is not achievable otherwise) I find indubitable."[9] A year later he wrote, "It is, for instance, a total misunderstanding of the U.S.A. to believe that it intervened in the World War [World War I] from such (imperialist) motives . . . I admit that the USA could be imperialist. I would not be surprised if in 20 years it would become so. But today it is not yet."[10]

This conviction that the United States alone could save the otherwise doomed European civilization from totalitarianism, whether the threat came from the right or the left, and avert the ushering in of a new Dark Ages stayed with my father throughout his life. Reinforced by the events of World War II and the Cold War that followed, it was a major motivation, along with a lively personal ambition, for his deep involvement in military matters. It also underlay his extremely hard-line ideas on US policy toward the Soviet Union, which included the possibility of preventive war on the latter. He made his feelings crystal clear in an interview with *Life* magazine: "If you say why not bomb them tomorrow, I say, why not today? If you say at five o'clock, I say why not one o'clock?"[11] This view sounds incredibly heartless and immoral today, but it should be judged in the context of the times: "It was widely held, especially by liberal intellectuals, that the French and British governments had behaved in a cowardly and immoral fashion when they failed to march into Germany in 1936 to stop Hitler from remilitarizing the Rhineland . . . To them, the idea of forestalling a terrible catastrophe by a bold preventive action was neither insane nor criminal."[12]

Not long after my arrival, as Europe was descending into chaos, my parents' marriage also began to fall apart. Although he genuinely adored my mother, my father's first love in life was thinking, a pursuit that occupied most of his waking hours, and, like many geniuses, he tended to be oblivious to the emotional needs of those around him. My mother, accustomed to being the center of attention, didn't like playing second fiddle to anyone or anything, even when the competition was her spouse's supercreative mind. She began to pay more and more attention to a graduate student in physics who was a regular at the von Neumann soirees. His name was James Brown Horner Kuper, as befitted the scion of a well-to-do New York family of solid Dutch ancestry and impeccable social credentials. But she whimsically called him Desmond, after a favorite china dog, and the name stuck with him for the rest of his life.

The cracks began to show in the summer of 1936, when Mariette extended her visit with her parents in Budapest and Johnny returned to Princeton without her. In 1937 she spent much of a six-week Nevada residency, required for a divorce there, on horseback at The Ranch at Pyramid Lake, some thirty-five miles through the desert from Reno. The surprisingly intimate letters she wrote from the Riverside Hotel in that city to my father back in Princeton are remarkable partly for the vehemence of her negative reaction to the Reno of the 1930s: "I believe that hell is certainly very similar to this place. It is indescribable, everyone is constantly drunken and they lose their money like mad 5–6 hundred dollars a day, the roulette table stands in the hall just as a spittoon some other place."

Aside from the availability of horses, the Ranch was apparently no better: "The place itself is terribly primitive . . . There is no telephone or telegraph, . . . mail once a day . . . [I]t is entirely crazy here . . . I believe I won't survive. I live in the midst of an Indian reservation there is a beautiful lake and the country is so divine that it is difficult to imagine.

But these horrible females it is impossible that there are so many kinds of women in the world . . . Riding is very beautiful but the evenings are deadly, imagine dinner at six and night goes until ten o'clock."

Even more revealing is the fact that she addresses the husband she is in the process of divorcing as "Johnny Sweetheart," and entreats him, "[D]o you love me a bit" and "If you have time love me a bit." She ends one letter with "I have the howling blues" and signs the other "Million kisses."[13]

The ambivalence reflected in these letters persisted throughout Johnny and Mariette's lives, creating puzzlement and pain for the spouses they subsequently married. Desmond pretended not to notice, but my father's second wife, Klari, was haunted by the lively ghost of a legally terminated relationship. In her unpublished autobiography, she wrote, "This [a meeting of the two couples at a party] was definitely a crisis—a crisis which was followed by many other similar ones for many, many years. Gradually I did get used to them and learned how to handle the situation, but Johnny and Marietta never ceased playing the game of detached attachment or vice versa, which ever fit best."[14]

I don't believe my father ever really understood why my mother left him for an unremarkable graduate student, and neither did anyone else. In her manuscript, Klari vividly described the paradox of Johnny and Mariette: "They were a perfectly matched pair; gay and gregarious, intelligent and witty—frankly and openly enjoying all the luxuries they could easily afford—but, above all, both of them being intensely ambitious. It is a pity that these two, who remained deeply attached to each other many years beyond their divorce and their respective marriages—it is a pity that they could not overcome their difficulties and stay together. Even separately, they went a long way towards their clearly pinpointed goals, but heaven only knows what further heights they could have attained if they had only stuck it out together—and so speaks the second wife, the successor of Marietta."[15]

As for my father, he wrote in a letter to his close friend, the Polish physicist Stan Ulam, "I am sorry that things went this way—but at least I am not particularly responsible for it. I hope that your optimism is well founded—but since happiness is an eminently empyrical [sic] proposition, the only thing I can do, is to wait and see."[16] Actually, he did nothing of the sort; by the time the divorce was final, he was already writing intimate letters to Klara Dan, who became Mariette's successor. Klari, a noted beauty from the same Budapest Jewish haute bourgeoisie as my parents, hid a first-class brain behind her flirtatious manner. Though not yet thirty, she had already been married twice before, once to a dashing young man who was "an incurable gambler" and then to a banker eighteen years her senior, a "kind, gentle, attentive husband" who bored her to tears, she wrote. I have always felt certain that my father married her on the rebound, both to assuage the hurt caused by Mariette's desertion and to provide himself with a helpmeet who could manage the everyday details of life that eluded him.

Klari was trapped in Budapest for much of 1938 by an inconsistency between Hungarian and American law that threatened to leave her stateless, and therefore unable to leave Hungary, as war appeared imminent. Tensions between the couple ran high as the distance between Princeton and Budapest appeared insurmountable. They were finally able to marry and leave Europe together just before war broke out. But her profound insecurity and the constant demands for expressions of devotion that his letters were trying to respond to would haunt their relationship throughout their marriage. In one, he pleads, "Darling, we *will* win . . . and I will make you very, very, very happy! It *will* be a happy marriage, . . . and I will be able to reconquer you."[17] In another he tries to reassure her and apologize at the same time: "You are frightened of life that has maltreated you, . . . you are terrified even of the breeze because you sense the storm behind it . . . I seared you, I bullied you, I hurt you!"[18] And, finally, his cry to her: "Please, please, give me a bit of faith . . . or at least 'benevolent neutrality.'"[19]

My father's lifelong desire to impose order and rationality on an inherently disorderly and irrational world was reflected in many of his handwritten letters to family and close friends. It was also, in the view of science historian Robert Leonard, one of the major motivators of von Neumann's return, after more than a decade, to the development of the theory of games. After publishing the paper containing the central tenet of game theory, the minimax theorem, in 1928, he had dropped the subject entirely until he began to discuss jointly developing the theory and its applications to economics with his friend the Austrian economist Oskar Morgenstern in 1940. Their collaboration over numerous breakfasts at the gentlemen-only Nassau Club in Princeton during the years 1940–43, while my father was deeply involved in military consulting and the development of the atomic bomb, culminated in the publication of the pathbreaking *Theory of Games and Economic Behavior.*

Even in the midst of this enormous project, squeezed into spare moments snatched from the frenetic pace of his secret and often hair-raising wartime missions, my father's puckish sense of humor didn't desert him. Klari collected elephants, and she had hundreds of them, from one hewn out of a solid chunk of pink alabaster to the one I carved for her in a bar of Ivory soap. She insisted that she would have nothing to do with the *Theory of Games* unless it tipped its hat to her with a drawing of an elephant somewhere in its pages. So there, on page 64, illustrating an abstruse proof in set theory, is a collection of dots and curved lines that clearly traces out an elephant in full pursuit, trunk aloft and ears and tail flying.

One reason for my father's dogged commitment to getting the book done was his (and his coauthor's) profound dissatisfaction with the standard assumption of neoclassical economics, the dominant school of thought at the time, that individuals make "rational" economic decisions without taking into account what other people's responses are likely to be. This totally contradicted reality as he saw it. His own emphasis on social context and the characteristics of the multiple possible outcomes of the strategic "games" played by individuals, businesses, or nation-states in a wide range of human interactions is reflected in the title of John McDonald's book on game theory written for a general audience: *Strategy in Poker, Business, and War* (1950).

The first applications of game theory, in fact, came not in economics but in simulations of possible scenarios of future military conflicts, strategic analyses conducted by the Rand Corporation for the US Air Force—a use entirely consistent with my father's ultrahawkish view of the world. It was decades before this theory became integrated into mainstream economics, but today political scientists use it to analyze countries' relationships in peace as well as war, anthropologists call on it to ferret out patterns of interaction among neighboring cultures, and biologists employ it to examine the effects living cells have on each other.

In this use of game theory to uncover previously hidden patterns, scientists in a wide variety of fields are spurred by motives not unlike those of the theory's progenitor. In Leonard's words, "It is difficult not to see in his [von Neumann's] efforts an element of perhaps subconscious resistance to the conditions of the time; an almost defiant willingness to see order beyond the disorder, equilibrium beyond the confusion, to seek an inevitable return to normality once the present transition, with its 'abnormal spiritual tensions,' was over."[20]

In the event, my father's domestic life would reach a new, if somewhat shaky, equilibrium long before his wider world returned to some semblance of normalcy. Indeed, near the end of his life, he seems to have concluded that such normalcy, like the Holy Grail, would remain forever beyond reach. That pessimism is certainly implied in an article he wrote for *Fortune* magazine in 1955, the year he was found to have the cancer that would kill him. Asked to give his views on America in 1980, he titled his response "Can We Survive Technology?" In it he predicted, "Present awful possibilities of nuclear warfare may give way to others even more awful . . . In the years between now and 1980 the (global) crisis will probably develop far beyond all earlier patterns. When or how it will end—or to what state of affairs it will yield—nobody can say."[21]

Despite the ambiguous wording, this last sentence reflected his fear that mankind might not survive another twenty-five years but instead would become the victim of its own self-destructive inclinations. He had quantified this fear in a letter to Klari in 1946 regarding the probable date of the *next* war: "I don't think this is less than two years and I do think it is less than ten."[22] It was not technology itself that my father feared but human nature: "It is just as foolish to complain that people are selfish and treacherous as it is to complain that the magnetic field does not increase unless the electrical field has a curl. Both are laws of nature."[23]

My father's belief in a coming Armageddon, and his firm conviction that the only hope for civilization lay in American victories over both nazism and communism, was born as the storm clouds gathered over Europe in the mid-1930s and lasted until his death. The result was a clear line of demarcation between the two halves of his life as a scientist. During the first half, which spanned his youth in Europe and his early days in the United States, he made fundamental contributions in the realm of pure mathematics and mathematical physics, involving himself in some of the major scientific issues that roiled European intellectuals in the early part of the twentieth century. In 1935, though, he symbolically put Europe behind him by resigning from the German Mathematical Society, writing, "I cannot reconcile it with my conscience to remain a member of the the German Mathematical Society any longer . . ."[24] He was equally emphatic twenty years later in explaining his reasons for coming to America: "I expected World War II, and I was apprehensive that Hungary would be on the Nazi side, and I didn't want to be caught dead on that side."[25]

As soon as he obtained American citizenship in 1937, von Neumann embarked on a collaboration with the US military that lasted the rest of his life, first with the Ballistics Research Laboratory of the Army Ordnance Department in Aberdeen, Maryland, then with the Manhattan Project and, after World War II, all three branches of the armed forces, the Department of Defense, and the Atomic Energy Commission. His work in such disparate areas as game theory, digital computers, intercontinental ballistic missiles, meteorology, and other kinds of mathematical modeling was united by their relevance to real-world problems, including military, economic, and political applications. Although he remained on the faculty of the IAS until 1955, the contemplation of pure mathematics in its tranquil surroundings was pushed aside by his involvement in crucial issues relating to the security of the United States, to the dismay of his mathematics colleagues. It was this second John von Neumann, a man of affairs in the most fundamental sense, that I knew as my father.

· 2 ·

$\mathcal{S}$aving Civilization

I am American born and bred, yet my earliest memories are of Budapest. My recollections are typical: sharp, concrete, disconnected images of particular objects—a bed and bedside lamp in the room where I slept and a very large, rough-hewn amethyst that stood by a decorative pool in the garden of my great-aunt's house. Of people and relationships I remember nothing, although, according to my mother, I learned during the course of that year to speak "perfect German to the family and perfect Hungarian to the servants."

These memories were formed because my mother, occupied during 1937–38 with divorce and remarriage, left me in the care of my grandparents and a nanny in the home where she herself had grown up. She brought her new husband, now permanently christened Desmond, to Budapest shortly after their marriage, partly to introduce him to her parents and partly to take me home to their new household in the United States. There was no question about which parent I would live with. After their separation but before their divorce became final, my parents had drawn up a carefully constructed document regarding my care. It provided not only that my father would contribute 10 percent of his income to my support, but also for an unusual form of joint custody. Until I was twelve, I would live during the school year with my mother and spend vacations with my father; after that, the situation would be reversed until I reached the age of eighteen, when the decision about how my time would be divided between the two households passed to me.

As my mother explained it to me, this arrangement was made with my intellectual and emotional welfare in mind. She felt that the child of a man as remarkable as John von Neumann should have the opportunity to live with him and get to know him well. At the same time, she believed that he would be better suited to parental interaction with his daughter once she had reached something approaching the age of reason and no longer needed physical care. It was a thoughtful and well-intentioned agreement, but they were too inexperienced to realize that adolescence is often the stage of life farthest removed from of the age of reason.

Because I had no memory of living with my parents together as a single family, I accepted the new household arrangements with equanimity as a natural state of affairs. In fact, I quickly came to regard Desmond as a loving parental figure, without his displacing my actual father in my affections—I just basked in being loved by both of them. But the emotional fallout of the arrangement on some of the adults involved turned out to be more painful than anyone could have anticipated.

By the time he and my mother were married, my stepfather had completed his PhD in physics at Princeton and had a job with the National Institutes of Health in Washington, DC. It was there that we settled into a rented house and I started nursery school, an environment that erased my multilingual abilities in short order. As rapidly as I had substituted Hungarian and German for English when I lived in Budapest, I now reversed the process. My desire to fit in, to be "just like everyone else," led me to insist, even at home, that the only language I would speak or understand was English.

Within a very few weeks, apparently, my stubborn insistence had become reality. When, some twenty years later, I tried to learn enough German to pass an exam in the language for my PhD, my mother was amazed to discover that I "couldn't even make the sounds correctly." My Hungarian vocabulary now consists of one sentence taught me by my grandmother, "I would like to speak Hungarian, but I don't know much," and a few stray bits of profanity.

The lengths I would later go to in order to shape my four-year-old's world by sheer force of will also showed up in other ways. Apparently concerned about my strong resistance to change in any detail of my life, my mother and Desmond followed the advice of a child psychologist and completely rearranged the furniture in my room. They were taken aback when they discovered, a few hours later, that everything was back in its original position. My only comment was "Please, dear Desmond, don't move it again; it's so heavy." Confronted with my stubbornness, the adults capitulated and the furniture stayed.

Expecting to live in the DC area more or less permanently, my mother and Desmond immediately hired an architect and built a house, with my mother playing a hands-on role in the design and Desmond supervising the construction almost day by day. Its location, on 30th Place just off Ellicott Street, was at the time right at the edge of urban Washington; just beyond their block were untouched woods. Today those same houses are very much in the midst of a city that has expanded well beyond the Maryland state line.

Of particular interest to me and my best friend, Mariana Moran, was the fact that J. Edgar Hoover, at that time at the height of his formidable powers as head of the FBI, lived next door. Mariana, a dark-haired, dark-eyed, Spanish-style beauty, daughter of an American naval officer and a wealthy Panamanian mother, grew up to be a fashion model and a pillar of Washington society. At the time, though, she was my partner in juvenile—very juvenile—delinquency. Looking for some excitement to spice up our lives, we delighted in thumbing our noses at the nation's most feared authority figure by spreading mud on Mr. Hoover's laundry hanging on the line and writing the naughtiest words we knew in chalk on his sidewalk. To our disappointment, he didn't call on the resources of the FBI to catch us in the act, probably because his housekeeper didn't bother to tell him about our desecration of his property. But we didn't escape unpunished; when my mother found out, she responded with a solid spanking for me and a sharp report to Mariana's parents.

On many weekends during the hot Washington summer, my mother, Desmond, and I would make the two-hour drive to the seashore at Rehoboth Beach for the day. Returning from one such outing in early September of 1939, we heard over the car radio that war had been declared in Europe. This didn't mean much to a four-year-old, but it clearly shook up the adults in the front seat. They knew then that the pleasant flow of their lives was about to be totally disrupted. My maternal grandpar-

ents and great-aunt were in the midst of a holiday visit, their first to the
United States, and my mother realized that they would be stuck on this
side of the Atlantic indefinitely, with only the clothes they had brought
in their luggage. Suddenly, she was responsible for finding them permanent housing and became their sole means of support. Their return tickets to Europe, booked for November in cabin class on the luxury liner
Normandie, still lie in my safe deposit box, "refundable only in Paris,"
where they had been bought.

As refugees in the United States, my grandparents reversed roles from
the domineering, philandering husband and bored hypochondriac wife
they had been in Budapest. My grandfather, too old to resume his profession in a new country and an unfamiliar language, became gentle and
passive, spending his days listening to his beloved classical music on the
radio with his dog at his feet. My tiny, fragile-appearing grandmother,
who for the first time in her life was needed and had something to do, became a first-class housekeeper and budgeteer (she was acutely conscious
that they depended on my mother for their livelihood), an outstanding
cook, and a social butterfly.

Among the elderly grandes dames of Washington, DC, Paulette
Kövesi was much sought after for her skills at bridge, which included
never arranging the cards in her hand, because that might give something
away, or inquiring sternly of her talkative companions, "Are we here to
chat or to play bridge?" The small but comfortable apartment on Connecticut Avenue—it even boasted a new innovation, central air condi-
tioning—became the scene of many elegant ladies' luncheons and bridge
teas. My grandmother, dressed in vintage black lace, was undaunted by
her triple role of hostess, cook, and dishwasher.

In October of 1940, soon after we moved into the new house, my
brother and only sibling was born. Christened George Henry Kuper III,
he was known to the family as Gorky until he was old enough to insist on
George as more appropriate to his dignity. Miss Levesconte, or "Vee," the
beloved French Canadian nursemaid who had cared for me from infancy
until I outgrew her by going off to school, returned to play a similar role
for the new member of the family. She had been my constant companion
and had relieved the restlessness of a precocious only child by helping me
learn to read when I was three. I was delighted to have her back in the

household again, even though the main focus of her attention was now my brother rather than me.

My mother was clearly delighted with this new infant; the fact that she now had a boy as well as a girl, and a child by each of her husbands added to her satisfaction. But, true to her hands-off parenting style, she left his care mainly in Vee's capable hands. Her role as the gracious and elegant hostess at frequent parties in her up-to-the minute new home continued undeterred by dishes or diapers. Some of my clearest memories are of her playing that role in flowing hostess pyjamas—a new and rather daring style at the time, and one that emphasized both her vivid persona and her graceful femininity. I was proud of having such a glamorous mother and yet discomfited by the certainty that I would never, even as an adult, acquire her aura of drop-dead elegance, her ability to turn heads in any room she entered.

I regarded baby Gorky as an interesting curiosity; it was not until he became the golden-haired darling of a succession of maids and nannies that I became fiendishly jealous. The contrast was particularly painful once I, five and a half years older, had turned from a Shirley Temple lookalike—I was occasionally mistaken for her in Hungary—into a plump, pigtailed, bespectacled little egghead, always at the top of her class in school but notably lacking in social graces.

My ambivalent emotions regarding this baby, who quickly developed into a boy of irresistible appeal, were reflected in a piece I wrote for a school assignment when I was a teenager: "His most endearing yet often most annoying quality is his charm, which makes women of any age love him at first sight. After being a little hellion all day, he can go down to a party and, with one smile, captivate everyone in the room. 'Isn't he an angel?' they all say. It is then that I feel a desire to wring his angelic little neck! . . . Gorky's thoughtful, unselfish nature makes me love him with all my might, but he's enough of a little boy to make me think sometimes he should be caged."

At about the time of Gorky's birth, the pleasant rhythm of my family environment was unsettled by the question of what role Desmond, a physicist whose specialty was studying the effects of various types of radiation on human health and designing instruments to measure it, would play in the fast-approaching war. The US Congress had authorized compulsory military service, even though we were not yet officially at war; at about the same time, the Radiation Laboratory, or RadLab, was established at MIT as a joint Anglo-American project for the further development and production of radar, which had recently been invented in England. After several months of cat and mouse between the highly placed scientists assembling a RadLab team and Desmond's local draft board, the civilians won, and we moved from Washington to an old but spacious rented house in Cambridge.

My mother wasted no time setting up her household and establishing our home as the social center for the group of scientists and their spouses who were rapidly being assembled in Cambridge from all over the country. But it soon became clear that the role of well-off housewife was not going to be enough for her quick brain or her boundless energy and dominant personality. As a European whose parents had just lost their home, their belongings, and their country, she was passionate about the importance of an American victory in World War II and felt an increasing urge to play a more direct role. She was egged on by her husband's half-teasing insistence that keeping household servants in wartime was downright unpatriotic; either the maids would have to go or she would have to justify their existence by going to work herself. And now that her parents and aunt were totally dependent on her for their financial support, she felt an obligation to earn much of their keep herself.

The question of what kind of job she should apply for was a real one, since nothing in her education or experience had equipped her for the world of paid work. So she joined the army of Rosie the Riveters who made up an increasing part of the civilian work force as their husbands and brothers went off to war. Risking her long, elegantly manicured fingernails, she started out assembling radar sets at the Harvey Radio Laboratories in Cambridge. "You're just another socialite who'll quit as soon as you're bored," was the response she recounted to a reporter who interviewed her for the women's page of a Boston newspaper. Instead, she was promoted to foreman within three months and, six months later, became the supervisor in charge of training women technicians at the same RadLab that had recently recruited her husband.

My mother was long on conviction and self-confidence and short on patience, a combination that made her a tough but fair taskmistress in the workplace as well as at home. When the women she supervised were asked to vote on whether they were willing to have "Negroes" as coworkers, she drew on the sheer force of her personality, along with some well-placed Hungarian profanity, to ensure that they voted yes. When she organized annual reunion dances for RadLab and Los Alamos alumni during the spring meetings of the American Physical Society after the war, she was equally adamant. These meetings were held at posh Washington hotels, which, at the time, were strictly whites only. Her insistence that a black physicist and his wife be included in the party meant that she had to find a different hotel every year in which to hold it. These events were, in the words of one of the participants, "the first unsegregated dances at first class hotels in Washington D.C."[1] Although her enormous energy had been focused virtually 24–7 on winning the world war against the forces of darkness, my mother also seized opportunities to conduct her own small battle against the injustices rampant in her adopted country.

While World War II was engulfing the world, my life in Cambridge was astonishingly, even embarrassingly, normal. Although the rationing of meat, butter, sugar, and gasoline may have made household management a bit more complicated for my mother, about all I remember of it is that mixing yellow coloring into the margarine, so that it would look more like butter and less like lard, was my job. And why was the margarine white? Because Wisconsin farmers, fearful that the substitution of margarine for butter might become a habit that persisted even after the war was over, managed to push through a regulation requiring that it be sold in its original, pasty-white state. Packagers, ever creative, promptly attached little cellophane packets of coloring to each container of margarine.

That manual mixing task, along with collecting tin foil into shiny round balls for recycling and remembering to pull down the blackout shades when the lights went on in the evening, constituted my contribution to the war effort. And, oh yes, I was responsible for pasting the ration stamps that ruled our lives as consumers into the proper booklets and keeping track of the piles of little round cardboard circles, some red and some blue, that represented fractional values of the rationing "points" assigned to each family. This last responsibility made me feel very important.

Most of my waking hours, of course, were spent in school. I had entered first grade, in the middle of the school year, at Shady Hill, at the time one of the leading "progressive" schools in the country. Its reputation arose from its uniqueness in a variety of ways. One was physical; Shady Hill consisted of a cluster of small wooden structures scattered about on its own campus, one for each grade. Running between buildings during the cold New England winter helped to toughen both bodies and minds, in the British tradition.

What really set the school apart, though, were the new ideas about children's education that underpinned it. The academic requirements were demanding, but much of the teaching and learning took the form of individual or group projects, with teachers acting as coaches and guides as much as authority figures standing at the front of the classroom. We reenacted the original Olympic Games as part of our third-grade study of Greek civilization, a project that included making our own garments and athletic props, after appropriate research to ensure authenticity. In the fourth grade, we had a contest—participation required—to see who could draw the best map of the world from memory. This sort of education had two very positive effects. It pushed me, along with my classmates, to value independent thinking over rote learning, to be active participants in our own intellectual development. And it opened our eyes—far more effectively than just reading and memorizing could—to the world's infinite variety, both in the past and in different places during our own time. Even today, when many of these so-called progressive approaches are no longer novel, the Shady Hill School continues to be recognized as one of the best of the breed. And it reinforced my own appreciation of all kinds of people, places, and experiences that I was already absorbing from my family life.

The richness of our school experience was enhanced by an unexpected fallout of wartime: the international element it brought into our classrooms. Most of my classmates were the offspring of successful local lawyers, doctors, professors, and businessmen. But scattered among us were a number of British children who had been packed off by their parents to escape the bombing they knew would strike their homeland, crossing the Atlantic alone on some of the last nonmilitary ships to make the voyage. Once landed in Boston, some of them lived with relatives, while others were taken in by volunteer families. Although these boys and girls were at first traumatized at finding themselves alone in a strange land, they soon fitted quite naturally into our world, and many of them have, in fact, maintained close relationships with their American families throughout their adult lives. But their initial panic at suddenly being torn from everything familiar brought home to us the reality of a war that was leaving the security of our own lives pretty much untouched.

My mother's first parental encounter with the formidable headmistress of Shady Hill, Miss Katharine Taylor, was not exactly felicitous. She was greeted by that lady's comment, "You know, Mrs. Kuper, I don't approve of mothers who work." The meeting continued for the appointed forty-five minutes, at the end of which, as my mother rose to leave, Miss Taylor fired her parting shot: "On the whole, Mrs. Kuper, it is probably better for your children that you are working." My mother laughed as she told this story, but Miss Taylor had a point. George and I were fortunate that our mother's boundless energy and fierce competitive spirit were not focused exclusively on us; surely we would have shriveled in the flame.

While I was going about my routine of school, dancing school, skating lessons, and playing with my friends, the adults around me were working harder, and playing harder, than they ever had in their lives. For my mother and Desmond, long workdays at RadLab were punctuated on most weekends by large, raucous parties at our house where they and their colleagues drank a lot, danced a lot, and made up clever, mildly dirty ditties about their lives. Mingling with the guests during the early hours of these parties, I got to know many distinguished scientists in their more relaxed moments. Margaret, the daughter of the Nobel Prize–winning physicist I. I. Rabi and, like me, a high-powered scientist's child dropped into new surroundings by the demands of the war effort—Rabi was a professor at Columbia University in normal times—became my closest friend and playmate, and remains my friend today.

Even this life of hard work and hard play did not exhaust my mother's boundless energy. To take up the excess, she volunteered with the Red Cross at least one night a week, serving coffee and doughnuts to policemen and firemen at the sites of fires or large accidents. Thus it was that she found herself at the scene of one of the most horrific fires in our country's history. The Coconut Grove, one of Boston's largest and most elegant nightclubs, was packed well beyond capacity on the night of November 28, 1942, when it caught fire. Many of the exit doors were locked, and the main revolving door was soon jammed with people, turning it into a death trap. Nearly five hundred people, many of them servicemen on leave celebrating with their girlfriends, died there.

Although my mother must certainly have edited out the most graphic parts when she recounted to us what she saw that night, the memory of the report she gave was burned indelibly into my brain. American civilians never experienced the carnage of World War II firsthand, but that fire gave us a glimpse of what people in many other cities around the world were going through on a daily basis.

My mother's penchant for benign neglect and the exigencies of wartime combined to give me a degree of freedom and independence unthinkable today. From the time we moved to Cambridge, when I was in the first grade and not yet six, I walked the mile or so to school and home again alone—my mother was too busy with work and rationed gasoline too scarce to expend either time or fuel on getting me back and forth. I wasn't much older when I began to take the streetcar to Harvard Square to attend Saturday afternoon movies at the University Theater with my friend Margaret. On one of those afternoons, we were so mesmerized by *The Song of Bernadette* that we sat through it twice. It was dark by the time we got home, and even my doughty mother was beginning to panic. Her fear turned to anger, though, when we showed up, and I was subjected to a sound spanking. I felt it was unjust that Margaret didn't get spanked also.

I was on my own for much longer trips as well. With wartime restrictions, there was only one way to go from my mother's home in Cambridge to my father's in Princeton, and that was by train. My brother and I had a nanny who might have been called on to escort me on these journeys, but she was Austrian and, classified as an "enemy alien," was forbidden to travel across state lines. So my mother would buy me a first-class ticket, tip the railroad car porter five dollars to keep an eye on me and make sure I got off at the right stop, and send me on my way. I didn't see anything remarkable about this; I thought the wartime trains, jammed with young soldiers and full of hustle and bustle, were rather fun. The independence I learned early from these experiences has been invaluable many times along my adult career path.

The unconventional family arrangements that defined my life had other profound effects on my growing up. At least in those days, most families were defined by parents and children together in a single household. For me, though, family meant two households, four adults, all brilliant and all emotionally complex, with me shuttling back and forth between them and adapting on the fly. Without being conscious of it, I became precociously adept at figuring out the soft spots in their personalities and relationships and exploiting them to my advantage.

Dealing with this complicated situation also developed in me an emotional self-sufficiency that was reinforced by my mother's parenting style. In some ways we were very close; she took me and my concerns seriously and never condescended. But she was prone to fly into sudden rages, and her humiliating slaps in the face, sometimes in front of other people, continued until I was well into my teens. Nor did she make any bones about the fact that, if the exigencies of wartime forced her to choose between being separated from her husband or from her children, she would leave us in the care of others in order to stick with the person who would be her lifetime companion after we grew up and left home. In the face of all these challenges, I developed a surface unflappability and unwillingness to examine my own feelings, traits that have lasted all my life and made writing this memoir inordinately difficult.

While my mother and stepfather were busy making their contribution to the war effort in Cambridge, my father's much higher profile role had him commuting between Princeton and Los Alamos, New Mexico. In that supersecret location, he was a major participant in the Manhattan Project and one of the very few people permitted to go in and out of Los Alamos while the war was on. He was even involved in selecting the sites in Japan where the two atom bombs then in existence were to be dropped, displaying in that task the cool rationality that dominated his thinking about any decision that affected the ability of the United States to win the war. In one of history's finest ironies, the signatures on a patent filed on the US government's behalf for a method to set off a hydrogen bomb were those of two Los Alamos colleagues, John von

Neumann and Klaus Fuchs, the German-born British citizen who, as a spy for the Soviet Union, gave the Russians crucial information about first the atomic and later the hydrogen bomb.

As if the Manhattan Project wasn't enough to keep him busy, my father made a secret trip to England in 1943 to apply his game theory to the problem of sweeping highly sophisticated German mines from the English Channel. This last assignment was extremely dangerous: not only was there the possibility of being blown out of the sky on the flight over or killed by a bomb in ravaged London, but there was also the danger of being taken prisoner should the Germans manage to invade Britain. With this latter exposure in mind, he was temporarily assigned a high military rank, so that he would fall under the rules of the Geneva Convention for officers if taken prisoner. The ever-present danger did not, however, prevent him from including the latest additions to his store of dirty limericks in the letters he wrote to his wife back in Princeton. All of them were clever, but most of them were not as clean as this one.

> There once was an old man of Lyme
> Who married three wives at a time.
> When asked, "why the third?"
> He said, "One's absurd,
> And bigamy, sir, is a crime."

All this activity meant that my vacation visits with my father were somewhat catch-as-catch-can as long as the war lasted.

The other half of the Princeton household, my father's new wife Klari, was an excellent writer, even in the English she learned only as a teenager at a British boarding school, and a remarkably perceptive observer of people. The chapter in her autobiography entitled "Johnny" captures the many aspects of my father's complex personality as no one else could. "I would like to tell about the man," she begins, "the strange contradictory and controversial person; childish and good-humored, sophisticated and savage, brilliantly clever yet with a very limited, almost primitive lack of ability to handle his emotions—an enigma of nature that will have to remain unresolved."[2]

Sadly, Klari was also profoundly insecure and intensely neurotic, as the letters my father wrote to her during their engagement attest. Her view of herself in relation to the world around her is reflected in the title she chose for her autobiography: "A Grasshopper in Very Tall Grass." From the very beginning of their relationship, this insecurity had imposed an enormous burden of constant reassurance on my father, one that continued to be reflected in the many letters he wrote to her during his frequent trips away from home during and after the war: "You are scared. Your fear is only to a very small extent based on reality . . . You are *not* old, you *are* attractive."[3] Apologies for some perceived misbehavior on his part and pleas for her forgiveness were also a recurring theme: "Why do we fight when we are together? I love you. Do you loathe me very violently? Let's forgive each other!"[4] These outpourings continued even when he knew that he was dying: "Let's not quarrel. Believe me, I love you and more than ever before."[5]

Despite the fact that her formal education had ended with high school, Klari wasted no time in finding a way to partner with my father in one aspect of his all-consuming work. As he was developing the modern stored-program computer, he trained her, at her request, to become one of the original programmers, writing instructions for different computational tasks in a form that the machine could understand. She was a quick study, and I remember the flowcharts she produced, filled with rectangles and arrows and circles, on huge sheets of white paper that spilled over onto the floor. The Princeton household, like the one in Cambridge, was totally consumed in the job of winning the war. And, by failing to pay attention and never learning to make sense of Klari's flowcharts, I passed up completely the unique opportunity to become an early expert in computer programming. To this day, I'm profoundly ignorant of what is going on inside my desktop computer, or how to fix it when something goes awry.

From my vantage point, the adults saw the war as an onerous task that required maximum effort from everyone, but one in which we would ultimately be successful. I knew nothing of the extent to which European civilization was being destroyed by the horrors inflicted on huge swaths of civilian populations—Jews, Poles, Russians—by the Nazis and their allies. It never occurred to me, listening to the conversations that swirled around me, that the conflict would end any way other than with a victory for our side. I was startled to learn years later, from old copies of *Life* magazine when I was helping to clean out my father's Princeton home after his death, that in the dark days of 1943 an Allied victory was by no means assured.

By the spring and summer of 1945, the job was finished. Although the radar and other electronic technology developed and produced at RadLab had played an important role in the Allied bombing attacks that inflicted huge damage on Germany's industrial structure and civilian population, it was the capture of Berlin by Russian infantry that brought about Germany's unconditional surrender on May 8, V-E Day. My friends and I joined in the shouting and hugging and banging of pots and pans in the streets until dark, when my mother, fearing for my safety in the general crush, made me come inside.

Although the war in the Pacific still raged, the general sentiment was that the outcome was a foregone conclusion. The big question, we learned later, was whether the United States should proceed with an invasion of Japan, which was sure to produce enormous casualties on both sides, or take the shortcut offered by the fearful new weapon my father and his colleagues had developed at Los Alamos, the atomic bomb. President Harry Truman authorized the dropping of two such bombs, on Hiroshima and Nagasaki, and a week later World War II was truly over.

I don't recall, though, the same unalloyed jubilation in August that had filled the streets in May. Whether this feeling of anticlimax arose from a sense that the issue was no longer whether we would win but when, or whether relief was clouded by a sense of foreboding regarding the new and terrible weapon we had unleashed, I don't know. But for one young lieutenant in the Army Air Corps, who had just received orders to leave for the Pacific as navigator, photographer, and nose gunner on one of the B-29s that would fly over Japan to map it for the invasion, there was no ambiguity. Facing an assignment in which the mortality rate was said to be 70 percent, Robert Whitman—the man who would become my husband a decade later—felt certain that the bomb had saved his life.

With its job completed, RadLab was disbanded and its scientists dispersed to old jobs or new ones. My mother and Desmond found jobs in New York, she doing for the Sperry Gyroscope Company the same kind of training of women technicians that she had pioneered at RadLab, he as a department head at the Federal Communications Laboratory. There was a severe housing shortage, but my mother, master networker that she was, managed through friends to ensconce us, in return for paying the annual tax bill, in the unoccupied brownstone mansion of an oil millionaire.

The house, fully furnished, reeked of the grandeur of a vanished age. The kitchen and dining room were just below ground level; the front steps led up to a first floor fully occupied by a reception room and a grand ballroom complete with crystal chandeliers and Louis XVI furniture. The master bedroom, sitting room, and bath were just above; then there were two more floors, each with two bedrooms and a bath, with the degree of luxury declining as one ascended successive flights of stairs. There was no elevator, but a small rope-and-pulley dumbwaiter was available for delivering necessities from the kitchen. The house stood on the corner of 70th Street and Fifth Avenue, directly across from the Frick Museum, and was an ideal vantage point for viewing the many colorful parades that passed beneath our windows.

Just as we were settling down to life in the big city and my mother and Desmond into their new jobs, my mother's reputation as a hostess, facilitator, networker, and people motivator led to a truly extraordinary job offer. A group of eminent physicists, led by I. I. Rabi of Columbia, had conceived the idea of a government-funded laboratory to do peacetime research in a variety of areas of physics and the nuclear sciences. The new entity would be managed by a consortium of universities and have as its core a nuclear reactor to be built in an as yet unspecified location near New York City.

The scientists and science administrators representing the nine participating universities quickly set out on a search for their first employee, a jack-of-all-trades (or a jill) who "would have to do everything: secretarial work, serving as liaison with [General] Groves and top-ranking scientists, investigating Columbia's government contract to see what costs it covered, and setting up the machinery to run the IUG [Initiatory University Group] accordingly."[6] It didn't take them long to find Mariette Kövesi von Neumann Kuper. Her dense network of friends and acquaintances in the world of physics, her I-can-do-anything self-confidence, and her irresistible charm, fortified by her exotic Hungarian accent—throughout her life, *thick* and *thin* became *sick* and *sin* on her tongue—made her the ideal choice.

My mother's first task in the challenging job she had accepted with alacrity was to figure out how to get herself officially on the employment rolls, obtain security clearance, and generate a paycheck. That done, she launched herself on a career as senior administrator, confidante, house-mother, and chief of protocol of the as yet unnamed laboratory, a career that would end only with her health-enforced retirement twenty-eight years later. Shortly after taking the job, she set out with a subcommittee of the IUG to find a site for the new venture.

Nuclear reactors do not sit well with neighbors, so a location with lots of empty space around it was essential. Various possibilities were eliminated, one by one, until only Camp Upton, an army base located in Yaphank, Long Island, some sixty miles from New York City, remained. When my mother and the new venture's only other employee went to look at Camp Upton, most recently a prisoner of war camp, they found that "Their future business address was a muddy army camp in the middle of rural Long Island, with pitched tents, temporary wood shacks, and drafty barracks with broken windows."[7] It required a stout heart and a vivid imagination not to be discouraged.

Nothing could dampen my mother's enthusiasm for her new job, though. In a radio interview she gave shortly after the new enterprise was under way, she described her response to the job offer: "I broke into what could best be described as a new type of Indian Victory Dance . . . Who wouldn't be exuberant when privileged to be in on the birth of a new venture which would have as far-reaching significance as I now know Brookhaven National Laboratory will have."[8]

Asked what impact she thought her job was having on her children (a standard question put to working women in those days), she replied, "As a mother, I consider myself unusually fortunate. When my children hear the words 'atomic energy,' their minds do not immediately jump to 'the bomb' . . . My seven-year-old is not building an atomic pile to blow up the neighborhood. Instead he pretends to treat the sick cat with radiation . . . My thirteen-year-old daughter commented to me '. . . Mother, I am glad you are not making hats, designing clothes, or other stuff like that. I like your job much better . . .' I am quite sure that the men who were smart enough to make the atom bomb will be smart enough to use it for something which is not only used in war, and I am glad we are all in on it."[9]

In a high-school graduation speech delivered that same year, she elaborated on the need for the younger generation to be actively involved in world affairs. Citing the mistake her own generation had made in believing, after World War I, that if "each nation paid strict attention to its own business . . . there would be no more war," she urged her listeners "to take an active, living interest in these two things, government and science."[10] The lessons of their youth were never far from the minds of either of my parents. My stepfather soon joined my mother in the new venture, first as a consultant and later as a department head. But until the site could be cleared and the necessary structures built, Brookhaven National Laboratory operated out of offices at Columbia University. So we stayed on for a year or so in our elegant digs in the heart of New York City. My new school was as dull and stuffy as Shady Hall had been open and stimulating. And the independence I had been so proud of in Cambridge now marked me as an outsider. I soon discovered that I was the only girl in the fifth grade who made it to school—a distance of three blocks—without either a chauffeur or a nanny.

While I was plodding my way dutifully but unenthusiastically through school days, intellectual stimulus arrived from an unexpected source. George Gamow, a brilliant physicist who was a friend of both my parents, had embarked on writing what he thought would be a book on modern science for children. After he had finished a draft of the first section, he looked around for a real child to try it out on and settled on me. I adored Gamow, a wild-haired Russian who suited perfectly a child's vision of a mad scientist, and I worked hard to carry out the task he set me. I spent evenings and weekends making notes on all the things I didn't understand, which was just about everything.

Gamow's acknowledgment in the preface to the published version of *One, Two, Three, Infinity* describes the outcome of my labors: "Above all my thanks are due to my young friend, Marina von Neumann, who claims that she knows everything better than her famous father does, except, of course, mathematics, which she says she knows only equally well. After she had read in manuscript some of the chapters of the book, and told me about numerous things in it which she could not understand, I finally decided that this book is not for children as I had originally intended it to be."[11]

This well-intentioned bit of teasing, aimed at my father as much as me, was to cause me painful embarrassment when, as a high-school senior, I started dating Princeton freshmen who read Gamow's book as a textbook. Talk about a reputation as a bluestocking—a female egghead—scaring off the men! But when it was published, I was only eleven. Concerns about boys and dating had not yet entered my head, and I was proud and delighted by such public recognition of my efforts.

My father may not have been a constant presence in my life during my first twelve years, but he clearly adored me and worked hard to create and maintain a father-daughter intimacy. His concern on this score had shown even in the letters he wrote to Klari soon after his separation and divorce from my mother, when I was a toddler: "Marina came over . . . she loved all the postcards I sent . . . she told me she put on her beautiful rosy dress for me."[12] And "In my role as a father I have some success because Marina shows some sentimentality toward myself."[13]

Once I could read, my father wrote to me often, and his letters were filled with terms of endearment and expressions of affection. They contained, as well, constant reminders of the relentlessly high expectations he held for my academic performance. Regarding one of my sixth-grade report cards, he notes, "I saw your report, I am very glad that you have shown in French and mathematics that you can do it well, but what about English?"[14] Nothing short of perfection would satisfy him, and it didn't take me long to internalize those standards. Oddly enough, though, his demands didn't cause me particular stress during my precollege years because I loved learning new things, was both very competitive and very successful where school was concerned, and found meeting his expectations an enjoyable challenge.

In many of these letters, my father included tidbits of information that he thought would interest me. In one, for example, he enclosed several samples of the paper money, with its endless strings of zeroes, issued by the Hungarian government during the postwar hyperinflation, explaining carefully the denomination of each. He took for granted that I would understand his precise, complex explanations: "Actually, the dollar went to something like a septillion pengos [the Hungarian currency]. Towards the end of the inflation the price of fat was over one pengo per molecule."[15]

In return, I wrote him affectionate letters telling him how much I missed him and, in one, describing my fascination, which I knew would please him, with a science assembly at school that had explained the workings of radar and the cathode ray tube and demonstrated the effects of fluorescent and incandescent light on various crystals.[16] In another, which Klari and I wrote jointly during one of his many wartime absences, every other sentence was signed "your neglected family (Klari); the slap-happy females (Marina)."[17] My ten-year-old view of the war's end is reflected in a letter I wrote to Klari a few days after Japan's surrender: "Isn't it wonderful that the war is over? . . . Is Daddy still going to travel so much now that the war is over? I hope not."[18]

During the summer of my eleventh year, my father and I drove alone across the country in one of his substitutes for a tank—in this case, a large Buick. Our ultimate destination was Santa Barbara, California, where Klari would join us and she and I would enjoy life on the beach while he went off on a secret trip somewhere in the Pacific, a "somewhere" that was later revealed as Bikini, a tiny atoll in the Marshall Islands group that had been captured from the Japanese. There, in the summer of 1946, the United States, having more or less forcibly removed the 167 residents to another island, conducted the first of a series of atomic bomb, and later hydrogen bomb, tests code-named Operation Crossroads. As one of the creators of these weapons, my father was there to observe the results.

Our cross-country trip was uneventful, miraculously unmarred by any of my father's notorious car accidents. We stayed in a series of prewar motels, unprepossessing strings of small cottages, a few of them still with outdoor plumbing, which we both regarded as a hilarious adventure. When we stopped in Santa Fe, he bought me two silver and turquoise belts made by local Indians. They would be worth a minor fortune today, if only I had managed to keep track of them. I felt snugly enveloped in a leisurely span of time that existed just for the two of us, in contrast to the hectic encounters, marked by hurried arrivals and departures, I had grown used to.

Once we reached Los Alamos, my father exuded boyish enthusiasm as he showed me around those areas I was allowed to enter—all the buildings where bomb-related work was conducted remained strictly off-limits—and introduced me to some of his colleagues from the Manhattan Project. Chief among them were Stan and Françoise Ulam. Ulam, a Polish-born mathematician who had arrived in the United States in 1935 and quickly become one of my father's closest friends, had stayed on to work in Los Alamos after the war was over. The secret city, whose existence had been revealed less than a year before, looked amazingly primitive to my citified eyes, with muddy paths instead of sidewalks and open stairs leading up to second-floor apartments in flimsy wooden buildings. I now began to understand where my father had been and what he had been doing during the war years, and the intensity of the residents' commitment to an Allied victory was brought home to me when I saw the physical discomfort his colleagues had been willing to put up with.

Not long after that trip, about the time Brookhaven Laboratory actually began to function on Long Island and the Kuper household moved from New York to the small town of Bayport on the island's Great South Bay, my twelfth birthday arrived. With it came the long-planned move from my mother's household to my father's during the school year. My parents, concerned about my likely reaction and perhaps each hoping that the other would break the news, had delayed telling me about this long-standing agreement until the move was nearly upon me. I had always handled the shuttling between two households with aplomb, but I was shaken on learning that my base would now shift from one to the other, and furious that no one had consulted me or even told me about it far enough in advance to allow me to get my mind around the idea.

Although I acquiesced without outward objection, not wanting to hurt or alienate any of the adults involved, the shift in households was an emotional wrench. Soon after moving to Princeton, I wrote nostalgically, in a school assignment, about the Long Island family I had just left: "The commander-in-chief is Mother. Good-looking, and with a wonderful flair for clothes, she seems to have energy enough for three, managing to hold down a full-time-job, run a household and, in her spare time, lead a dazzling social life . . . Her nature is a wonderful mixture of contradictions; her unreasonable temper is as terrifying as her warm-hearted generosity is gratifying."

"My stepfather . . . is quite different from Mother, quiet and cautious, seeming to take a very serious view of life but often bursting forth with something really funny when we least expect it . . . Although usually quiet and undemanding, he really comes into his own on the boat, where he is complete master and a stern tyrant. It is there, watching the delighted little boy playing with his marvelous toy, that we love him the most."

Although my mother's dominating personality and my stepfather's response through what would today be termed passive aggression were creating tensions in this marriage even as I wrote, they did not come to the surface until much later. My view at the time, doubtless heightened by the fact that blessings brighten as they take flight, was that "as a unit, they are one of the happiest, most closely-knit families I know." I was both angry and apprehensive at the thought of leaving this comfortable nest for one less familiar and, I already foresaw, more complicated.

· 3 ·

Walking on Eggs

"How do you like your eggs cooked, Daddy?" I asked on one of the first mornings of my new life at 26 Westcott Road, the big white colonial house in the elegant western section of Princeton that was now my home during the school year. This homely question about his breakfast was my awkward attempt to start building a normal father-daughter relationship with a parent who had so far moved in and out of my life with unsettling frequency. Neither one of us knew exactly how to go about it, but we were both determined to try. I sensed that every aspect of our relationship—his genuine affection for me and his yearning for it to be returned, his stratospheric expectations for my academic achievement, his treatment of me as an intellectual equal even as he played the role of an old-fashioned father in matters relating to my behavior, my social life, and even my allowance—were going to be at the center of my life for the next few years. On his side, my father wanted desperately to make up for lost time in creating the emotional bond that should have been building gradually over the years.

It didn't take me long to figure out that I had walked into an emotional minefield. Despite his brilliance and outward sociability, my father was both inept and insecure in handling the intimacies of marriage. I couldn't ignore the tensions in his relationship with Klari, tensions that leaped from every page of the letters he wrote almost daily, throughout their nearly twenty-year marriage, whenever they were apart.

A painful theme ran through nearly all these letters, which I read only long after they were both dead: his despair over the fact that they seemed to quarrel whenever they were together, his assurances that he adored her, and his vacillation between self-defense and self-flagellation for whatever sin of commission or omission she had most recently taxed him with. In her eyes, it seemed, he could do nothing right. Yet he worked constantly to bolster her fragile ego: "You are nice and clever and intelligent, believe in yourself." Beset by the chronic depression and profound insecurity that would haunt her for the rest of her life, she could not be reassured. Once I had intruded on this already fragile relationship, both Klari and I found ourselves competing for my father's attention not only with each other but with what remained throughout his life his central preoccupation: the output of his brilliant mind.

As the threat to American security shifted from the defeated Axis powers to the increasingly menacing Soviet Union, my father's focus shifted as well. As he described it to his friend and colleague, physicist Freeman Dyson, "I am thinking about something much more important than bombs. I am thinking about computers."[1] He had first become seriously involved with computers when he was introduced to an early electronic version, the ENIAC, being built at the Moore School of Electrical Engineering at the University of Pennsylvania under contract with the Army's Ballistics Research Laboratory (BRL) at the Aberdeen Proving Ground in Maryland.

The original goal was to use the machine for the incredibly complex calculations required to develop mathematical tables to guide the trajectories of guns and bombs, but it was eventually enlisted to study the feasibility of a variety of ideas generated at Los Alamos, including the development of an effective trigger for the hydrogen bomb. The ENIAC could perform in hours or days calculations that required hundreds or thousands of person-hours when performed by hand by the large group of women, actually called "calculators," whom the army had recruited as civilian employees.

The ENIAC was a huge advance, but it still couldn't keep up with the computational demands placed on it, primarily because it had to be physically rewired, a time-consuming process, every time a new problem came along. In a 1945 paper, a group led by my father proposed changes in the logical design of the computer's memory to turn it into an "electronic brain" that could store not only data but instructions (programs, later called software) to perform different kinds of logical functions. This design, known ever since as the "von Neumann architecture," was used to retrofit the ENIAC into a primitive version of the modern stored-program computer. Computer-related conversations filled the adults' dinnertime conversations at home, and Klari even named her Irish setter puppy Inverse, after one of the computational problems that weighed on my father and some of his close colleagues.

Now my father was determined to build a machine embodying the von Neumann architecture from scratch, and to do it on his own home ground, the Institute for Advanced Study. It was not an easy battle. Money had to be found, a team assembled, and above all, he had to overcome the determined opposition of his colleagues on the IAS's Mathematics Faculty. They regarded his dream as an engineering project, totally inappropriate in an institution devoted to abstract thought. And once he was able to get the project under way, the practical obstacles were formidable. The transistor that made miniaturization possible had not yet been invented, so the machine had to be constructed from bulky vacuum tubes. The result was that the completed computer, with only a millionth of the computing power of the flash drive we hang on our keychain, filled a brick building of its own. It overheated at the slightest provocation and quit functioning for a thousand different reasons—once because a mouse had gotten inside and chewed on some wires. My usually irrepressible father often came home for dinner tired and discouraged, but as determined as ever to see the project through.

Although my father had hoped that his computer could be built in three years, it actually took six, from 1946 until 1952, before a celebratory cocktail party was in order. The party at our house had as its centerpiece an ice-carved model of the computer, which my father dubbed the MANIAC but later was given a less playful designation as the IAS machine. The vacuum tubes were represented by silver thumbtacks, which of course started falling out as the ice melted. Margaret Rabi and I kept busy for a while replacing the fallen tacks, but eventually entropy defeated us and the computer became a formless puddle.

The fate of the celebratory ice carving was, in a way, emblematic of the fate of the IAS machine itself. Opposition on the part of much of the institute's faculty never really faded, and, once my father had gone to Washington in 1955 to serve on the Atomic Energy Commission, some members of his team departed and the ones that remained were poorly treated. At his death, in 1957, the computer project was closed, and the institute's faculty passed a motion decreeing that henceforth no experimental science would be conducted there.

The machine itself, superseded by newer and faster models with the same basic von Neumann architecture, was dismantled and the brick building in which it was housed became a storage unit for cleaning and maintenance materials. Today it is shared by a fitness facility and a preschool for the offspring of visiting members at the institute. Until recently, a segment of the machine, which had been donated to the Smithsonian, was on display in one of its buildings, the National Museum of American History. With the latest remodeling, that, too, has been consigned to attic storage. But its millions, nay billions, of progeny shape nearly every moment of our waking lives.

My father had no inkling of the ways in which his invention would revolutionize our world. He expected that the whole world wouldn't need more than a few, perhaps a dozen, computers, since their purpose was cutting-edge research with huge computational requirements. His immediate goal was more accurate weather forecasting; he saw it as the first step toward control of the weather, which, he believed, would become a more effective weapon than bombs in future conflicts. But the notion that computers would sit on millions of desktops and in millions of pockets, would be used to transmit business documents, love letters, and pornography instantaneously across the miles, and would set adults to fulminating about the time their children waste on computer games—all this was beyond his wildest imagining, although the ubiquity of computer games might have appealed to the childlike, playful side of his nature.

When he was at home, the main private time my father and I had together was in the morning, before his workday and my school day began. Klari generally slept late in her own bedroom; she was so grouchy in the morning that waking her up before I left for school was a task I dreaded. So I would fix breakfast for both of us, and we would talk as we ate. My father enjoyed teasing me, and he fell into the habit of calling it "a dying father's last request" when he asked me to fetch him the newspaper or toast him a second English muffin. When he really was dying, and the requests he made of me took on a new urgency, he never used this phrase, but the memory of its use in happier times sharpened my pain and, very possibly, his.

It wasn't easy to penetrate the surface cheerfulness and bonhomie with which my father armed himself against the world, to reach the deeply cynical and pessimistic core of his being. Indeed, I was frequently confused when he shifted, without warning, from one of these personas to the other—one minute he would have me laughing at his latest outrageous pun and the next he would be telling me, quite seriously, why all-out atomic war was almost certainly unavoidable. But I enjoyed being talked to as an equal and cherished the glimpses he gave me into the complex, fascinating world in which he lived. I could not, and still cannot, begin to penetrate the realms of higher mathematics that occupied so much of his thoughts, and to which he made such major contributions. But I could follow and relish his humor-laced accounts of his dealings with a wide range of people and institutions, and his opinions on world affairs.

Just in time for these breakfasts, my father would change from his striped pajamas into the three-piece banker's suit, complete with watch chain across the vest, that he habitually wore, no matter what the occasion. In all our years together, I never saw him wear anything else. There is even a famous photograph of him—first published in a *Life* magazine article just after his death—in a train of people descending the Grand Canyon on mules. Whereas everyone else is wearing blue jeans and sitting on a downward-facing mule, my father, dressed in his usual three-piece suit and necktie, is perched on a mule facing in the opposite direction.

His mode of dress, however incongruous at times, suited him well and lent dignity to his rotund frame, which Klari described in her autobiography as "roly-poly . . . babyishly plump and round, like a child's drawing of the man in the moon."[2] Sometimes, at a particularly lively party, he would top the outfit with some sort of funny hat. Especially memorable was the half pineapple, immortalized in a photograph, that sat comically atop his round face and balding curly head.

That picture reflects yet another aspect of my father's complex personality: his love of children's toys. Three of his particular favorites sat on his desk, and he often studied them intensely for long periods of time. These were a bird perched upright on a metal stand that would lean over to drink from a water glass and then right itself on a precise schedule; a handblown glass tube filled with soap bubbles; and a wooden disc with everyday objects (a heart and a four-leaf clover, for example) painted on its face and a metal pointer that, when spun, would land on one or another of them.

When I asked him why he found these toys so fascinating, he explained that each embodied some principle of mathematics or physics. Watching the changing pattern of the soap bubbles after he shook the glass tube, he contemplated the effect of surface tension in making them obey the law of entropy; noting where the pointer on the wooden disc landed on spin after spin stimulated his ideas about the laws of probability. Had LEGOs been available at the time, he might have built a model of his computer from them.

Because my father traveled so much, a great deal of my time was spent with Klari. She had the best of intentions toward me, and I had had fun with her during the years when I was just visiting; but her neurotic personality and profound sense of insecurity had ill-prepared her for her new role. To make things tougher, her new charge was neither infant nor toddler but an awkward near adolescent, already taller than she, who arrived with a very clear view of how a mother should look and act and sent unspoken but clear messages that she didn't measure up. Her sometimes clumsy attempts at discipline infuriated me, and I found her frequently tense exchanges with my father emotionally wearing. She persuaded my father to buy elaborate gifts for me when I was a teenager—a fur coat, an evening gown from Paris, even a small car for my sixteenth birthday—but somehow these fell short of the mark, embarrassing me because they marked me as different from my friends.

Once I was an adult and had children of my own, I felt considerable sympathy toward Klari and her efforts at parenting. This sympathy increased when I learned two secrets that had been assiduously kept from me: that her father had committed suicide by jumping under a train shortly after her marriage to my father; and that she had had a late-term miscarriage, which she blamed on my father for not having been around to help her lift a heavy garage door. But at the time, ignorant of these tragedies, dealing with the emotional turmoil of adolescence, and struggling to adjust to a new and different home life, I had little thought to spare for other people's emotional problems. In fact, when Klari became too irritating, I would tell my father bluntly, "If you don't get her off my back, I'm going back to Long Island," despite what the divorce agreement said. Today I'm ashamed of this emotional blackmail, but at the time I used it as the only weapon I had in the struggle to keep my home environment emotionally tolerable.

Whenever my father and Klari were both traveling, Granny Gitta came down to Princeton from New York. She had been living with my father's younger brother Mike ever since Johnny, the oldest sibling, had persuaded his widowed mother and two younger brothers to come to the United States shortly before war broke out in Europe. She had been a beauty in her day, the adored wife of her husband Max. When the patent of nobility bestowed on my grandfather by the Austro-Hungarian emperor in 1913 entitled the family to its own heraldic crest, the one Max designed was emblazoned with three daisies—or marguerites—in honor of his wife, Margaret.

My father and his mother were very close; in fact, I sometimes think that he was more emotionally attached to her than to either of his wives. By the time I knew her she was a tall, thin, chain-smoking lady, still elegant, though given to wearing too much bright-red lipstick, which bled into the wrinkles bordering her upper lip. Now that I am about the age she was then, I take inordinate pains to prevent my own lipstick from creating that same effect, which was imprinted on my child's mind as one of the more unattractive symbols of old age.

Still, I loved having Granny Gitta in charge. She did wonderful handiwork—knitting, crocheting, embroidery—and, although none of these talents rubbed off on me, I delighted in going through fascinating books of Hungarian designs that she brought with her to choose the right pattern for her next project. She cooked odd but delicious things for dinner, like fried bread, a staple of the Hungarian peasant diet. And, above all, she didn't shout. My memories of this period in my life are filled with parents and their partners shouting at one another, constantly caught up in some emotional Sturm und Drang. Granny Gitta was as tightly wound and tense as any of the others, but she was outwardly calm and gentle with me.

The move to Princeton gave me the opportunity, once again, to go to a truly remarkable school. The quality of education delivered at Miss Fine's School for Girls totally belied its prissy, finishing-school name. Within the walls of a converted mansion in the middle of town, the environment was one of an intellectual intensity that could perhaps be achieved, in the 1950s, only in a single-sex institution. Many of our teachers were brilliant women who today would be doctors, lawyers, or, most likely, professors at first-class colleges or universities, but for whom already-limited opportunities were narrowed further by the fact that they were faculty wives or otherwise tied geographically to the Princeton area.

Not only did we get first-class instruction in the usual basic high-school subjects, but if three or more students wanted a more advanced class in Latin or Greek or calculus, one of the faculty members would teach it. We read Racine and Molière in French class, Virgil and Ovid in Latin. But what really stretched us to our intellectual limits were the history and English classes taught, in alternate years, by Anne Shepherd.

Mrs. Shepherd, a Vassar graduate divorcée with a brilliant only son (who, tragically, grew up to become one of the first American casualties in the Vietnam War), was the sort of teacher who comes along once in a lifetime. Surely everyone in our class could not have been geniuses, but she somehow inspired us to think and probe and imagine as if we were. When, in 1965, Miss Fine's School merged with its male counterpart, Princeton Country Day School, to become the Princeton Day School (PDS), Mrs. Shepherd's intellectual passion and brilliance proved as effective with adolescent boys as it was with adolescent girls. When she died, at the age of ninety, she was still teaching, as a volunteer in the Princeton Adult School. And today plaques in the library, the computer center, and an assembly hall, as well as a bust in an outdoor garden at PDS, honor her memory.

The results of this nurturing were amazing. Four of the twelve members of my senior class applied to Radcliffe College, the women's branch of Harvard, which in those days conducted a nationwide test in English literature for all applicants. One day in the spring of our senior year, the headmistress of Miss Fine's received a phone call from the president of Radcliffe, inquiring about the school. She told him it was a private school for girls in Princeton, New Jersey, then asked why he wanted to know. It turned out that the four applicants from Miss Fine's had placed something like first, third, sixth, and ninth in that competitive exam (I placed third).

Some of us not only stretched our minds for Anne Shepherd but we also opened our hearts in candid outpourings of our hopes and fears. In one essay, written loosely in the form of a poem, I described the stage of life I was going through.

> Adolescence is a bittersweet hour
> Between childhood and the time
> When we meet the world face to face,
> And become a part of it. Now all
> Is new, confusing, the joys so strange,
> So sharp, that they are almost pains.
> . . .
>   . . . Now the warm,
> Close security of childhood dissolves
> And we see the world, a frightening place
> But, oh, so tempting, promising success,
> Yet warning of a thousand pitfalls on the way.
> Will we succeed or fail, will happiness be ours,
> Or grief? Will we even have a chance to try
> This world, or will everything end tomorrow
> In a blinding ball of flame? No one knows.
> We can only work, and hope, and think.
> And, in the dark, become children again,
> And dream.

Also stashed in my attic is a yellowed copy of a paper I wrote in tenth grade, tracing the literary history of a classic morality tale, the battle for his soul between Dr. Faustus and the Devil, which had grown and developed in several languages over hundreds of years. When, as a college freshman, I went out for coffee with a Harvard PhD candidate in English whom I had just met at an informal dance, the man who was to become my husband swears that it was my ability to talk knowledgeably about such an arcane subject that first made him take serious notice of a seventeen-year-old. And there is no question that the intellectual challenges my classmates and I received and rose to at Miss Fine's, and the self-images they nurtured, created a firm foundation for the intellectual self-confidence that I carried into adulthood. As an early and often lonely entrant into professional arenas dominated by men, that faith in myself was an absolutely essential ingredient.

My classmates and I spent a lot of time in earnest discussions about the dangers of another global conflict; my own pessimism regarding the inevitability of war reflected my father's views, spelled out in the letter he had written to Klari in 1946 predicting another world war within the next decade. Hoping to avert catastrophe, several of us joined an idealistic organization called the World Federalists, whose goal was to create a world government, a gesture that doubtless earned me a spot on some FBI list of members of subversive organizations. Even then I admitted in a school essay how naive the movement was, but concluded, "There seems to be only a very slight chance that the idea will work, but even that slight chance is worth working for if it could mean the prevention of the almost inevitable next war." My efforts to bring about world government did not survive my adolescence, but a commitment to greater coordination of national policies in a world grown increasingly interdependent has infused my entire career.

The people and the conversations around my father's dinner table were even more important than my school environment in expanding my teenage horizons. Some of them were leading mathematicians and scientists, many were fellow Hungarians transplanted to the New World, and all of them were brilliant. Among them were two friends from his high-school years in Budapest—the physicists Edward Teller and Eugene Wigner. The gruff, beetle-browed Teller, who spoke in staccato sentences that called to mind the firing of a repeater rifle, had been a colleague of my father's at Los Alamos. There he had not only played an important role in the development of the atomic bomb but became the major proponent of building the even more powerful hydrogen bomb. Slight, balding, soft-voiced Wigner, whose rabbitlike buck teeth made him speak with a lisp, also worked on the Manhattan Project, and he eventually won a Nobel Prize for his work on atoms and elementary particles.

In his later years he went a bit batty, becoming a supporter of the Unification Church, which he hoped might offer a path toward world peace and thus an escape from the vision of wholesale destruction that his work had helped create.

These three men were linked not only by their Jewish Hungarian backgrounds and their scientific achievements but also by the vehemence of their anticommunist views. In this they were joined by yet another Hungarian, Arthur Koestler, the dark, brooding former communist whose novel, *Darkness at Noon,* became one of the most powerful exposés of the cruelties of Soviet communism ever written. In a paper I wrote at the time, tracing the evolution of communism through the lens of three political novels (*Man's Fate* by André Malraux, *Bread and Wine* by Ignazio Silone, and Koestler's *Darkness at Noon*), I noted that Koestler's was "the most hopeless of the three," a reflection of his deep pessimism and, probably, chronic depression.

Another Hungarian who appeared often at our house couldn't have been more different from the brooding Koestler. He was short, urbane, wise-cracking Emery Reves, a close friend and confidante of Winston Churchill, whose last-minute escape from his Nazi pursuers was worthy of an episode in the *Perils of Pauline.* The most frequent dinner guest of all was yet another refugee from the former Austro-Hungarian Empire, Oskar Morgenstern, the tall, rigidly handsome, and forbidding-looking economist and Princeton professor who coauthored *The Theory of Games and Economic Behavior* with my father. Unlike the others, Morgenstern had deserted Austria for the United States not because he was Jewish—his mother was an illegitimate daughter of the German emperor Frederick III—but because he couldn't stand the thought of living and working under Hitler's regime after Germany annexed Austria in the Anschluss of 1938.

Regrettably, we never had all these men gathered at Klari's elegant glass-topped dining table at the same time—what a conversation that would have been! But even one at a time, their rapid-fire interchanges with my father, whether in the form of "can you top this" joke contests or sophisticated discussions of geopolitics, expanded my horizons far beyond the purview of an American teenager. Still, I often chafed at the adults' long, drawn-out conversations over coffee, which kept me from getting back to my homework and endless phone calls with my friends. I found Koestler's unrelieved pessimism much harder to take than the ever-merry Reves's anecdotes about his narrow escapes or Winston Churchill's foibles, but it certainly inoculated me against any belief in easy solutions to the precarious state of the world in the 1950s. This was a time when people were building bomb shelters in their basements or backyards and schoolchildren regularly ducked under their desks or filed into cellars in drills to prepare for an atomic attack.

A lot of what I learned, though, had less to do with science or politics or world affairs than with intimate human relationships. The formal, correct, "confirmed bachelor" Oskar Morgenstern courted his beautiful redheaded wife Dorothy in our living room, and Emery Reves's tall, bottle-blonde girlfriend from Texas, Wendy, made no bones about her efforts to enlist my father and stepmother's aid in persuading Reves to make an honest woman of her. Eventually they were married, and, despite her brassy looks and smoke-roughened voice, she proved a devoted helpmeet, attending to his every need and whim throughout the rest of his life.

Perhaps the most startling lesson of all came from Arthur Koestler, who lived only a few miles from Princeton and was a frequent dinner guest. Despite the fact that he was unusually short, with a perpetual scowl and a face only a mother could love, he often appeared with a beautiful young woman in tow. I was appalled to learn, a few days after one of these visits, that his companion that evening had committed suicide. I was even more horrified when, only a week or two later, Koestler came to dinner again, this time with an equally lovely lady who, I later learned, had become both his secretary and his mistress. My sensibilities were so outraged that I refused to speak to either of them, despite my father's and Klari's pleadings that I stop being so rude.

That mistress, Cynthia Jeffries, eventually became Koestler's third wife and died with him in a suicide pact in 1983. Why Cynthia, much younger than the terminally ill Koestler and apparently in good health, chose to die with him has never been explained. But, remembering the sheer force of Koestler's personality, his well-known ability to press his girlfriends and wives into performing as his secretaries and maids, and the ferocity of his emotions, I wasn't surprised.

The long, serious dinner conversations exposed me to one face of my father's social world; the cocktail parties at 26 Westcott Road showed me a different one. My father and mother had hosted legendary parties in Princeton before the war, my mother and Desmond had done the same in Cambridge during the conflict, and now my father and Klari carried on the tradition in their large, handsome house ideally suited to entertaining. These events brought out my father's fun-loving side, displayed in his enjoyment of children and children's toys, his renowned stock of dirty limericks, his ability to down a remarkable number of martinis without any sign of impairment, and his fondness for ridiculous party hats. But the serious side of his nature was never far below the surface; he was known to disappear suddenly from one of his own parties to work on some mathematical problem, then reappear as suddenly as he had vanished and resume his good-fellow role.

Occasionally my father would take me to the ritual four o'clock tea in the institute's vast and elegant common room, where the resident geniuses would gather daily for cookies and conversation. Albert Einstein generally stood off in one corner, either alone or in close conversation with his one good friend, the brilliant but mentally unbalanced mathematician Kurt Gödel. My father didn't try to intrude on Einstein's isolation. The two had once been both socially and scientifically intimate, but they had grown increasingly apart, both personally and in their views on developments in physics—whereas my father had embraced quantum mechanics, Einstein rejected the uncertainty that was fundamental to that theory with the much-quoted comment, "I am convinced that He [God] does not play dice."

My father had become an insider in both the world of mathematics and physics and the American military-industrial complex, as comfortable speaking and writing in English as in Hungarian. Einstein, a steadfast pacifist during the heat of the Cold War, remained "an outsider in his adopted country, never accepting the professional mores or mastering the national language."[3] This outsider status was solidified by his widower status and his growing frustration over his inability to achieve his life's goal—the development of a unifying theory to explain within a single framework the four fundamental forces that bind all matter.

My attitude toward the unique experiences afforded by living under my father's roof was ambivalent. I was stimulated by the range of intellects and personalities I encountered there, but I was discomfited by the growing recognition, as I compared my world to that of my classmates, that ours was hardly a regular American family. I relished opportunities to visit households very different from my own and become part of them, however temporarily. I spent every moment I could with one particular friend, Leslie, even though she lived in a cramped apartment where I had to sleep on the couch when I spent the night and it was difficult to escape the presence of her alcoholic parents. The offbeat casualness of their world attracted me, and it was only in adulthood, as I saw Leslie's own life gradually destroyed by alcohol, that I recognized I had been witnessing not an enviable family life but a multigenerational tragedy.

While I was absorbing the complexities of social interactions among grown-ups, I was having the usual adolescent struggles over my own relationships with the opposite sex. My Miss Fine's classmates and I were labeled "townies" by Princeton undergraduates, potential dates when older and more desirable female companionship, imported from Smith or Vassar or other points north, was unavailable. We knew full well how we were regarded, but that didn't prevent us from responding eagerly to invitations to parties at the eating clubs that were, in those days, the center of undergraduate social life at Princeton. By the time I was a senior, my father and Klari succumbed to my unrelenting pressure and, somewhat reluctantly, allowed me to participate in these events as long as I obeyed the curfew they set.

I soon figured out how to turn my position of weakness into strength. Princeton undergraduates were not allowed to have cars and, given the tendencies of many of them to overimbibe, a number of lives were doubtless saved as a result. I, on the other hand, did have a car and was by nature abstemious. The party evenings often ended with me unceremoniously depositing my inebriated date on the sidewalk in front of his dormitory. This early role reversal reassured my parents and may well have helped stiffen my spine for future academic and professional competition with the opposite sex.

My mother may not have been the custodial parent during my adolescence, but she remained a forceful presence in my life and was the source of some very mixed signals I was getting about what was important and what my priorities should be. The example she set by her life was of a smart, strong, energetic woman who could not only succeed in a man's world but also leave her mark on it. Yet she was constantly anxious that I not "let my brains show too much," lest I scare off the boys and find myself a permanent wallflower. Always glamorous herself, she put a heavy stress on physical attractiveness, and her very efforts to improve mine made it clear that she wished she had better material to work with.

She made that clear when she was helping me to get ready for a dance at the country club near their home on Long Island, where I spent my summers. I was an awkward sixteen, mildly overweight and recovering from a bad case of poison ivy that had left my face red and scaly. She had bought me a very pretty dress—white, off the shoulder, and sprinkled with dainty flowers—and worked what magic she could with my makeup and hair. When she was done, she stood back to survey her handiwork and commented, "Jesus Christ, I'm glad I'm not sixteen!" I got the message and went off to the party feeling more than ever like a clumsy cow; my social self-confidence, always shaky, took a steep downward plunge. Between my father's expectations for academic performance and my mother's about appearance and social success, I had my work cut out for me.

During the summer vacation before I started college, I bowed to my mother's pressure to improve my appearance and had cosmetic surgery done to change the shape of my nose. I hesitated to tell my father because I was sure he would disapprove. But the letter he wrote in response to my news reassured me. After congratulating me, as he always did, on my excellent report card, noting that "of course, we have grown used to this," he added, "I also think that it [the nose job] was sillyness [sic], 200 proof, but then that's the normal condition of the world. It must be admitted, though, that at least according to one usually well informed source, had Cleopatra's nose been half an inch longer the course of whatever it was would have been different."

In that same letter, he replied to one I had apparently written him, thanking him for the years I had spent under his roof: "For me, too, the years that we spent together are unforgettable, and the more so, because that phase of our lives is past. It has all the heartrending quality of a very fine and delicate thing that is gone. The future might be good—for you it should be better—but it will not be the same. Yet, since we will now both be "adults" (Heaven knows what that means . . .) we will have more to say to each other, and I hope that we will say it. There is a well-defined limit up to which I should interfere or appear in your life, but I hope that we will, even so, have much in common."

I was deeply moved by my father's marking this rite of passage with such tenderness, and such a touching sense of vulnerability. At the same time, now that I was going off to college, I was relieved that I would no longer have to cope full time with the emotional whirlwind at 26 Westcott Road. And I was exhilarated by my newly acquired independence from my parents' divorce agreement, which gave me the freedom to make my own choices about where and with whom I would spend my time. Both my father and I believed that we had used the years together to establish a solid basis for our relationship as two adults. We could not foresee that this relationship would be cut mercilessly short, and that it would be marred by a more painful conflict than either of us could imagine.

· 4 ·

$\mathscr{E}$ngaging Head and Heart

"May I cut in?" With this courtly, old-fashioned request, Bob Whitman entered my life. The occasion was an informal dance, innocently called a "jolly-up," at Holmes Hall, my dormitory at Radcliffe College, where I had started as a freshman a few weeks earlier. Among the Harvard undergraduates who came to try their luck at meeting a new crop of girls were two somewhat older graduate students, both veterans of World War II, who had "gone slumming" to unwind and celebrate having just passed the dreaded oral exam for the PhD in English. One of them, Bob Ganz, was my graduate instructor in the writing course required of all freshmen. He dutifully asked me to dance but was clearly uncomfortable fraternizing with one of his own students. Seeing his discomfort, his friend gallantly relieved him by cutting in.

Bob Ganz's rescuer was Bob Whitman, with whom I danced most of the rest of the evening and went out for coffee with afterward. I don't remember exactly what we talked about, but I do remember how taken I was not only with his blond good looks and obvious erudition but with his understated Yankee manner, so different from the explosive Hungarian interchanges I was used to. It didn't take me long to discover that, although not particularly religious, he had a strong commitment to the moral life, which he interpreted as having a positive impact on the lives of others, as well as a reluctance to let his emotions show, both inherited from his Puritan ancestors.

64

Bob was, in fact, related through both his paternal and maternal lines to five of the voyagers on the *Mayflower*, including the military leader, Miles Standish, and the spiritual leader, Elder William Brewster. His parents were both Whitmans (very distant cousins) and both social workers; they had met when they were seated alphabetically, next to each other, at a professional conference. The family was rich in education and culture but not in worldly goods. Bob told me that, during the Depression, his father would often make some excuse to stay home from a family outing to the movies in order to save a quarter, while his mother would never turn away empty-handed the homeless, penniless men who knocked so frequently at their backdoor. These habits, so different from the spendthrift ways of my own family, stayed with the senior Whitmans throughout their lives and were firmly imprinted on their son.

Back in my dorm room at the end of the evening, dazzled by the intensity of my reaction to a man I had just met, I told my roommate, "I've met the man I'm going to marry." She replied with something like, "Oh, you're just a starry-eyed seventeen-year-old freshman impressed by an older man." That same evening Bob wrote in a spiral notebook, which he still won't let me see, "have I finally found her?" Improbable as it may seem, the stars we both saw that night were real. Bob followed up in that same journal a few weeks later, "and now I am mooing like a love-sick calf until I see Marina again . . . She can wrap me around any finger— including 4th finger, left hand." In 2006, Bob Whitman and I celebrated our fiftieth wedding anniversary. And that same roommate was among the guests at the elegant dinner party our children hosted to celebrate the occasion.

When I entered Radcliffe—the women's division of Harvard—in the fall of 1952, I returned to Cambridge, the city of my childhood. But contained within it was a world I hadn't known anything about during those earlier years, a world that, in the richness of its offerings and the protection it gave its inhabitants from the problems and tragedies of the world outside, seemed like a modern Garden of Eden. In these new surroundings, linked to family only by an infrequent phone call, I could begin to define myself and my goals in my own terms, rather than struggling to meet my parents' expectations.

Radcliffe women of the 1950s were among the last beneficiaries of a special privilege, the freedom to enjoy learning for its own sake without much concern about what it was useful for or how it would enhance our job opportunities, which we knew would be limited by our gender, no matter how smart we were. And we exercised this privilege in the most stimulating intellectual community in the world, guided by a brilliant faculty and surrounded by Harvard/Radcliffe classmates who were—as we were frequently reminded by our teachers and each other—the cream of the crop. This perspective faded in the upheavals of the 1960s and 1970s, as women began to challenge the cultural barriers that had prevented them from entering the man's world of career competition and advancement. Although I was one of the earliest and most determined of those challengers, I still look back nostalgically on the freedom my classmates and I enjoyed to pursue whatever subjects we found interesting.

Established in 1879 as an experiment in "separate but equal" education for women, giving them access to Harvard faculty while keeping them in a strictly single-sex learning environment, Radcliffe College had become increasingly integrated with Harvard. Finally, in 1999, it was fully merged into Harvard University, becoming the Radcliffe Institute for Advanced Study and ceasing to exist as an undergraduate institution. In the 1950s, Radcliffe was in the midst of that long transition. Thanks to the pressures of World War II, all our classes, with the exception of gym, had become fully shared with Harvard, and our instructors made no distinctions based on gender when they admitted students to courses or handed out grades. But the Radcliffe dormitories were at least a mile away from the Harvard campus, and women were not part of the social and intellectual world of the Harvard Houses, as the handsome living quarters strung along the edge of the Charles River are called.

The gracious, protective cocoon of Holmes Hall would look like an alien planet to today's students. We sat down to dinners served formally by our freshman classmates, at polished dark wood tables set with real china and flatware. After dinner, we drank coffee from demitasse cups, poured by our elderly but gracious housemother, in a living room that looked for all the world like an enlarged version of those in the affluent suburban homes many of us came from. We lived under strict parietal rules, signing in and out when we were going to be absent after 6:00 p.m., and alert to the fact that we would turn into pumpkins at midnight. During daylight hours, when the front door was unlocked, a bell desk, guarded on a rotating basis by the hall's residents, prevented any male, including our fathers, from penetrating above the first floor without special permission.

Partly because of the physical separation of our living quarters, but even more because of long-standing tradition, women were allowed to participate in Harvard's rich extracurricular life only on a very limited basis. Radcliffe had its own Choral Union, its own Dramatic Club, and its own newspaper, the *Radcliffe News*. This last was an amateurish effort, vastly inferior to the royalty of all college newspapers, the *Harvard Crimson,* and as female undergraduates were somewhat grudgingly beginning to be allowed to work on the latter, my coeditor Jody Fisher and I were delighted to preside over the dignified demise of the *News*.

The blatancy of the many gender-based barriers to Radcliffe women's full participation in Harvard's undergraduate life was matched by the passivity of our response. We never thought to question why we were not allowed to study in Lamont, Harvard's undergraduate library, or be admitted to the Harvard Business School. When the overweight French graduate student with bad teeth who served as my thesis adviser made clumsy amorous advances, it never occurred to me that the problem of fending him off without jeopardizing my chances for a summa cum laude was anyone's but mine. My success in doing both turned out to be good practice for dealing with the episodes of sexual harassment—although the term had not yet entered everyday vocabulary—that I encountered during my professional life.

This achievement gave a boost to my self-confidence, but I still meekly accepted put-downs that would be unthinkable today. When an IBM recruiter abruptly terminated a job interview by remarking curtly, after a glance at my left hand, "We have a policy of never hiring engaged girls," I stood up, smoothed my skirt, apologized for taking up his time, and left the room.

As I recounted this episode to my daughter and her closest friend shortly after they graduated from college, their faces fell in disappointment—they had expected a sharp departing put-down from me, at the very least. How could I make these children of the postfeminist era understand that arguing or making a scene would have been futile? No laws existed to prohibit such policies, and there was no Equal Employment Opportunity Commission with which to lodge a complaint. Luckily, I didn't take this dismissal as an indication of my own inadequacy, but rather as an example of the idiocy rife in a world where I would soon have to make my own way. I was to call on this self-confidence many times as I elbowed my way into a man's world, though always with a smile on my face that belied my stubborn ambition.

We Radcliffe women were, in fact, curiously detached from the world outside, oblivious to the sexism and racism that marked the era. No one I knew ever disrupted the smooth academic rhythm to do volunteer work on another continent or work in an election campaign. The only student protest I can remember was aimed at winning the right to wear jeans instead of skirts to dinner—and we lost. And when the college rented television sets for the dormitories so that we could watch the Eisenhower-Stevenson election returns, it never occurred to any of us to ask why the sets had to vanish once the returns were in.

Part of the reason we were so oblivious to the gender-based limitations that surrounded us is that we were the good girls of the 1950s, members of the "silent generation" that was swept away by the upheavals of the 1960s and 1970s. But the arbitrary boundaries that limited our full access to Harvard's offerings were also obscured by the richness of what *was* available to us. We studied with the greatest academic stars of the era, whose lectures and questions expanded our intellectual horizons as far as they would stretch. My senior thesis adviser in the Government Department, Carl Friedrich, periodically left my supervision to that amorous graduate student because he was off in Europe, writing new constitutions for several of the war-torn countries there. My graduate student instructor in Government 1 was Zbigniew Brzezinski, who later headed the National Security Council under President Carter; Henry Kissinger was a graduate student in the same department. Many of my generation of government majors at Harvard remember Brzezinski's impersonation of a Soviet commissar, with a brush of blond hair, piercing blue eyes, and a genuine accent (he was Polish, not Russian, although the distinction was lost on us). Most of his listeners were convinced that he was the real thing, only to discover later that he was, and remained, a fiercely anti-communist Cold War hawk.

The professor who had the greatest impact on me, fixing his laserlike gaze on the students as he outlined the roots of American democracy and why it is such a fragile plant, in need of constant nurture, was the political scientist Louis Hartz. He combined professorial rigor with a romantic streak. I will never forget wrestling on his final exam with an analysis of a couplet by e.e. cummings.

> While you and i have lips and voices which are
> for kissing and to sing with
> Who cares if some one-eyed son-of-a-bitch
> invents an instrument to measure Spring with

At the peak of a brilliant academic career, Hartz vanished. I learned from reading his obituary in the *New York Times* some thirty years later that he had spent the rest of his life wandering in Europe, homeless, alone, and mentally ill—evidence of the unsettling truth that creativity and madness can be closely linked.

Some of the most mind-stretching experiences I had in college, to my surprise, came in one or another of the three much-maligned Gen Ed (General Education) courses every student was required to take during the first two years. I chose Natural Sciences 1, widely dubbed "science for poets," as well as a quick trip through the history of philosophy and a survey course in intellectual history. In them I wrote papers on such varied subjects as "Science as an Agency of Social Change," "Religious Truth and Its Relevance for Mankind," and "Freedom and Security: The Problem of Planning in a Free Society." Such courses have often been criticized as encouraging dilettantes rather than serious scholars. But for me, at least, they succeeded in their goal—to expose me to some of the greatest thinkers and most difficult questions of all time—and thereby laid a foundation for the sort of critical thinking and analytical dissection of issues that have proved invaluable in every facet of my professional life.

In fact, along with many of my friends, I took what might be called a "smorgasbord" approach to the whole of undergraduate education, sampling tastes of whatever subjects interested us, without worrying about how it all hung together or whether it was preparing us for working lives, which, in any case, were expected to end with marriage. One area I left largely untouched, to my later regret, was math and science. And at least part of the reason was the burden of the expectations I carried as John von Neumann's daughter.

My progress through the first term of freshman calculus was uneventful; I did the work that was required without either huge effort or great enthusiasm. But just after the term ended, two things happened. First, I learned through the grapevine that the young teaching assistant, cowed by my name, had assumed that whenever I asked a question in class I was baiting him. He didn't realize that I was simply a conscientious Radcliffe student who wanted to make sure that I had understood everything.

Even worse, I ran into the chairman of the math department, a renowned mathematician named Garrett Birkhoff, who was both a coauthor with and a sometime adversary of my father in the world of higher mathematics. Making what he thought was pleasant conversation, he commented, "Well, Marina, I'm glad to see that you've upheld the family tradition by getting an A in calculus." I smiled and said nothing but thought, "Good Lord, what would happen to the family honor if I ever got an A–?" I vowed not to risk it, and that chance encounter ended my formal study of mathematics on the spot. Although I eventually worked my way through a book on mathematics for economists while giving my firstborn his late-night bottle, and informally audited a math course or two after beginning my own teaching career, I remain surely the most mathematically illiterate economist of my generation.

Even though my father may have, indirectly and unwittingly, truncated my education in this particular direction, he continued to contribute to it in others by the intellectual dialogues he carried on with me in his letters. In one he responded at length to a question in my previous letter to him about whether the indeterminacy at the heart of the quantum mechanics description of reality supported the idea that human beings do have free will, and that we must therefore take responsibility for the decisions we make. He had clearly thought long and hard about the question, and had changed his mind about the answer somewhere along the way.

I did work on causality, free will and quantum mechanics in 1927 and thereafter, up to about 1931. I belonged—and still belong—to the "extreme" denomination who think that quantum mechanics points the moral that the laws of nature are not strict, but in most cases only prescribe the probabilities for otherwise "free" events. At that time I also thought—which I don't think now—that human "free" will may be due to such causes. What I now think is that the quantum mechanical indeterminacy may affect some physiological matters, e.g., a lot in genetics and most in mutations, but not necessarily "free" will. I would be more inclined to think that the "freedom" of will, at any rate as experienced, is a subjective illusion, which means primarily that we are not conscious of the sources of our decisions . . . I think that W. James pointed out that the Great Unknown, that we feel so often so close to us, and to which we are inclined to attribute such esoteric significance, may be nothing more than our own subconscious. That would make it very physiological, non-wonderful and home made.

The letter concludes with typical self-deprecatory skepticism: "Such is life. Of course it may well be that it is not such. Much love, Daddy."[1] Along with my expensive Harvard education, I continued to receive a complementary one for free.

Once Bob Whitman and I had accidentally found each other, we got together nearly every day. That meant I had to make sharp choices about how I spent my time. Three major occupations vied for my dorm mates' waking hours: studying hard enough to get good grades, going out on frequent dates, and joining the endless games of bridge that went on day and night in the small kitchens on each floor of our dormitory. I figured I could successfully pursue only two of the three, so I foreswore bridge.

I managed to handle the two balls I had chosen to keep in the air pretty well. In a letter I wrote to Bob after the end of my first exam period, I enthused, "I got two A's and two A–'s, which all goes to prove that it is not study but inspiration (yours) which does the trick, and I shall make it a practice for the rest of my academic career to go out every night of exam period."[2] I did have some awkward stumbles, though. Right at the beginning of our freshman year, a friend and I met with the director of volunteers at Mt. Auburn Hospital to offer our services; I had been a candy striper, as junior volunteers were called, at Princeton Hospital and had thoroughly enjoyed it. But our schedules soon overwhelmed us, and we never returned to follow up. It was only after I had been dating Bob for a while that it dawned on me that the elegant, white-haired Mrs. Whitman to whom I had made an unfulfilled promise at Mt. Auburn was his mother.

As Bob and I got to know each other better, my conviction that I had been right in that first snap judgment about him grew firmer. He treated me as an intellectual equal—for once, I didn't have to try to downplay my bluestocking tendencies—and, at the same time, showed a sensitive appreciation for the gap in life experience created by the ten-year difference in our ages. I appreciated his positive reaction, promising to encourage and support me in whatever career I chose, when I voiced my own ambitions, which had put off more than one prospective swain in the past. And, unlike some of the other young men I met, he was in no way influenced by my father's fame, which was particularly notable in the Harvard environment. When he chanced to introduce me to a friend in the math department, the immediate response was "Not *the* von Neumann?" When I responded with a modest nod, Bob's silent reaction was "Who on earth is this von Neumann?" His puzzlement must have showed, because the friend quickly launched into a brief biography.

Bob cemented his romantic stature in my eyes with all kinds of gestures during that first year. To celebrate my eighteenth birthday, he single-handedly mounted a perfect dinner for ten, complete with roast beef and Yorkshire pudding; the only store-bought item was the cake. To this day, he is the chief cook when we entertain, although he leaves the baking to me.

After taking me to a production of *Der Rosenkavalier,* Bob presented me with a lovely silver pin in the shape of a rose. I admired its beauty but failed to recognize its significance as a proposal, despite the fact that, in the gloriously romantic poem that accompanied it, he referred to it as a symbol of "The multifoliate roses of our love," writing, "It's just to mark the passage of a year / Since I became your Rosenkavalier." A couple of years later, while we were planning our engagement party, I mockingly complained that he had never formally proposed to me. Appalled that I had missed the point of his gift, he insisted that I read the libretto of Richard Strauss's opera. How could I have been so dense?

Much more significant than dinners and jewelry was the powerful emotional support Bob gave me through a variety of crises, physical and emotional. When I totaled my car in a frightening accident on the over-crowded Merritt Parkway during an Easter Sunday return from Prince-ton to Cambridge, with five classmates along, it was Bob who insisted that I "get right back on the horse" by getting behind the wheel of his own car the next day. And when he realized how much my father's pres-sure on me to get stellar grades weighed on my self-confidence, he took it upon himself to write a letter to a formidable figure he had never met. In it, he urged my father to stop putting pressure on me to excel academi-cally, telling him that I was already putting quite enough pressure on myself. It was this unstinting offer of emotional support, from the very beginning of our relationship, that underpinned me every step of the way as an adult, enabling me to take the chances and make the decisions without which my career could never have taken the path that it did.

Despite my immediate conviction that Bob was the man I wanted to spend my life with, seventeen seemed a bit early to commit myself to an exclusive relationship. The shy, quiet Princeton student who escorted me at the white-tie-and-tails Debutante Assembly and New Year's Ball, an elegant if anachronistic New York ceremony I participated in mainly to please my mother, visited Cambridge at my invitation. But, in the course of that weekend, I managed to maneuver him back-to-back with Bob to assure myself that the sweater I had been endlessly knitting for this first steady boyfriend could be successfully transferred to my new love inter-est. In another brief relationship, I found myself helping a student at the Harvard Business School finish up his case analyses—always due on Sat-urday evening—in time for us to go out. The fact that I could participate successfully, if clandestinely, in one of the most dreaded assignments in an MBA program that women were not allowed to enter nourished my growing awareness that arbitrary barriers based on gender were ripe for breaking, and that I just might have what it took to do it.

Two of my three college summers were spent at my mother's new home, the Villa Francesca in the quaint village of Old Field on Long Island. It was a turn of the century mansion overlooking Long Island Sound, designed and built by William de Leftwich Dodge, an American impressionist painter and one of the artists who had decorated the inte-rior of the Library of Congress. Inside its dour gray stone exterior were a living room fireplace and mantel imported from France and one in the dining room brought over from Spain, with ersatz plaster columns painted to match, ornate ceilings painted by the artist-owner himself, and faithful replicas of Greek caryatids holding up the side balconies. The house nicely reflected my mother's flamboyant side; the real estate broker had shown it to my stepfather only after he mentioned that his wife was a "crazy Hungarian."

They were able to pick up the house at a fire-sale price, partly because it was so eccentric but also because the bank that had attempted to repossess it when the owners failed to make mortgage payments was desperate to unload it. Those owners, former circus performers, had bought the house with a fortune acquired by making and selling fake French perfume during World War II. Once the real thing became available again, their business collapsed. After selling off everything in the house that wasn't nailed down, including a little Italian statue that topped the mosaic fountain on the sun porch, they stubbornly resisted the bank's efforts to evict them by holding off any possible purchaser with a shotgun. Undaunted, my mother somehow penetrated the firearm barrier and made a deal: the besieged owners would vacate the house in return for cash equivalent to three months' rent on a New York apartment and a promise never to reveal their whereabouts to the many creditors who would surely come looking for them. With that, the derelict mansion was ours, and my mother wasted no time restoring it to its former elegance, although the fountain's statue was never replaced.

I spent a lot of time during these summers swimming, sailing, playing tennis, and partying, trying to ignore the fact that, in all of these activities, my brother's talents cast my own lack of them into sharp relief. By the time George reached adolescence, he was already a first-class sailor, horseback rider, dancer, and tennis player and, at the age of sixteen, manager of the major horse show that took place annually just down the hill from our house. I, on the other hand, was famously clumsy. My family never let me forget the time that Desmond put me in charge of tying our boat up as he docked it. I jumped nimbly ashore and tied the ship's line neatly to the metal cleat provided for the purpose, only to discover that I had neglected to tie the other end to the boat, which was drifting steadily away from the dock. And my "clumsy cow" view of myself was reinforced by my mother's shout from the top of the bleachers, "Get the lead out of your ass," when I missed a shot during a local tennis tournament. She meant to spur me on to do better, but she had a laserlike capacity to hone in on the gaps in my self-confidence and didn't seem to recognize how much such public humiliation hurt.

By the time of these humiliations, I had ceded the field to George in the athletic and social arenas, while regularly besting him in academic performance. It was only as adults, each with our own successful and rewarding career, that we became close friends and mutual supporters and could commiserate with each other on the way in which our parents—that is, our mother and my stepfather—had unwittingly made each of us feel inferior to the other. The sense of personal inadequacy that has dogged each of us throughout our lives, the feeling that we have failed to live up to their expectations, was surely implanted by the messages, spoken and unspoken, that pervaded our growing-up years.

A quite different humiliation was caused not by my mother's outspokenness but by her irresistible charm. As I came downstairs to greet Paul, the wealthy, debonair Frenchman I went out with a few times one summer, I surprised him trying to make out on the sofa with my still glamorous mother. She was resisting valiantly, but the scene was too much for me, and that was our last date. As a wedding present when I married Bob, Paul sent a set of very expensive French crystal sherry glasses. They're meant to wipe out his guilt, I explained to Bob.

I had a real job during those Long Island summers. I earned my first paycheck—forty dollars per week—working as a summer replacement at a weekly newspaper in Huntington called the *Long Islander,* whose major claim to fame was that it had been founded by Walt Whitman. Because my job was to fill in for whoever happened to be on vacation, I got a taste of every aspect of the newspaper business, from writing up wedding announcements to taking classified ads over the phone. Once or twice I was even allowed to write an editorial, which I did with my fingers crossed behind my back, since the editor-publisher's views were a lot more conservative than my own.

Mostly, though, I was a reporter, and it was in that capacity that I discovered my enthusiasm for journalism as a profession. The accounts I gave in my almost daily letters to Bob sounded a bit jaded: "I get to write up such fascinating items—weddings, silver weddings, golden weddings (my God, what a rut), Lion's Club elections, old men honored after 179 years with the Podunk Manure Co., etc. Also such fascinating meetings as that of the stockholders of the Hotel Huntington Corporation, which lasted 2 ½ hours and was all Greek to me. I wrote it up under the theory that no one else understood it either so it didn't matter if I mixed up par and market value." (Luckily, by the time I became an economist, presidential adviser, and corporate director I had learned the difference.) But in the next sentence I wrote, "In all seriousness, I'm having lots of fun."[3]

Somewhat later I wrote, "I also find myself police reporter, which is one helluva job. I know the inside of every police station for miles around, the life history, tastes and 'line' of every cop, and drew a rather caustic comment from the Judge yesterday when I fell asleep in the jury box [where reporters were allowed to sit during nonjury trials] in Justice Court yesterday."[4]

Beneath the mock insouciance of a would-be sophisticate, the enthusiasm of a young woman thoroughly enjoying her varied perspectives on the everyday world comes through. And I actually admitted to being impressed, not to say frightened, when I found myself peering down the barrel of a shotgun wielded by an angry landowner, who was not at all pleased by my effort to write an investigative story on his employment, and mistreatment, of the itinerant farmworkers who tended his cucumbers.

Bob visited as frequently as he could during those Old Field summers and fitted in easily with my family—Mother, Desmond, and George. That meant a lot to me, since the three of them had made subtle but merciless fun of earlier boyfriends who, in their view, did not measure up. Bob's visit to my father's home in Princeton was a different matter. Once we had settled into what promised to be a long-term relationship, we both felt that Bob should get acquainted with the other side of my family as well. It was a visit that he looked forward to with real apprehension, partly because of my father's renown and even more because he knew how much I yearned for paternal approval.

In preparation for the visit, Bob went to the Widener Library to look up some of my father's writings. Among the many impenetrable mathematical titles, one offered a ray of hope: *The Theory of Games and Economic Behavior.* Encouraged by the fact that he was pretty good at both bridge and poker, Bob started to read. With some effort, he told me later, he got all the way to page fifteen before a thicket of equations stopped him.

When we got to Princeton, my father must have sensed how tense Bob was and did his best to put him at ease. He offered to show Bob the computer he had built at the Institute for Advanced Study, and Bob, curious to see this revolutionary machine, agreed enthusiastically. Once they got to the building, however, my father pulled out a large ring of keys, muttering as he went through it, "Here's the key to my office at Los Alamos, and here's the one to our house in Budapest." He was unable to locate the proper key on that ring, however, and Bob never did get to see the construction of vacuum tubes that marked the dawn of the computer age. But my father was a gracious and amusing host throughout the weekend; Bob relaxed, and I sensed that the two had gotten along much better than I had feared.

While I was absorbed in my busy but sheltered college life, my father was caught up in a whirlwind at the center of which was Robert Oppenheimer. Oppenheimer, who, as head of the Manhattan Project, had successfully led his team to victory in the race against Germany to produce an atomic bomb, was enjoying the adulation of a grateful nation. In 1947, he had become both the director of the IAS and chairman of the General Advisory Committee (GAC) of the newly formed Atomic Energy Commission (AEC), "the group which, more than any other, made the government's decisions about atomic weapons."[5] But, in the process, he had made two mortal enemies: Edward Teller and Admiral Lewis Strauss. Both men were strong proponents of building a hydrogen bomb (also known as the H-bomb), which Oppenheimer was known to oppose. But both had personal reasons for wanting to bring him down as well. Teller felt that Oppenheimer had never given sufficient recognition to his, Teller's, role in Los Alamos's success, and Strauss had never forgotten that he had been made to look foolish by Oppenheimer in the course of a 1949 government hearing.

While the nation was glued to its television sets in 1954, watching the Army-McCarthy hearings that ended Senator Joseph McCarthy's anticommunist witch hunt, another drama was being played out behind closed doors. That was a hearing on whether Oppenheimer should be stripped of his security clearance, which was essential to his participation in any matters related to national security. In fact, Lewis Strauss had been working behind the scenes for some time to bring Oppenheimer down. Strauss, a retired navy admiral, wealthy businessman and banker, and confidant of President Eisenhower, who made him his White House adviser on atomic energy shortly after his own election, had quietly arranged Oppenheimer's ouster from the chairmanship of the GAC when his term was up in 1952. But the following year when Strauss, now chairman of the AEC, threatened to have him stripped of his security clearance, Oppenheimer refused to acquiesce without a fight. The result was a hearing before a three-person personnel security board, whose members were selected by Strauss himself.

Oppenheimer's vulnerability to allegations of disloyalty to his country stemmed primarily from his well-known association with members of the Communist Party and his own membership in a number of communist front organizations prior to World War II—indeed, these had very nearly prevented his appointment as head of the Manhattan Project, and the FBI had had him under surveillance ever since. His opposition to the H-bomb project was also raised against him, and he was forced by a bullying prosecutor to confess to a lie he had told in 1943 to protect a communist friend.

One after another, members of the scientific elite who had worked with Oppenheimer on the Manhattan Project attested to his unquestionable loyalty to his country, as evidenced by his untiring labors in its defense. Among them was my father, who pointed out how innocent of any knowledge of espionage and counterespionage they had all been at the beginning of the project. "We were little children," he said, "we had to make up . . . our code of conduct as we went along." He wasn't surprised at "how long it took Dr. Oppenheimer to get adjusted to this Buck Rogers universe, [but] . . . he learned how to handle it and handled it very well."[6]

Edward Teller, on the other hand, drove the final nail into Oppenheimer's professional coffin with his reply to a question from a member of the three-person board that served as the jury as to whether he thought the nation's security would be endangered if Oppenheimer were allowed to keep his clearance: "[I]f it is a question of wisdom and judgment, as demonstrated by actions since 1945, then I would say it would be wiser not to grant clearance."[7] In destroying Oppenheimer, Teller also damaged himself. He became a pariah to most members of the close-knit physics community, many of whom shunned him ever after, even to the point of refusing to shake his hand.

Drawing on his skills in interpersonal relationships, my father remained friends with both Teller and Oppenheimer and maintained a good relationship with Admiral Strauss. He had been unable to prevent Oppenheimer's expulsion from the world of decision making on national security matters in which he had played such a central role. He did succeed, though, in persuading Strauss, who was also chairman of the institute's Board of Trustees, not to oust Oppenheimer from the directorship there as well, thus salvaging a role for his devastated colleague, albeit a truncated one, in the world of physics that had been his universe since childhood. Oppenheimer proved himself worthy of my father's intervention on his behalf by building the IAS into one of the world's great centers of physics, as he had done twice before at other institutions—at the University of California, Berkeley, before the war and then at Los Alamos.

In the fall of 1954, hard on the heels of both the Army-McCarthy and the Oppenheimer hearings, my father was himself nominated for a seat on the AEC—later superseded by the Department of Energy—which had regulatory control over all activities involving the development and use of nuclear energy. It was a prestigious post, and one that required a spotless record of loyalty to the United States. My father's scientific prominence, his central role in the Los Alamos project, and his hard-line stance against Soviet communism won him Senate confirmation with flying colors. The congratulatory letter I wrote him was enthusiastic, but it also had a less straightforward subtext. Heavily influenced by my mother's desire to conceal our family's Jewish origins, over the years I had internalized her fear that the truth might somehow detract from my social acceptability. In my letter, I expressed concern that his sudden prominence in the public eye might "out" our ancestry.

His reply addressed both his attitude toward the nomination and my awkward, as well as naive, request that he keep up the pretense of what he called, with his flair for a good pun even when discussing serious matters, "pseudo gentility."

The job isn't mine yet, I have to be confirmed by the US Senate and in view of my doings in re: Oppenheimer this might yet lead to a bust, but I think that is less probable than 50%, although not at all impossible. The job is of course horribly tempting for an ambitious SOB like I am . . . It is interesting to come to close quarters with some of the most Buck Rogerian technical jobs, and with some of the weirdest things of the so-called "contemporary scene." I would be lying if I did not admit that it is—to put it mildly—very stimulating.

Now to the Aryan business . . . Dear, I love you even if you decide to pass as a Chinaman. I don't despise you for trying to appear mildly Episcopalian, for a man who tries to get along at the same time with R. Oppenheimer and L.L. Strauss, the foundations of quantum mechanics and the hydrogen bomb, I couldn't take exception to such a matter even if I wanted to. I do think that you are taking unnecessary chances for an inadequate return. You are a talented girl, and you could probably get along in this silly world without indulging in such marginal operations. However this is no mortal sin.[8]

I accepted his mild rebuke in the loving spirit in which it was offered, but it would be a good many years before I saw the wisdom of my father's words and abandoned any effort to conceal my ethnic origins, although I remain to this day a communicant of the Episcopal Church I grew up in. This is not because I share the Christian belief in the promise of life after death, although, as the end of my eighth decade draws inexorably closer, I sometimes regret not having this psychological bulwark against mortality. But the older I get, the more I am convinced that when I die my body will return to the elements and a shrinking number of my genes will be passed down from one generation of my offspring to the next, but that my individual consciousness, my "self," will be forever extinguished. Why, then, do I remain a participant in the traditional Episcopalian service? It is because I find the familiar liturgy of the *Book of Common Prayer* a helpful framework within which to "keep myself constantly mindful of *la condition humaine*," as I once wrote to my mother.

My father took a much more serious view, however, of my declared intention to marry Bob as soon as I graduated from college. In writing to me about his concerns, he bemoaned the fact that he hadn't told me his feelings when we were together.

I was quite melancholy afterwards, isn't it symbolic of how I always managed my affairs with you—lots of hemming and hawing, and an occasional emotional burst, always very, very late. Perhaps it is not too late each time, I am afraid it is too little.

Dear, I am very worried about your plans. I may be seeing ghosts, but I think I don't.

Don't misunderstand me. I like Bob, I could, if I saw more of him, like him a great deal more. Also, he is clearly able, for many good reasons, e.g., otherwise you would probably not pass the time of day with him, nor could he have landed the Princeton job [where he had just been appointed an instructor in English, beginning in the fall of 1955].

But . . .

Dear, do not misread your own character. You are very, very talented and then some. You absorb information like a sponge, you have sense and charm, you can handle the most highly desired task in the world: dealing with people, influencing people. You are God's own chosen executive, and I am not joking. You would also make a damn good journalist, and a few other things.

Besides, you like money. Whether you show it or not . . . you have expensive tastes. You are "genetically loaded" from both sides, both Mariette and I adore money . . . [so] it would be a pity, a misery to see you in petty, straightened circumstances, and worst of all, cut off from using your talents and acting your proper role in life.[9]

Then, fearing that he hadn't expressed his feelings sufficiently clearly, he wrote me less than a month later, repeating his previous concerns and spelling them out at greater length.

[T]his marriage will set you very straight and narrow financial limits for good and ever. Also, the accidents of academic promotion are not unlikely to land you in remote and otherwise unrewarding places, where you have no means to do anything, to be anything, but a "Hausfrau." And—all of this has such a desperate finality and ineluctability, right from the word go, right from the age of 21 on. Do you really believe that the mood in which you do this, at 21 or 22, will last at 30 at 40 at 50? It seems to me a desperate chance.

"Don't—for heaven's sake—imagine that we are so very different.

In spite of my curses about the human race, I have been as happy as I can constitutionally be, most of the time, with Mariette and with Klari. But I could have never existed—not with a female angel—without external success and some strong intellectual interest . . . I doubt that things with you are fundamentally different.[10]

I was deeply moved by the love and concern expressed in this letter. But, even as I recognized the truth of many of my father's observations about me, I remained firm in my belief that Bob was the person I wanted to spend my life with, and that I would somehow manage to avoid the limitations and frustrations the letter had described. Wanting to respond positively to my father's outpouring of emotion, I tried to reassure him by saying that a year's separation, while I finished my senior year in Cambridge and Bob spent his first year teaching at Princeton, would give us time to test our relationship.

For my father, happiness was found first and foremost in the world of the intellect; for my mother, its wellspring was social relationships. True to form, she was as delighted with my marriage plans as my father was horrified. Her fear had always been that, by "letting my brains show," competing with men in the intellectual sphere, I would reduce my chances of finding a mate, which in any case would become more difficult after the college years were over and there were fewer single males at hand. Whereas my father's mantra was "Don't marry until you have established your own professional persona," hers was "Marry early, even if it means marrying often." Her enthusiasm, tinged with relief, was enhanced by the fact that my chosen mate was a certified New England Yankee, whose *Mayflower* pedigree laid to rest her fears about my Jewish origins by guaranteeing my social acceptability and that of our future children.

Soon after my exchange of letters with my father, I went off to Europe for six weeks with four of my college classmates, including my old friend Margaret Rabi. We had a fine time on our mini–grand tour, visiting all the major tourist sites in England, France, and Italy that we could cram in, engaging in a variety of mild flirtations while fending off the more annoying amorous advances of French and Italian males, and discovering that if we ate enough croissants and drank enough café au lait at our "free" breakfast, we could make it until dinnertime, thus saving the price of lunch.

We even survived without mishap the ocean crossings over and back on a creaky Italian ship called, euphemistically, the *Castel Felice*. We didn't tell our parents until we were safely back home that we generally slept on deck in preference to the crowded, smelly dormitory to which we were assigned, or that a couple of the young ladies in other groups who did likewise became pregnant by members of the ship's crew.

Hoping, once again, to give my father pleasure, I picked up a couple of mementos to bring home to him. One was a statue of a rotund, smiling ivory Buddha, the symbol of wisdom, which bore a more than passing resemblance to its intended recipient. The other was a slim volume of pornographic limericks to add to his vast collection—*Count Palmyra's Book of Verses*—whose cover left no doubt about what was inside. By the time I delivered these gifts, neither one of us had much heart to laugh together over them.

I had just returned to my mother's house from our European jaunt when a call came from my stepmother, telling me that my father had just been operated on for a malignant tumor so large that it had led to a spontaneous fracture of his collarbone. On hearing the news, Desmond, whose career in health physics had made him wise to such matters, immediately told me to ask whether the tumor was primary or secondary. On hearing that it was secondary, he gently explained to me that the cancer had metastasized from some other site. In the days before chemotherapy, such a diagnosis was a certain death sentence.

My father knew only too well what he was facing, but he told the truth to as few people as possible and carried on with his busy life as before. When I visited him and Klari in Washington, he clearly preferred to avoid any discussion of what lay ahead. I went along with his unspoken desire to pretend that everything was normal, although I cried myself to sleep many nights after I returned to my final year of college. But at the same time, I asserted my growing independence in a particularly painful way, by truncating the "test year" I had promised him. The summer's brief separation had only strengthened my conviction that I wanted to be reunited with Bob as soon as possible; we made plans to announce our engagement at Christmas and marry in June, as soon as I graduated.

Confronting both his imminent mortality and the knowledge that I was determined to take the step he had so vehemently argued against, my father wrote me a letter that was both angry and anguished.

> I feel thoroughly shocked . . . A person of your intelligence and sensitivity cannot fail to know that you are breaking a gentleman's agreement. Your lightness in glancing over this does you very little credit . . .
>
> I am sorry, but I must mention one more thing. At the time of the rather depressing episode of your worries, that my nomination to the AEC might lead to a public disclosure of your jewish origin, I wrote you . . . that I would, if you wish, put up and cooperate as far as I can with your desire to "pass" as gentile. However, I also wrote you, that there is one exception to this. I would consider it as definitely unconscionable if you concealed—by commission or by omission—from your future husband the fact *that you are 100% jewish on both sides and no nonsense about it.*[11]

On this score, at least, he had no reason to worry. It had never occurred to me not to tell Bob everything I knew about my origins, and he regarded my ethnicity as just one interesting but not particularly important piece of the mosaic that made me the person I was.

After his long cri de coeur about what he regarded as both a personal betrayal and a seriously unwise decision on my part, my father drew a line in the middle of page 8 of his letter and launched into a long, detailed, scholarly discussion of the proposed topic for my senior thesis. I was planning to write on the political theories of an obscure seventeenth-century theologian called Bossuet, a proponent of the absolute divine right of kings. In his response to my query, my father wrote knowledgeably about that bishop's theory of history, monarchism, and anti-Protestantism and suggested that I compare his theory of the state to that of Calvin, quoting in French, from memory, the essence of the latter's views on the subject. Never once, in a letter that ranged from outraged anguish to an intellectual tour de force, did my father refer to his own dire situation.[12]

Despite the pain he felt at my unshakeable decision, my father acquiesced in our plans with the outward graciousness that was his hallmark. Although by the Christmas vacation of 1955 he was confined to a wheelchair, he traveled from Washington to New York, where we had arranged to hold our engagement party in a hotel rather than at my mother's home on Long Island, in order to make the logistics easier for him. He captivated the guests with his wit and charm, never referring to his condition or revealing his true feelings about the event.

Soon after the beginning of the New Year, my father entered Walter Reed Hospital, where he was to spend the remainder of his life. Given the gravity of his illness, both of my grandmothers urged me to postpone our wedding, feeling that such a celebration would be inappropriate while he lay dying. Although I respected my grandmothers' traditionalist views, I didn't see that waiting for him to die before going ahead with our plans would either give my father comfort or show him respect. And I certainly didn't intend to deceive him by pretending that I had followed his wishes by breaking the engagement.

Despite my firmness, or rather because of it, I was an emotional wreck during the last term of my senior year at Radcliffe, knowing that I had reneged on a promise to the father I had spent my whole life striving to please. What's more, I had done it when we both knew he was dying. I actually took my final exams in the college infirmary, having been felled by a variety of symptoms that, though real enough, were almost certainly emotional in origin. No one from my family was there to see me receive the prize for the highest-ranking academic record in my class at graduation; my mother was also ill at the time, my stepfather was recovering from major surgery, and my stepmother was looking after my father in Washington. But Bob and his mother provided my cheering section, and I did the same for him when he received his PhD from Harvard the following day.

Our wedding took place just ten days after these academic rites of passage. The Episcopalian service was held in the beautiful, whitewashed, eighteenth-century Caroline Church, which my mother and stepfather attended in Setauket, a few miles from their home. That, too, had its complications. During one of the premarital sessions with the rector that were required of all couples intending to be married in the Episcopal Church, Bob mentioned that he was a Unitarian. This threw the good clergyman into embarrassed confusion; apparently baptism in a Trinitarian sect—one that accepts the reality of Father, Son, and Holy Ghost—was a requirement for an Episcopalian church wedding.

Bob responded that if rebaptism was a requirement for us to be married in the church of my choice, he would go through with it, but he would regard it as a meaningless ritual. The rector was, naturally, appalled, and at our next session he reported triumphantly that he had obtained permission from the bishop to waive the rebaptism requirement. When Bob told this story to his mother several years later, she burst out laughing. It turned out that, although he had been raised a Unitarian, he had been baptized in the Congregational Church, which was acceptably Trinitarian, so the whole imbroglio had been totally unnecessary.

Every detail of our very traditional ceremony seemed perfect: I wore my mother's heirloom Brussels lace veil, attended by six bridesmaids in the excessively bouffant pastel (in my case pink) dresses that were the fashion of the day. And the mountain laurel was in full bloom at the reception, held on the patio and in the garden of my mother's home with its stunning view of Long Island Sound. But there was one painfully discordant note. Although my father couldn't be there, his mother, my beloved Granny Gitta, was. The guests were shocked, though, that as we were reciting our vows, she turned her back to the altar. She died of cancer herself a few months after the wedding, and those who saw it tried to attribute her peculiar behavior to the fact that she was already ill. But I believe she knew exactly what she was doing: exhibiting a silent protest at the joyous ceremony that was taking place as her oldest and favorite son was dying. Fortunately, my back was to her as I faced the altar, so I didn't learn of her silent protest until much later, when it could no longer mar the joy of the day.

After I changed into the matching blue and white dress, coat, and remarkably unbecoming hat that constituted my going-away outfit, Bob and I ran down the front steps of the Villa Francesca through a shower of rice. Our wedding trip consisted of a hurried one-day drive to Camp Chewonki in Maine, where Bob would be in charge of the junior division of the camp. Only the dead fish that my brother and Bob Ganz had thoughtfully wired to the car radiator as a going-away gift marked us as newlyweds. It was discovered when we stopped for gas and asked the attendant to track down the source of the odd smell coming from under the hood of the car.

Our summer as Mama and Papa Woodchuck to a bunch of eight- to ten-year-old boys took the place of a honeymoon, which would have to wait until we could afford it. But, in an odd way, that summer served as a kind of prolonged honeymoon, by providing an interlude that postponed the beginning of real married life together, with its attendant routines, roles, and responsibilities. It also gave us the leisure and privacy to explore together, for the first time, the delights of sexual intimacy.

The camp provided us with our own little cabin off in the woods and excused Bob from having to spend more than a few nights in a cabin with the campers. His duties were not onerous and left us with a good deal of time together, without any of the pressures of a career-oriented job. We ate all three meals every day in the camp dining room, consuming institutional food in a huge hall filled with more than a hundred shouting, jumping, food-tossing boys. But it postponed for a couple of months the need to test my nonexistent cooking skills. My housekeeping consisted mainly of sweeping out our tiny cabin with a broom, and about all the camp expected of me was to give the nurse an occasional hand in the infirmary and, once in a while, drive into town on an errand. I was also asked to give a weekly bath to some of the junior boys, but that job came to naught when the boys protested violently. Somehow they sensed that I wasn't a legitimate stand-in for their mothers.

All in all, I had plenty of time to write thank-you letters for wedding presents and think about what the future held. I was determined to make a success of my brand new marriage without the tensions I saw in those of both my parents, and Bob and I definitely wanted to have children. At the same time, I knew my father was right. Unlike most of my classmates and female contemporaries, I also wanted a career that would carry the opportunity for both high impact and high earnings. But I hadn't the slightest idea what that career would be or how to go about finding it.

· 5 ·

*Y*ou Can't Go Home Again

"I regret, Mrs. Whitman, that it is impossible for us to accept a student of your caliber into our graduate program, but we just don't have facilities to accommodate women students." With this apology for its lack of sufficient bathrooms for women, Princeton's president shot down my plan to begin graduate work in economics at the university where my father had begun his American career and my husband was now teaching. Frustrated and furious, I couldn't foresee that the world of the 1950s, reflected in President Dodds's response, would be swept away by seismic changes in the national culture before the next decade was over, opening up new opportunities for me. Even less could I imagine the public violence and serial assassinations that would mark these changes' bloody birth.

Arriving in Princeton after our honeymoon summer, Bob at last carried his bride over the threshold. As we kissed, I tried to hide my dismay at my first glimpse of our new home, a sharp contrast to the large, gracious one of my Princeton adolescence. I was standing in the visible, tangible evidence of our lowly status on the academic totem pole, a cramped apartment far on the other side of town, in a group of wooden military barracks (bachelor officers' quarters, Bob insisted, but the distinction was lost on me) hastily constructed on the university's polo fields during World War II. They had been built to last only as long as the war did. Instead of tearing them down, though, Princeton took them over and today, more than sixty-five years after the war's end, married graduate students and members of the university's maintenance staff still inhabit both the original buildings, shored up with aluminum siding, as well as look-alike new ones built to house the overflow.

The apartment's two miniscule bedrooms—one served as Bob's study—had no doors; we separated them from the living room with sackcloth curtains hung on wooden poles. The floors were cement, painted red, and the bathroom, which housed a grimy galvanized metal shower along with a sink and toilet, was cut off from the living room by a louvered door that let every sound through. The paper-thin walls that separated our unit from the one next door made us an unwilling audience for our neighbors' constant fights and the orders and admonitions they barked at their children. And, as we were trying to get to sleep, we could watch the smoke from their cigarettes curl over the top of the wall that separated our bedroom from theirs.

Most daunting of all was a large black kerosene heater, the only source of heat, which sat against a living-room wall. The previous occupants of our apartment had installed a gravity feed, bringing the kerosene in from outside; without it, we would have had to go outdoors every morning and carry in the day's supply in a bucket. This convenience feature very nearly caused my premature demise. On the first cool day, I flipped the switch on the heater to activate it. When nothing had happened after several hours, I called Bob at his office to complain and ask for advice. "Well," he asked, "did you light it with a match?" I'd never before encountered a furnace that required a match but said I'd go do it immediately. "Good Lord, no," he shouted. "Don't touch anything, and I'll come home right away." When he did, he bailed several cooking-pots full of kerosene out of the heater, enough to have burned the place down if I had tossed in a lighted match.

I didn't know whether to laugh or cry at the incongruity as I set out our elaborate wedding presents, heavy on sterling silver and leaded crystal, against this drab background. But I got a new perspective when my mother brought as guests a family of Hungarian refugees, including two teenagers. The four, led by their sixteen-year-old son, had risked their lives to walk across the Austro-Hungarian border in the midst of the 1956 revolution in Hungary and had wound up in a hastily established refugee camp at Camp Kilmer, New Jersey. Fresh from communist Hungary and several stopovers as refugees, the whole family couldn't stop exclaiming how wonderful it must be to start off married life in such a cozy apartment of our own. Seeing it through their eyes gave me a new appreciation of our surroundings.

Our summer as Mama and Papa Woodchuck had postponed a test of my abilities as a homemaker, but now that honeymoon was over. Things had gotten off to a bad start on our first morning together in Princeton, when I attempted to make coffee for my husband, even though I never drank it myself. He thought the result had a rather peculiar taste but attributed it to the exotic Hungarian brand of coffee my grandmother had given us at the end of our brief visit to Washington. Only as I was washing the dishes did I discover that every drop had been filtered through the cardboard packing that I had neglected to remove from our new coffeemaker.

Like many university towns, Princeton had more bright, well-educated young faculty wives than there were interesting jobs for them. In the usually brief interim between marriage and motherhood, these women were expected to occupy themselves with "little jobs," most of which were excruciatingly boring and made inadequate use of their intelligence and education. I considered myself fortunate to have been hired as an administrative assistant in the planning department of the Educational Testing Service (ETS), the producer of the College Boards and a variety of exams required for graduate school admission. But I soon chafed at the vague, ill-defined nature of my job and the fact that I was sent off to perform technical tasks, like time-motion studies, for which I had absolutely no expertise. I felt both that my talents were being underutilized and that I wasn't doing a very good job on the assignments I was given.

Most of my friends from high school had moved away by the time I returned to Princeton, and my father's friends belonged to a different generation, so our social life tended to center on the English Department faculty. A few of the other junior newcomers became good friends, but the Princeton English Department was not a very welcoming place to our small cohort. Many of the older members of the faculty had started teaching at Princeton when it was a traditional WASP institution that reflected its southern origins—most of the town's black residents were the descendants of slaves that undergraduates had brought to college with them before the Civil War. That ambience was reflected in the stir created when, the same year we arrived, the English Department hired Princeton's first black faculty member.

Some of the senior faculty members, with private sources of wealth, owned elegant homes, while others rented one of the large Tudor houses that had been built for Princeton faculty decades earlier. They were an ingrown, clubby group, without the cosmopolitan diversity that had characterized my father's intellectual circle. I was relieved to learn that the wives of senior faculty members had recently abandoned the tradition of a formal visit to newcomers, with white gloves and calling cards. Being condescended to by people who would have sold their souls to be invited to one of the von Neumann cocktail parties while I was growing up would have been bitter medicine.

By the time Bob and I arrived in Princeton, my father had already been in Walter Reed Hospital for several months. He and Klari had moved to Washington when he became a member of the AEC, and he continued to try to carry out his duties as his physical condition steadily worsened. Knowing that time was short, Admiral Strauss, the chairman of the AEC, saw to it that my father was awarded two of our nation's highest honors. He went in a wheelchair to the Oval Office, where President Eisenhower presented him with the Presidential Medal of Freedom. As the president was pinning the medal on him, my father commented, "I wish I could be around long enough to deserve this honor." "You will be with us for a long time," the president replied, glossing over the obvious, "we need you."[1] That same year, 1956, my father became the first recipient of the government's highest accolade in science and technology, the Enrico Fermi Presidential Award.

Despite his illness and the overly full schedule demanded by his AEC appointment and his membership on a number of military advisory committees, my father somehow managed to find time to start preparing his Silliman lectures, a prestigious series originally scheduled to be given at Yale in the spring of 1956. This project was particularly important to him because in it he extended the insights that had made the development of the modern computer possible into what was for him a totally new area, neurobiology. The lectures were to be a comparison between the logical processes of the human brain and those of the stored-program computer.

When he entered Walter Reed Hospital for the last time, in April of 1956, the notes for these lectures went with him, and when I visited him that same month he gave me bits and pieces of his ideas. I found these conversations an enormous relief, a positive note in his world, which was becoming increasingly dark. And they helped us avoid a discussion of personal matters, especially my approaching wedding, which gave him so much mental anguish and me such a deep feeling of guilt at being the cause of it. It is one thing for a daughter to defy a father who is in good health, quite another to defy one who is dying.

The Silliman lectures remained unfinished because, as Klari put it in her touching preface to the published version, eventually "even Johnny's exceptional mind could not overcome the weariness of the body."[2] But the unfinished manuscript set forth the reasons for his conclusion that the brain's method of operation is fundamentally different from that of the computer; that while the computer's "von Neumann architecture" means that it operates sequentially, one step at a time, the human brain is "massively parallel," that is, it performs an enormous number of operations simultaneously. Increasingly intensive explorations in neuroscience over the last fifty-plus years have shown this insight to be not only pioneering but prescient. One of my father's most overwhelming fears as he lay dying was that his work would not endure and he would be forgotten; the unfinished Silliman lectures are but the final addition to a body of work that has given the lie to his fears, though too late for consolation.

We had been in Princeton only a few months when, in February 1957, my father died. Many of his friends and colleagues had been amazed when, a few months before his death, he had expressed a desire to return to the Catholic Church, in which he had been baptized many years before, and asked for the assistance of a Catholic priest. He and Father Anselm Strittmatter, a Benedictine monk, spent many hours together while he could still communicate, and even after he fell silent. His brother, my uncle Nicholas, believed that his request arose primarily out of a desire to talk about the world of Greece and Rome with a fellow classics scholar, but I knew differently. My father had told me more than once that Catholicism was a difficult religion to live in but the best one to die in. Terrified of his own mortality, he found comfort in the promise of personal immortality in an afterlife. Although I didn't share that belief, I had never argued with him about it; I was grateful that he could find some comfort in the midst of his despair.

The funeral mass, held in the chapel of Walter Reed Hospital, was attended by a considerable array of the city's notables and scientific colleagues from around the country. In his homily, Father Anselm spoke eloquently of my father's inquietude of soul: "But as he came more and more to realize that the control over the physical forces of nature which he and his co-workers had placed in the hands of their fellow men could be used for evil as well as for good, that as the world is moving today this control might quite possibly be used for destruction rather than up-building, he felt with steadily increasing intensity the moral problems bound up with the greatest of scientific triumphs . . . It was not easy for one who had never known frustration, still less failure, to submit to the designs of an inscrutable Providence, to say 'Thy Will be done,' once he had come to realize that science could not check the progress of his disease."[3]

In contrast to the very public service in Washington, my father's burial next to his mother in the Princeton cemetery was a brief, quiet ceremony, attended by family and a small group of intimates, including both Robert Oppenheimer and Lewis Strauss, who delivered the grave-side eulogy. I was dry-eyed at both events. I had done my mourning months earlier, when the father I knew had already slipped away, leaving only a shrunken shell of a body to linger a little while longer. Although I had long known that it was coming, the finality of his death left me with a lingering sadness and sense of deep regret that my last conversations with my father had been marked not by the epiphany of mutual understanding that so often marks deathbed scenes in novels and plays but by tearful intransigence on my side and a profound sense of disappointment, tinged with betrayal, on his.

During the spring following my father's death, and perhaps accelerated by it, my dissatisfaction with the job at ETS, and with the unfamiliar and humiliating second-class citizenship in Princeton's intellectual circles it represented, crystallized into the recognition that if I wanted to prepare myself for the kind of challenging and rewarding career that was a rarity for married women in the 1950s I had better go to graduate school. During my brief time in the Planning Division, I had discovered that most of the more interesting problems that crossed my desk seemed to relate to economics. Combining that interest with the enthusiasm for journalism nurtured during my college summers at the *Long Islander,* I decided to pursue two master's degrees, one in economics and another in journalism. The combination, I fancied, would prepare me to write insightful articles on business and economic issues for the *New York Times* or some equally respected journal.

By the time these plans had crystallized in my mind my new boss at ETS, John Valentine, had been on the job only a week or two. I didn't know him very well, so it was with some embarrassment that I told him I was going to resign and become a graduate student. In a well-meaning if slightly condescending way, John tried to persuade me not to do anything so rash but rather to stay on at ETS and, if I was really serious about a long-term career, work my way up the ladder there. But I held firm; the emotional turmoil caused by my father's decline and death had only intensified my determination to equip myself for professional achievements that lived up to his, and my own, expectations, while at the same time fulfilling my commitment to a family life with my husband and our future children at its center.

As it happened, ETS's Planning Division was abolished shortly after my departure, so I don't think it would have made a very promising launching pad for the career I envisioned. Many years later, when I was a vice president of General Motors and a trustee of Princeton University, Polly Bunting, who had successfully led Radcliffe as its president through the tumultuous 1960s, asked me if I remembered John Valentine. When I replied "of course," she said John, who was by then president of the College Board in New York, had given her a brief, cryptic message for me. In its entirety, it was "tell Marina Whitman she was right."

The upshot of my decision was that a good friend, Burt Malkiel, and I applied simultaneously to the graduate program in economics at Princeton. The departmental faculty looked with favor on both our applications but pointed out that, in my case, there was a technical obstacle to overcome. I would have to persuade Harold Dodds, then in the final year of his thirty-five-year career as Princeton's president, to change the university's rule against the admission of women.

As I've described, my interview with President Dodds did not go well.

Two years after my vain attempt, Princeton, led by a new young president, Bob Goheen, accepted its first female graduate student. But by that time I was preparing to take my doctoral qualifying exams and start writing my dissertation at Columbia University.

My choice of Columbia was entirely pragmatic; I simply picked out the closest school on the Pennsylvania Railroad that was well known and had an excellent reputation. I was not only accepted but received a generous fellowship, despite the fact that when I walked into the office of Columbia's financial aid officer wearing the fashionable going-away dress from my wedding, along with white gloves, he told me that I looked much too well dressed to need financial assistance. When, as a faculty member, it came my turn to handle admissions and financial aid for the economics department at the University of Pittsburgh, I realized that I would never have admitted myself, let alone awarded a fellowship to a student whose entire preparation for the graduate program had been Harvard's Economics 1. But, fortunately for me, the requirements were more elastic when Columbia decided to take a chance on me.

Commuting daily by train from Princeton to New York, and then taking a long subway ride from Penn Station to the Columbia campus and back, made for very long days, and it wasn't easy to study on the jerky, overcrowded commuter trains. But Bob, who worked long hours himself both in intensive research and in crafting little jewels of lectures that met his perfectionist standards, did everything possible to make things more manageable for me, providing a strength of support that was virtually unheard of among husbands in the 1950s. And I had one of my closest friends from Miss Fine's School for company on the daily trek to New York and back.

Petite Daisy Harper, whose enormous blue eyes and fetchingly tousled curls had been attracting a male following ever since she was a little girl, had started at Radcliffe with me but dropped out at the beginning of her junior year to get married. By the time we moved to Princeton, she had had two children and a divorce in quick succession. She was muddling along as the single mother of two active toddlers, a very different life from the one she had anticipated when, as a talented teenaged violist, she had played string quartets with her family's next door neighbor, Albert Einstein. Determined to finish her college education, she had applied and been accepted to Barnard College, then the women's division of Columbia. We made the daily trek together and often studied together at home over endless cups of coffee.

I was entering uncharted waters when, despite my lack of undergraduate preparation, I signed up for a full load of graduate courses in economics, and I had to work harder than I ever had in college to catch up. The course I found both most challenging and interesting was the required one in microeconomics. It was taught by a brash, brilliant young professor named Gary Becker, whose pathbreaking work in applying formal economic analysis to such decisions as marriage and childbearing eventually won him a Nobel Prize.

Becker's innovative approach to teaching microeconomics gave me a whole new way of making sense of a wide range of questions. It was what I thought of as a mental filing cabinet that enabled me to take real-world questions apart for systematic analysis and then reassemble them into a coherent whole, an approach that has proved invaluable to me not only as a teacher and researcher but as a corporate executive and board member as well. At the end of the term, I was amazed to discover that only two students had received A grades: the sole undergraduate in the class and me. When I asked Becker how that could be, he replied, "That's simple. You two had the least to unlearn."

My one venture into a course given by the Columbia Business School, on corporate finance, was not such a happy experience, although it was a useful one. The instructor was both boring and unhelpful; when I asked a naive question, he told me I had no business taking his course without the prerequisites and, if I didn't withdraw, he was going to fail me. I replied boldly that I might be ignorant but I wasn't stupid, and I intended to stick it out. When Bob learned about the B+ I got as a final grade, he bought champagne. For the first time in my life, I had broken through the A barrier on the downside, a long-overdue lesson in humility.

Early in my second year at Columbia, Gary Becker called me into his office and asked me if I had considered going on for a PhD in economics. I answered no, that I intended to stop with a master's degree and then move on to a master's in journalism in preparation for the career I envisioned. He commented that he was prepared to offer me a doctoral fellowship if I should chose to go in that direction. The fellowship, underwritten by the conservative Earhart Foundation, carried no teaching duties; its only requirement was a good-faith declaration that I believed in the superiority of a market-oriented economic system.

I had always resisted being pigeonholed politically as either liberal or conservative, but my parents' views, the Cold War environment in which I grew up, and my own research on alternative systems during my high-school and college years had all engendered in me a deep suspicion of statist regimes. So the commitment required by an Earhart fellowship came quite naturally to me. And Becker's proposal intrigued me. I was thoroughly enjoying my study of economics, and I was beginning to think that writing about economic developments as a journalist might not be as satisfying as actually having some impact on those developments. So with little more reflection than a "sure, why not?" I accepted his suggestion and the offer that went with it. With that decision, I took a big step toward defining the direction my intellectual and professional life would take, rather than drifting in a sea of choices, as I had done with my dilettante's selection of undergraduate courses and then with the plan to get master's degrees in two different fields.

In the middle of my second year of doctoral study, I discovered that I was pregnant. We had really meant to wait until I was further along in my studies, but Bob and I were excited at the prospect of becoming parents. There was no way, though, that we wanted to introduce a third person, however small, into our crowded quarters—I had seen too many lines filled with damp diapers strung across the living rooms of other apartments like ours. Armed with money inherited from my father as a down payment, we went looking for our own house. We found one a few blocks away from where we were living. It was a Christmas-card white ranch, small but with a lovely, tree-filled backyard, on a quiet street. We bought the little house and lovingly painted each room a different color—the only do-it-yourself project we have ever successfully completed. Now we had a bathtub, a furnace properly located in the basement, and a nursery for the upcoming addition to our family.

I was uncomfortably aware of the disdain felt by a number of my professors for a married woman, "who would drop out as soon as she became pregnant," taking up a place "that might have gone to a man" in the PhD program. That knowledge, combined with my natural impatience to get on with it, made me determined to take the doctoral exam before my pregnancy started to show. This meant advancing to the end of my second year an ordeal that most students preferred to delay until the third, after they had completed all the necessary courses and had time for review. The exam, a two-hour oral inquisition on four different subjects, would determine whether or not I would be allowed to go on to write the dissertation required for a PhD. Horror stories abounded about students who, in the stress of the moment, couldn't remember the name of John Maynard Keynes. And the fact that I intended to take the exam early created even more pressure.

As I plunged into intense hours of cramming for the dreaded orals, no amount of coffee could keep me from falling asleep. Guessing that this had something to do with my pregnancy, I tried to make an appointment with a highly regarded obstetrician. He indicated that he had no interest in seeing me until I was a further six weeks along but, told of my difficulty, said he would phone a prescription in to my drugstore. I picked it up, took one pill from the unlabeled bottle every morning (in those days prescription bottles gave no hint as to their contents), and, miraculously, had no more trouble staying awake. Only much later did I find out that I had been popping amphetamines. Given what we have since learned about fetal vulnerability, hardly a day has gone by that I haven't given thanks that such an irresponsible act did no harm to our unborn son. And I've never again taken unidentified pills.

By the time my oral exam came, I could barely squeeze my expanding waistline into a regular suit—if I had sneezed, the crucial button would surely have popped. I was nervous enough anyway, confronting the serious miens of four of my professors across a seminar table. Most terrifying of all was Arthur Burns, the economic forecasting pundit whose mop of iron-gray hair, rasping drawl, and interminable pulls on a pipe between sentences had become familiar outside, as well as inside, the academic establishment. Eventually, he and I would meet again, as near equals, when he was chairman of the Federal Reserve Board and I was a member of the President's Council of Economic Advisers. But I never quite conquered my fear of him, nor got away from the feeling of being student and professor again, as we sat across from each other at monthly meetings in the Fed's elegant lunchroom.

I honestly don't remember how I managed to answer the variety of questions that were put to me during those endless two hours. I only remember the huge sense of relief I felt when I was called back into the room and congratulated on having passed. I had gambled and won my high-stakes bet.

Having passed that hurdle, the next one was to hone in on a subject for my dissertation and find an appropriate supervisor. My long-standing interests pointed to an international topic, and my teacher of international economics, Ragnar Nurkse, a wise and kind Estonian who had previously worked for the League of Nations, would have been my chosen supervisor. But that spring, while hiking in the mountains near Vévey in Switzerland, the fifty-two-year-old Nurkse had suddenly dropped dead of a heart attack. Fortunately for me, Albert Hirschman had just come from Yale to join the Columbia economics faculty. A specialist in international trade and economic development, he was already well known for his innovative ideas on political economy.

What made Hirschman a true original among academics, though, was his heroic past, concealed by his merry blue eyes, calm demeanor, and courtly manner. When war broke out in Europe, shortly after he had completed his PhD, the German-born Hirschman joined the underground in German-controlled Vichy France. There he worked with the American journalist Varian Fry, head of a rescue network that helped many Jewish artists and intellectuals escape the Nazis and the Holocaust. Surviving numerous narrow escapes, Hirschman made his way to the United States and joined the American army, before settling into a career as a financial adviser and then a professor. His underground code name was Beamish—which means "beaming with optimism, promise, or achievement"—a name that suited him very well indeed.

Hirschman readily took me on as an advisee, and we talked about how I might focus a dissertation in international political economy, reflecting my long-standing interest in both relationships among nations and the interactions between economics and politics. There was then a great deal of interest in the question of how government loans and guarantees could be used to attract private money into economic reconstruction and development projects abroad, with the goal of shifting more and more of such funding from the public purse to private investors. I had observed that, although proposals for new programs to implement the goals of public policy abounded, much less attention had been given to careful evaluation of how well the programs already in operation were working. So I decided to investigate how effective the existing loan and guarantee programs were at pump priming. When, several years later, a revised version of this study was published by Princeton University Press, I took it as a sign that I was beginning to be heard in the public discourse on policies affecting international relationships.

While I was doing this research, I received another badly needed lesson in humility. I could do a lot of my work at home, but one hot, late summer day, in an advanced stage of pregnancy, I went to New York to keep an appointment with Gary Becker, whom I still regarded as a mentor. I arrived at Penn Station from Princeton in the midst of a subway strike and had to battle a huge crowd, all trying to get taxis.

When I finally arrived at Becker's office, hot, disheveled, and out of breath, I found that he wasn't there. Filled with righteous indignation, I stomped into the office of the department secretary and unburdened myself of a long soliloquy on the irresponsibility of faculty members who didn't keep appointments with students, particularly in light of all I had gone through to get there. When I finally paused for breath, she asked quietly if I would like to know why Professor Becker hadn't showed up. "I certainly would," I replied. It turned out that his wife, who suffered from postpartum depression, had attempted suicide that morning. My self-righteousness evaporated in an agony of embarrassment.

A few weeks after this incident, our son Malcolm was born. My friends had been amused at the thought of bluestocking Marina becoming a mother, but like many first-time parents, I couldn't believe how enchanted I was by this newborn creature. Fortunately Bob, who had diapered more than one young cousin, could fill in for my total lack of experience where babies were concerned, and it didn't take me long to catch on. My brain, which seemed to have gone into hibernation toward the end of my pregnancy, stayed there for several months afterward, and Bob and I spent much of the time in the happy but sleep-deprived daze common to new parents. It was clear from the very beginning that Bob regarded himself as an equal partner in the parenting adventure, long before such an attitude was fashionable or even socially acceptable.

My husband and my parents were totally supportive of my intention to finish the PhD and then combine motherhood with an academic career. But in the world of the late 1950s my decision was more generally regarded with surprise and, often, disapproval. During my pregnancy, acquaintances and even strangers would respond with raised eyebrows when they learned, in the course of a cocktail party conversation, that I intended to lead a double life as both mother and scholar.

I could take these reactions in my stride, but my mother-in-law was a different matter. A strong and intelligent woman, herself a college graduate at a time when that was rare for a female, she was also an old-fashioned lady closer in age to my grandmother than my mother. Although I liked and admired her, I had always felt that she didn't entirely approve of me. When she learned of my plans, she was horrified. Convinced that I would ruin my health, make my husband miserable, and neglect my children, she told me I was being selfish to insist on going on with a career outside the home. I was upset at the effect that the tension between us was having on Bob, trapped between the views of the two strong-minded women he loved most. I was also terrified that there was a chance she might be right.

Without Bob's staunch support, I might have succumbed to the then-current view of the proper role for a married woman with a family. As it was, I cried a lot and demanded constant reassurance from my husband but stuck to my course. My first publication, my master's thesis revised into a monograph, came out at about the same time that our son was born. In response to my mother's long-ago warnings that I shouldn't let my brains show too much, I inscribed her copy "As evidence that blue stockings don't necessarily form a chastity belt." I thought I was being terribly clever, but as usual she had the last word: "I think you've married the only man in the world who would put up with you." The longer Bob and I have been married, the more convinced I am that she was right.

When I resumed my monthly trips to Columbia to discuss the latest chapter of my dissertation with Professor Hirschman, he commented that he hadn't received either a chapter or a visit from me in several months and asked why. When I told him that I had recently had a baby, he looked surprised. Although I had last seen him less than a month before Malcolm's arrival, he had never noticed. Inured as I was to the apprehensions with which other professors regarded the possibility of pregnancy in female students, Hirschman's cheerful insouciance and the genuine warmth with which he congratulated me made me want to hug him. At last someone seemed to recognize that a woman could exercise both her brain and her uterus at the same time.

During all the time that I was going to graduate school and embarking on motherhood, I was in a constant state of anxiety about my husband's career prospects. I nagged him constantly to write more and publish faster in order to enhance his chances for promotion in a department that put a heavy emphasis on scholarly output. But Bob, who preferred to let his ideas germinate at their own pace before committing them to paper, and who devoted as much care and time to the preparation of a lecture for his students as on research for his next journal article, felt that I was trying to impose on him priorities different from his own.

Having grown up in two households where emotions were quick to surface in shouts and arguments, it took me a while to realize that Bob's New England reserve was suppressing the tension and unhappiness created by my nagging. I, on the other hand, assumed that his lack of overt response meant that he didn't share my concerns, increasing my fears about the future. If he didn't get the promotion required for tenure, he would have to leave Princeton, and heaven knows where we would end up. Perhaps my father's fears about exile in some academic outpost, far from the world with which I was familiar and offering little or no professional opportunities for me, might come true.

As it turned out, Bob didn't get tenure at Princeton and had to start looking for a job somewhere else. Over the next few months, he received several job offers and decided to accept one at the University of Pittsburgh, whose ambitious new chancellor, backed by Mellon money, was determined to raise it from a largely commuter school to national status as a research university. My mother, who believed, along with the *New Yorker* magazine, that civilization stopped at the Hudson River, was appalled. She asked if I would come back to New York to buy my clothes. But I took comfort from the fact that we were going to a good-sized city with several universities, offering the possibility of interesting friends and decent opportunities for me.

One of the first things I discovered about my new hometown was that it didn't deserve its bad rap. Like almost everyone else, I had an image of Pittsburgh as the city where coal-fired steel mills and home furnaces belched smoke that produced actual "darkness at noon" on winter days. Stories about executives going through two white shirts a day and housewives washing their window curtains every week were legion. My own memory of Pittsburgh, where my father and I had spent a night on the homeward leg of our cross-country car trip in 1946, was of a darkened sky and black smoke belching from the "dark satanic mills" that ringed the city's downtown.

By 1960, though, Pittsburgh had undergone the first of several transformations: a drastic cleanup of its polluted atmosphere. What emerged from the murk was a very livable city that converged on a compact downtown located at a point where two rivers, the Allegheny and Monongahela, meet to form the Ohio. Approached from the west, the first view of the city as one emerged from the Fort Pitt tunnel onto the Fort Pitt bridge was—and is—positively stunning: a city bordered by rivers, with high hills on one side and a downtown of landmark corporate headquarters, which became increasingly elegant as the building boom progressed, on the other.

By the time moving day came, I had started to lock on the bright side: we were starting the next chapter of our lives in a new city, where no one knew me or my family. "Here's the first chance I've ever had to establish myself as my own person, on a blank slate rather than a template formed by other people's expectations," I told myself. It was an exhilarating thought. As for my own next steps toward a career, as I commented years later, "I had this kind of innocent, sublime self-confidence that something would turn up."[4]

We had been in town only a few weeks when unexpected good fortune walked into our lives in the form of Josephine Pierce. Josephine was a divorced African American single mother of two school-age daughters, girls who called her faithfully every day when they got home from school. It seemed perfectly natural to both of us that she should take on the washing, ironing, and housecleaning, on top of taking full charge of first one and later two small children while Bob and I were at work—a set of duties that would require two or three different people today. She stayed with us for twenty-three years, even moving with us to California,

Washington, and Princeton, once her daughters were grown. By the time she retired our own children were adults and, sadly, she was in some ways the only child left, having suffered a series of small strokes that neither she nor we were aware of. In the days before widespread day care, I could never have achieved my twin goals of career and motherhood without such loyal assistance.

While I was still in the midst of finishing my dissertation, I met Benjamin Chinitz, a senior faculty member in the economics department at the University of Pittsburgh. Ben was teaching a course in econometrics at the time and asked me if I would be his teaching assistant. Although my knowledge of econometrics could have gone through the proverbial eye of the needle and left room for the thread, I saw the offer as an interesting challenge, as well as a potential learning experience, and said yes. By dint of some late nights poring over the textbook, I managed to stay a chapter ahead of the students and apparently did a good enough job to persuade Ben to offer me a much more ambitious assignment.

Ben was not only a professor of economics; he was also codirector of an ambitious multiyear study of the economy of the six-county Pittsburgh region, which was beset by a steady decline in employment in the steel industry, the traditional core of its economy. Money for the project was running short, and the academic economists who had been brought together in Pittsburgh to do the research were scattering back to their home institutions before the final volume of the study, a forecast of the region's economic future, had been written. Desperate to finish the project within their rapidly shrinking budget, Ben and his codirector, Ed Hoover, took a chance on an unknown with a PhD completed only a few months previously (in 1962). They asked me if I would be willing to pull together the pieces of the forecast, the work of several different researchers, into a coherent volume.

Never one to just say no to a new challenge (my stepfather Desmond once said I needed "a chastity belt for the mouth"), I took on what all three of us thought would be a fairly simple job of assembling and editing the material. Actually, the task was more complicated; I had to do most of the writing and even fill in some of the gaps in the research. I was driven to the edge of despair several times, but the book, *Region with a Future,* was completed and published in 1963.[5] The two directors of the project were relieved and delighted that I had been able to pull it off. And I could say, only half jokingly, that I written one more book in the field of regional economics than I had read.

With that project completed, Ed Hoover and Ben Chinitz returned to full-time teaching at Pitt, and they took me along with them into my first academic job, as a part-time lecturer teaching the introductory course in international economics to evening students. Most of these people, all men and usually in midcareer, came to class after a full day's work, and it wasn't easy to hold their attention. The fact that I was female, and younger than any of them, made it all the harder to establish my classroom authority.

Just as the first class began, a tall, gray-haired man near the front said, "Excuse me, but are you the teacher?" My yes was followed by a pause. Then he blurted out, "Oh. You see, at U.S. Steel, we don't pay women to think." Covered with confusion, he tried unsuccessfully to backtrack. I'm sure he blamed his mediocre grade in the course on that revealing gaffe, but I hadn't taken it personally. He had simply stated a fact; an accurate reflection of the culture that prevailed, not only at U.S. Steel, but at other big industrial firms as well. And Pittsburgh, then one of the country's main manufacturing centers, had cleaned up its air but not its social structure, represented not only by its attitude toward women but by the fact that it was a town divided into bosses and workers; there wasn't a group of middle-class professionals large enough to buffer the city's "us against them" mentality. Up until that moment, I had studied and worked in academic environments. When the man from U.S. Steel blurted out his surprise, the extent of male domination in the "real world" hit me full force.

With a toddler at home and now another child on the way, I found part-time teaching was just the right amount of professional involvement. But on the first day of the fall term in 1963, the senior professor in my field dropped dead of a heart attack in the departmental office. Desperate to fill the holes in the teaching schedule, and without knowing that I was pregnant, Ben, the department chairman, asked me to change my status from part-time lecturer to full-time assistant professor and take on the two courses now without a teacher. With some misgivings, but with the "I can tackle anything" enthusiasm of youth, I agreed.

It turned out that hiring the spouse of a faculty member into a full-time position violated the university's strict nepotism rules, but by the time the bureaucrats in the personnel department noticed I was settled into my courses, and no one wanted to do battle with the economics department to dislodge me.

The course I was most excited about was one on the interactions between international trade and economic development that I developed and taught with a friend and colleague, Jerry Wells, who had spent several years in Nigeria doing field research for his PhD. Jerry and I both were committed to the idea that being open to economic relationships with other countries was a distinct plus for countries trying to mount the ladder of economic development. Ours was a contrarian view; the theory of development popular at the time called for government dominance of economic activity, high import barriers, and an economy as self-sufficient as possible. We were ahead of the curve, but the mainstream began to move gradually in our direction. And we pulled at least some of our students along with us, although we didn't find out how successful we'd been till decades later. One of the most radical and anticapitalist of those students, who later became a distinguished professor and department chairman at Bryn Mawr, teaching courses in business, as well as economics, wrote me that "the seminar the two of you taught changed my life."

While Bob and I were settling into our family and professional lives in Pittsburgh, all hell was breaking loose in the world around us. Two events in 1961 escalated the temperature of the Cold War with the Soviet Union: President Kennedy's failed invasion of Fidel Castro's Cuba through the Bay of Pigs; and the Soviets' construction of the Berlin Wall, which isolated the population in the eastern part of the city from their counterparts on the western side. The Cold War very nearly boiled over into a hot one the following year, when American ships blockaded Cuban ports in order to prevent the Russians from placing missiles with atomic warheads in that country, only sixty miles from US shores. I walked into Ed Hoover's office when we got the news, to ask him if he thought this meant the onset of atomic war. Ed, ever calm, was reassuring, but it was a couple of days before the nation was sure that the Soviets had backed down.

Worse was yet to come. I was sitting under a hair dryer on the Friday before Thanksgiving 1963, heavily pregnant with our second child, when word came that President Kennedy had been shot. As our disbelief was gradually replaced with horrified acceptance, my colleagues and I wandered around the department offices in a daze, trying to figure out how to respond to a national tragedy far beyond our experience. At home, Bob and I struggled to explain to four-year-old Malcolm what had happened. He found the permanence of death a hard concept to absorb and, at one point, shouted triumphantly, "Mommy, Daddy, he isn't dead; I just saw him on TV."

In the days that followed, Jack Ruby emerged from obscurity to shoot and kill John F. Kennedy's assassin, Lee Harvey Oswald, in full view of millions of Americans glued to their television sets. And, in La Jolla, California, my father's widow, my stepmother Klari, now remarried to a research physicist, fulfilled her father's legacy of suicide by walking into the Pacific Ocean to her death. Sadly, there could be no question as to her intentions. In ruling that her death was attributable to "suicide by drowning," the Coroner's Office of San Diego County noted that the skirt of her elegant black cocktail dress had been rolled up to hold "approximately 15 pounds of wet sand."[6]

Although her emotional demands had driven my father crazy throughout most of their marriage, Klari had turned into a dedicated caretaker, closely attuned to his needs, exhausting herself both physically and emotionally after he fell ill. I had hoped that in her marriage to the gentle, low-key Carl Eckart she would at last find the tranquility that had eluded her throughout her life. For a time, she thought she had. In one draft of her autobiography, she describes her life in California: "I have met and made friends with many new people, I also get to see many of my old pals, Carl works at his desk, I swim and loaf and, for the first time in my life, I have relaxed and stopped chasing rainbows."[7]

I will never know what happened to move Klari from satisfaction to suicide. Whatever it was, her death revived my guilt at having unwittingly contributed to her deep-seated insecurity, by rejecting her efforts to serve as a stand-in for my mother during my teenage years. By the time Thanksgiving arrived, the pileup of tragedies made the idea of a day commemorating our blessings seem like a cruel irony.

True to her academic heritage, Laura Whitman was born during

Christmas vacation, on January 3, 1964. Her timing allowed me to finish the teaching term, despite my mother-in-law's admonitions against exposing myself to "the young people" in such a delicate condition—then a common view among the older generation. From the start, Laura was a placid and cheerful baby; a good thing since, thanks to her brother's vulnerability to childhood illnesses, the circumstances surrounding her arrival were anything but.

Just before Christmas, Malcolm had come down with chicken pox. My obstetrician told me, first, that my eighty-five-year-old grandmother, who was visiting for the holidays, might contract the disease in the form of painful shingles and, second, that if I hadn't had chicken pox and did contract it, the baby might actually be born with it, which meant I certainly wouldn't be allowed to deliver at the maternity hospital. Fortunately, I did have the disease in childhood, and Laura was born in Magee-Women's Hospital without incident.

On the day that she and I came home from the hospital, though, Malcolm developed scarlet fever. He wasn't dangerously ill, but it meant that an infant who was fed every six hours had to be awakened to take a preventive dose of penicillin every four, rendering her parents even more sleepless than usual. Malcolm topped off the plague-house syndrome by coming down with German measles when his sister was less than a month old. It was a mild illness but dangerous to the fetuses of pregnant women, and no vaccine was yet available, so I thought it might not be a bad idea for Laura to get it over with early in life. My mother-in-law was horrified at the idea, and, despite my efforts to expose her, Laura remained robustly healthy.

When I returned to teaching from maternity leave, the economics department had a new chairman. Mark Perlman was an economist with an impressively broad knowledge of history, literature, and philosophy, in addition to his own field. He was also a deeply religious Conservative Jew, who viewed the world through a moralistic lens without the narrow-mindedness that is so often associated with the word. The formality of his dress and manner of speech was leavened by the brightly colored bow ties he habitually wore and by sudden, surprising bursts of humor.

Mark was a wise and generous professional mentor to me, the first person who took seriously my goal of climbing the academic ladder, and gave me practical advice on how to go about it. He asked me to spend a year as the department's associate chairman, handling all the applications for graduate admissions and financial aid, while he got his bearings in a new environment. In return, he promised to guide and encourage me through the steps required for promotion. He was as good as his word; within two years of his arrival I was promoted to associate professor and received the lifetime job security of tenure that went with it.

At a time when women were first entering this man's world, managing my relationships with male colleagues was not always so smooth. Over several years, I wrote a series of articles with a somewhat younger junior colleague. As coauthors, our skills were complementary: I was good at formulating ideas about how international monetary interactions worked, and he had the statistical skills needed to test how well these hypotheses fitted the facts. But after we'd been working together for a while, he started touching me "accidentally" and hinting that we should make our relationship more than professional. "Back off," I growled. When he didn't take the hint, I told him that he would have to behave or our collaboration would stop. Our joint articles, which appeared in several leading economics journals, were an important part of the publications portfolio he needed to be promoted to tenure, so my threat had the desired effect. But this was neither the first nor the last time, beginning with my evasive action to keep my senior thesis adviser at Radcliffe at bay, that I had to use my wits to keep relationships with male colleagues from straying off the reservation.

As I was climbing the academic ladder at the University of Pittsburgh, Bob was moving upward a couple of rungs ahead of me. Recruited as an assistant professor in 1960, by 1967 he had become both a full professor and chairman of the English department, having published a well-received book on dramatic literature the preceding year. During the four-plus years of his chairmanship, he rejuvenated that department, recruiting a number of talented young PhDs from leading universities, many of whom became widely recognized scholars during their careers at Pitt.

In the second half of the 1960s, three developments together transformed American culture: the civil rights movement, the emergence of feminism in the form of a definable women's movement, and the mass protests against the escalating Vietnam War. The coalescence of these three movements—which spurred a broader economic, social, and cultural radicalism in many professors and students—permanently altered the face of American college campuses and, ultimately, of the nation itself.

No one knows exactly how and when mass movements originate, but two events, both in 1963, were important markers. The Reverend Martin Luther King Jr articulated the goals of the civil rights movement in his unforgettable "I Have a Dream" speech, delivered to some two hundred thousand demonstrators in front of the Lincoln Memorial on August 28. At about the same time, Betty Friedan's book *The Feminine Mystique* struck a chord with many American women as she described the frustrations and limitations of the housewifely role that postwar American culture defined as a return to normalcy. This consciousness-raising, together with the increasing availability of the Pill, which enabled women to make individual decisions about birth control and the connection between sex and motherhood, created a powerful launching pad for the developments that, over the succeeding decades, vastly broadened women's choices in shaping their own lives. And I, who had started out without role models for encouragement, gradually acquired more company in knocking down gender barriers and had to spend less time defending the path I had chosen.

While the impact of the women's movement built gradually, in an evolutionary and nonviolent way, the civil rights movement spurred powerful responses. The positive response was the passage of the Voting Rights Act of 1965, the brightest spot in the legacy of President Lyndon Johnson. The negative responses were both numerous and horrifying. They included the murders of three civil rights workers in Mississippi during the "freedom summer" of 1964; the brutality with which local police responded to the peaceful marches for civil rights in Birmingham, Selma, and Montgomery, Alabama; and the Ku Klux Klan's assassination of one participant in the latter march, a white wife and mother from suburban Detroit named Viola Liuzzo, because she was riding in a car with a black man. And the mid-1960s were scarred by riots in the black ghettos of many large American cities that caused deaths, injuries, and widespread destruction of property. The worst one was in Detroit in 1967; after more than forty years, the city has still not recovered.

I blush now to admit that I never took part in the marches or other public protests that marked these tradition-shattering developments. Although I was a trailblazer for feminist goals in the conduct of my own life and career, I never tried to advance feminists' political aims, or those of the civil rights movement, through public declarations or actions. In later years, I came to regret this passivity, wishing that I had spoken out more forcefully against the wrongs these movements were committed to righting. I came to recognize that being the mother of two small children (Viola Liuzzo had five), preoccupied with work and family, was not an adequate excuse.

It was years before I fully acknowledged how much the political and cultural changes stimulated by the women's movement had spurred my own professional advancement. And throughout my life I have exerted pressures for reform by working inside established institutions rather than protesting against their failings from the outside. I genuinely believe that both kinds of behavior are essential for change, but I can't deny that my desire to be liked rather than reviled, included rather than excluded, shaped my own choices.

There was no escaping, though, the impact of the Vietnam War and the escalating protests it engendered. American troops were first sent as combatants to Vietnam in the summer of 1965, and by 1966 teach-ins, sit-ins, and more violent forms of protest were erupting on college campuses all over the country. In many cases, protests against the war melded with black students' grievances. On my own undergraduate campus, a black Harvard student named Franklin Raines called for revolution from the steps of Widener Library, and at Bob's alma mater, Cornell University, a black student named Tom Jones, leader of a group occupying Willard Straight Hall, was photographed on the building's steps, a rifle over his shoulder and a cartridge belt filled with bullets across his chest. No one could have foreseen that, in their middle years, both these men would become pillars of the establishment as top executives of major financial institutions, nor that Frank Raines would chair the Harvard Board of Overseers.

The storm of violence at our leading universities became minor ripples when they reached the University of Pittsburgh. Pitt students, many of them the first in their families to go to college, were more interested in joining the establishment than tearing it down. But there were noticeable reverberations in our university environment. I wasn't particularly shocked by the eruption of four-letter words in students' everyday conversation (my mother had been expert in the use of profanity, after all), but I was taken aback by the fact that they didn't seem to have any other vocabulary at all. There were also more serious pressures on the faculty. Male students had to maintain a certain grade-point average to avoid losing their student draft deferments, and more than one student informed me ominously that the C grade I had just given him could be signing his death warrant. Thus grade inflation was born, and, though I tried to resist it, I soon found myself giving more As and fewer Cs and Ds than ever before.

Several of my colleagues in the economics department, along with some of the graduate students, joined the Union of Radical Political Economists, better known as URPE. Their rebellion was cultural, as well as political, and faculty-student pot parties became regular events. My husband, God bless him, showed himself deserving of a medal for squareness; at one such party, he mentioned to me that it smelled as if dinner was burning. I explained to him that the sweetish odor came from burning marijuana.

At one point a group of URPE members, joined by like-thinking colleagues from other departments, went downtown to picket the Duquesne Club, the city's dining club for the all-white, all-male business leaders of the community and their families. The picketers were humiliatingly driven off by members of the service staff brandishing dishtowels and other household implements. But, to simplify security measures, the club decided to close permanently the side door through which visiting women had to enter. After it was all over, I teased my colleagues who had been involved, "The net result of your picketing has been to allow me through the front door of the Duquesne Club."

With the rapid-fire disasters of 1968, the ugliness of the turmoil in the world outside broke with full force into the relative calm of our own environment. Jerry Wells and I had just brought our seminar students back to my house on the evening of April 4 for an informal pizza party to celebrate the end of the winter term. His wife, Nancy, who had been setting out food and drink, met us at the door, looking even paler than usual, to tell us that Martin Luther King had just been fatally shot. Our celebration rapidly turned into a wake. Riots broke out all over again in a number of cities as their black residents reacted to the wanton murder of their leader in the struggle for full recognition as human beings and citizens. Barely two months later, Senator Robert Kennedy, President Kennedy's younger brother and his attorney general, was gunned down in a passageway of the Ambassador Hotel in Los Angeles, where he was campaigning for the Democratic nomination for the presidency.

Lyndon Johnson, reviled by some for his support of the civil rights movement and by others for the escalation of the Vietnam War, had announced in the spring of 1968 that he would not run again, putting the nomination of a Democratic presidential candidate up for grabs. At the party's August convention in Chicago, the public fury that had been building on both sides of the Vietnam War issue erupted into terror when police responded to antiwar demonstrations by using billy clubs, tear gas, and Mace on just about everyone in sight, resulting in numerous injuries but, fortunately, no deaths.[8] Even inside the convention hall, surrounded by barbed wire, journalists were roughed up by security forces. The battle for the nomination between the strongly antiwar Eugene McCarthy and the more moderate Hubert Humphrey was virtually submerged by the spectacle of a nation tearing itself apart.

Bob and I, like almost everyone we knew, viewed these events through the lens of our black-and-white TV set, the horror of the images in no way mitigated by their small size and fuzzy resolution. What was happening to our country, one of whose proudest hallmarks for more than a hundred years, since the end of the Civil War, had been its ability to effect orderly political transitions? I never dreamed that I would soon be observing antiwar protests not on a television screen but from the windows of a large stone building next door to the White House.

· 6 ·

$\mathcal{H}$e's Going to Drop a Bomb

The grim, gray, granite face of the Old Executive Office Building (EOB, later renamed the Eisenhower Executive Office Building) on the corner of 17th Street and Pennsylvania Avenue wasn't made any more welcoming by the stern gun-toting Secret Service guard who scrutinized my temporary access pass before letting me through the gate. Everything about the building's massive Victorian exterior, decorated with ornamental ironwork, exuded power and permanence. Built shortly after the Civil War to house the three cabinet departments focused on foreign affairs, the building now contained most of the Executive Office of the President, including my destination, the offices of the Council of Economic Advisers (CEA). The inside of the building was every bit as imposing as the outside, with nearly two miles of black-and-white-tiled corridors and eight monumental, curving granite staircases whose cantilevered construction made them appear to float. If one step were to break or be removed, the whole structure would collapse—a bit of knowledge that at first made my children afraid to use the stairs.

It was 1970, and I was inhaling this heady atmosphere on my first day as a senior staff economist with the CEA. I had actually visited the same offices a couple of years before, when President Johnson had invited a group of young economists to spend what had been billed as a day of informal, interactive meetings with members of his Executive Office, which included the CEA, but which had turned out to be a disappointing session of listening to these members describe their jobs and defend the president's economic policies. Now, though, I was going to settle into one of those offices for a year as an insider, albeit a very junior one, in the Executive Office of the President. That prospect was exciting enough; had I been told that this was only the first of several increasingly significant and visible jobs I would fill as a pioneering female policy maker, against a backdrop of mounting economic and political crises confronting the Nixon administration, I would have crossed my eyes in disbelief.

A few weeks earlier I had been invited by the CEA's chairman, professor Paul McCracken, to spend a year on his staff. One of the smallest government agencies, the CEA had been created after World War II to provide economic advice and analysis to the president. Whether under Democratic or Republican administrations, the economists at the council prided themselves on being defenders of economic logic and the long-run effects of policies against the more short-term views of government departments often dominated by political considerations or special interests. Because of this role, an apprenticeship at the CEA was an opportunity any rising young economist would jump at.

The nonpolitical nature of the job was a major selling point as I pondered McCracken's invitation. Although the chairman and the other two members of the CEA were always political appointees requiring Senate confirmation, these staff positions were deliberately nonpolitical. Senior staffers were generally young academic economists who had established scholarly reputations in their particular areas of specialization, as I had in international trade and finance. I saw myself as a moderate Republican in the mold of Dwight Eisenhower and Nelson Rockefeller, an economic conservative and social liberal on most issues. Above all, though, I prided myself on my political independence. I would have been put off if anyone had asked about my political views or affiliation as a prerequisite for the job, but no one did.

Even so, I had some qualms about joining the administration of Richard Nixon. In foreign policy, Nixon had long been known as an anticommunist hawk and had acquired a reputation as "tricky Dick" when he painted his opponent as a communist "fellow traveler" during his successful race for a Senate seat in California in 1950. Memories of Senator Joseph McCarthy's anticommunist witch hunt in the early 1950s, brought home to me by some of my father's mathematics colleagues as they sat in our living room recounting how they had been hounded out of their academic positions for refusing to sign the loyalty oath required of all public employees in California, were still vivid in my mind.

My worries on this score were offset, though, by Nixon's behavior during the first two years of his presidency. He had apparently become convinced early in his first term that there had to be some alternative to the horrors of mutually assured destruction (MAD) in our relations with the communist world. In line with this thinking, he signed the Nuclear Non-proliferation Treaty (NPT) in 1969 and, some months later, announced a US-Soviet accord on the scope of the first Strategic Arms Limitation Talks (SALT 1) and the end of the trade embargo against communist China, moves toward easing tensions that set the stage for his historic visits to both countries in 1972.

On the domestic front, the president had proposed dramatic policy innovations during his first two years in office, measures that coincided with my own views about good public policies. Two that he put forward in 1969, the Family Assistance Program, guaranteeing a minimum income to every American family, and revenue-sharing with the states, failed to pass the Congress but became templates for later, more successful efforts. Other measures he introduced became landmark pieces of legislation. These included the creation of the Environmental Protection Agency, the National Oceanic and Atmospheric Administration, and the Occupational Safety and Health Administration. These Nixon initiatives, followed in 1972 by the Equal Employment Opportunity Act and the Consumer Product Safety Commission, added up to a program so progressive that, as former senator Bob Dole observed in a 2007 television retrospective on the Nixon presidency, "I doubt that Nixon could be nominated today under the Republican Party. He'd be perceived as too liberal, too moderate."[1]

All in all, despite my earlier downbeat introduction to President Johnson's CEA and my initial concerns about the president whose White House staff I would be part of, I was tantalized by the chance to play a role, however modest, in the making of the nation's economic policies. But I worried that uprooting the family for a temporary assignment could threaten the delicate balance between work and family life that was never far from my thoughts.

As he had before, and would many times again, Bob reassured me that together we could figure out how to make the move work for all four of us. Each of us requested and received a year's sabbatical leave from the university, which Bob planned to spend doing research in the Library of Congress for a book on George Bernard Shaw. We rented a pleasant house in Montgomery County, Maryland, noted for the excellence of the public schools our kids would be attending. I knew I would be working long hours, but the flexibility of Bob's schedule, together with the fact that our housekeeper, Josephine Pierce, had volunteered to come with us, persuaded me that my more demanding responsibilities wouldn't disrupt Malcolm's and Laura's lives too much.

By September 1970, when I started my stint at the CEA, Richard Nixon was halfway through his first presidential term. By this time, the dark side of his personality—his secretiveness, his paranoia, his focus on political "enemies," and his willingness to use a variety of methods, both legal and illegal, both petty and terrifying, to harass them—had taken deep root, although the public did not learn about most of its manifestations until much later. He ordered the secret bombing of Cambodia in 1969 and, despite his announcement of US troop reductions and the "Vietnamization" of the war (neither of which came to pass) that same year, followed up with ground attacks on the enemy sanctuaries in Cambodia that bombing had failed to eradicate.

As the war escalated, so did the protests against it. There were mass demonstrations and arrests in Washington; at one point, National Guard troops were billeted on the marble floors of the Old EOB. Their presence, unavoidable evidence of the war that was going on beneath our windows, made all of us eggheads who were trying not to think too much about it acutely uncomfortable, and not only because, without access to showers, the soldiers smelled. In my enthusiasm for my new job and the exciting policy world I now felt a part of, though, I focused much more on the goals and accomplishments of the administration in both the foreign and the domestic policy arenas than I did on the big dark blot: the escalation of the Vietnam War.

One of the reasons that we young economists serving as the CEA's senior staff were largely unruffled by the mounting tensions between the White House and the world outside was the personalities of the men we were working for, the three politically appointed council members. The chairman, Paul McCracken, was a longtime professor at the University of Michigan Business School, a highly regarded macroeconomist who had himself once served on the council's senior staff. A wisp of a man who looked as if he would blow away in a high wind, McCracken had the courage of a lion. Not only was he totally candid in the economic advice he gave the president, even when he knew it was unwelcome, but he was also fiercely protective of the staff economists who worked at the CEA. Unlike the members, we were not political appointees, and McCracken took the position that, as long as we broke no laws, our political views should be irrelevant in judging our job performance.

In at least one instance, his willingness to act on this principle was severely tested. Paul Courant, a junior staffer fresh from his PhD studies at Princeton, was playing a game of chicken with the Old EOB's security guards, the Secret Service. Every night the guards would tear the antiwar posters from the walls of Paul's office, and every morning Paul would put them up again. After this had gone on for a while, one of the president's minions ordered McCracken to summarily fire the miscreant. McCracken refused, and Paul Courant completed the term of his staff appointment. He eventually became a chaired professor, and for a time provost, at the University of Michigan and thus a colleague of Paul Mc-Cracken, whose courage in defending him the younger man never forgot.

Herbert Stein, a macroeconomist who had spent his entire career at a Washington, DC, think tank rather than a university, was the council member primarily responsible for macroeconomic issues. I soon longed to emulate his graceful writing style and the dry wit that contrasted sharply with his ponderous body, owlish expression, and drawling speech. McCracken was in many ways a father figure during my stint as a council staffer; Herb was more like a wise, lovable uncle.

The member in charge of international economic issues, and thus my immediate boss, was Hendrik Houthakker. A short, compact Dutch-man with rapidly disappearing blond hair and clipped Dutch-accented speech, Henk looked and sounded every inch the Harvard professor that he was. He was the most ideologically rigid of the three members, firmly committed to the virtues of free markets and liberalized trade and unwilling to compromise for the sake of achieving consensus among different government agencies.

The atmosphere of the council was collegial; hierarchy had little impact on the lively economic conversations that went on more or less continuously. But the pace was much faster than I was used to; the time horizon of assignments was days or even hours rather than weeks or months, and the pressure undermined my self-confidence. One of my duties was to write a "Report to the President on International Finance," for McCracken's signature, late every Friday afternoon. It was nothing more than a few factual paragraphs on what had transpired in the US balance of payments and foreign exchange markets during the week, but in my early days on the job I was unnerved by having only an hour or less in which to meet a very tight deadline.

At the end of my second or third week, feeling not only insecure but beset by conflicting loyalties because this task would keep me from getting to the rehearsal dinner before my brother's wedding in St. Louis, I burst into McCracken's office on the verge of tears and confessed that I wasn't sure I was up to the job. I missed the dinner, but McCracken's calm reassurance about my competence quickly restored my equanimity, setting up a mentoring relationship that proved critical in every one of my subsequent career moves. Like my real father, he made clear his expectations of me and his belief that I had the ability to succeed. But his expectations, which, unlike my father's, reinforced rather than threatened my own life plan, were all the more influential because they did not have to do battle with my rebellion. Now in his nineties, McCracken until recently came to his University of Michigan office several days each week, and I cannot see him without being reminded of the impact he has had on the course my life has taken.

My training as an economist was key to my work on the CEA staff. But what I had learned outside the classroom while I was growing up was just as important. My parents' backgrounds and the conversations around my father's dinner table had taught me how lives could be disrupted when countries' behavior toward each other turned hostile, and I had tried to promote peaceful relations, however naively, by joining the World Federalists during high school.

I brought both kinds of learning to bear on the two big issues that commanded most of my attention at the CEA. One was the buildup of congressional pressure for increased import protection, particularly against textiles from Japan, whose growing success was making textile manufacturers in the South feel increasing competitive heat. The administration, meanwhile, was trying to move forward on liberalizing trade while expanding a program of adjustment assistance for American workers and businesses adversely affected. True to my cosmopolitan upbringing, I entered the fray enthusiastically on the side of freer trade and more generous adjustment assistance and against restrictions on imports, and I shared the mood of triumph when protectionist legislation failed to pass.

The administration was also confronted with growing problems with the so-called Bretton Woods Agreement on exchange rates, that is, the value of one country's currency in terms of another's. Hammered out during negotiations led by the British and Americans during the waning days of World War II, this arrangement provided that other nations would, with rare exceptions, maintain a fixed relationship between their own currencies and the US dollar, while the United States agreed to convert dollars held by foreign governments into gold, when asked, at the fixed price of thirty-five dollars per ounce.

This system worked extremely well for a while; other countries' war-devastated economies recovered, and international trade and investment, gradually freed from the constraints of the Great Depression and World War II, expanded rapidly. But by the beginning of the 1960s, the system was coming under increasing strain, made inevitable by an inconsistency at the heart of the Bretton Woods system—a situation that troubled me, partly because I shared my father's passion for order in relationships among people and nations, as well as in the realm of ideas, and partly because it was causing tensions with European countries and Japan, our most important Cold War allies.

The problem was that as foreign holdings of dollars, created by a persistent and growing deficit in our balance of payments, became ever larger compared to our supply of gold, the US promise to redeem dollars for gold on demand grew less and less credible. As these concerns escalated during the 1960s, the United States imposed a variety of restrictions on outflows of capital to hold down our payments deficit. These measures, inherited from previous administrations, went against the free-market predilections of President Nixon, who had promised during his campaign to abolish them. But, with concerns about the US balance of payments deficit mounting, 1970 was clearly a poor time to try to make good on that promise. I understood the political constraints, but the economist in me found the situation very frustrating, and I was eager to be involved in finding a way out of it.

The opportunity came when I was invited to participate in a working group, chaired by Treasury Undersecretary Paul Volcker, that had a mandate from the president to make recommendations on US international monetary policy.[2] The Volcker Group's discussions were focused on figuring out how to persuade other countries to implement two recommendations designed to alleviate the fundamental inconsistency that was threatening to destroy the Bretton Woods system. One was to make changes in exchange rates less difficult, smaller, and more frequent and, therefore, the whole process less disruptive. The second was to create a new type of "global money," issued by the International Monetary Fund, which would enable countries to acquire increased reserves without relying on continuing US payments deficits. At the time, the United States won on the second proposal and lost on the first, but the changes came too little and too late to keep the Bretton Woods system from being blown apart a few months later.

Writing briefing memos and taking part in interagency discussions of these issues gave me an exhilarating sense that the lectures I had given in my international economics courses back at Pitt had leaped off the pages of my notes and come to life. The pieces I wrote for CEA members were penned in an informal, even breezy style that attested to the easy relationship I felt with my immediate superiors. In one memo to McCracken, describing the perverse effect on capital markets of various US moves to shore up our balance of payments, I concluded that maybe the opposite of benign neglect is indeed malignant concern![3]

Much more formal were my drafts of shorter communications to the president or cabinet members, or written responses to questions posed by legislators in the course of various committee hearings. I soon discovered that McCracken or Houthakker were wont to send these memos forward, over their own signatures, more or less unchanged. Their demonstrated faith in me bolstered my self-confidence while at the same time deepening my sense of responsibility for the words I wrote. Writing memos to the president of the United States, even if they bore someone else's signature, gave me a heady sense that I really did have my finger on the pulse of world affairs. By Thanksgiving I, along with my senior staff colleagues, was spending ten or twelve hours a day drafting chapters of the *Economic Report of the President,* published annually at the end of January. Our efforts were so intense because this document reflected both why the CEA existed and what it had been doing during the preceding year. Because every word of the text had to pass the scrutiny of each government department or agency involved, it clarified and codified the administration's positions on issues that might otherwise have remained ambiguous. It also explained and defended the administration's views and actions on both domestic and international economic issues, first of all to the Congress but also to the interested public, or at least to the members of the press who digested and interpreted the material.

Although I came home every night exhausted, meeting the challenges posed by the report's purposes kept my adrenalin flowing. In drafting the chapter "The United States in the World Economy," I drew on all the skills I had honed, while teaching wide-eyed freshmen and tired businessmen, of making complex issues clear to nonexpert audiences. And I enjoyed figuring out how to express the CEA's often controversial views in terms that would pass muster with the many different members of the executive branch, representing widely varied constituencies, who would have to sign off on the report before it was printed. Both my parents were gifted—in their professional if not their personal lives—at bridging opposing viewpoints. I had watched and learned and was delighted to have an opportunity to play this game of skill myself.

I deeply appreciated my superiors' faith in my judgment, but sometimes the results left me red faced with embarrassment. The worst such moment came after Henk Houthakker asked for my comments on a comprehensive review of the US position in the global economy. It had been put together by Peter G. Peterson, a hugely successful businessman who had just been appointed as the first executive director of the Council on International Economic Policy, created by the president "to assure coordination at the highest level of all aspects of our foreign economic policy and to provide consistency with domestic economic policy and basic foreign policy objectives."[4]

Expecting that my observations would be seen only by Houthakker, I filled the margins with typically academic caustic notations, such as "nonsense" or "this guy is really paranoid." Instead, he passed my unvarnished comments directly to Peterson, and I soon received a phone call in which a booming voice at the other end said, "Well, young lady, why don't you come down to my office and tell me what's wrong with my report?" Far from reprimanding me, he asked questions, listened patiently while I explained my concerns, and incorporated a number of them into the final version of the "Peterson Report," which became a pathbreaking document. Widely circulated within the administration, it both explained and dramatized our weakening trade and competitive position, forcing policy makers to recognize for the first time that the global economic dominance the United States had enjoyed in the aftermath of World War II had begun to erode and that Japan was fast becoming an industrial power and economic competitor.[5]

Peterson moved on to become secretary of commerce, but his relationship with the president quickly soured and he left the administration, a departure immortalized by his remark that his loyalty had been questioned because "my calves are so fat that I couldn't click my heels." From our mortifying first encounter, a friendship was born between Peterson and me that has lasted through the decades, as he has gone from triumph to triumph in the business and financial world. He has also become one of our most prescient and influential public intellectuals, persistent in warning the nation about the dangers created by our skyrocketing government deficits, a crusade he has institutionalized by establishing the Peterson Foundation with a billion dollars from the fortune he had reaped in the world of finance.

Despite the intensive efforts to avert it, the US balance of payments position worsened throughout the spring of 1971, as our payments deficit rose, other countries continued to accumulate dollars, and our gold losses increased. In response, Undersecretary Volcker prepared and passed on to Treasury Secretary John Connally a supersecret memorandum suggesting that "we should take the initiative and close off our gold sales as a prelude to a large exchange rate realignment and necessary reforms in the [international monetary] system. Moreover, those decisions should be combined with a price freeze and complementary fiscal and monetary policies at home to restrain inflation."[6] Secretary John Connally took these suggestions as his own, and, after several discussions with the president and George Shultz, director of the Office of Management and Budget, a supersecret meeting was held at the president's Camp David retreat over the weekend of August 13–15 to finalize these plans and put them into effect.

Although I was well aware of the deepening balance of payments crisis and the increasing disorder in foreign exchange markets, I knew nothing of these policy initiatives as my year at the CEA drew to a close. I finished my usual end-of-week memo from McCracken to the president on Friday, August 13, a date fraught with ominous symbolism I was much too busy to notice. On Sunday morning, as we were in the throes of organizing our return to Pittsburgh, I received a call from McCracken's special assistant, Sidney Jones. "Be sure and listen to the president's speech tonight," he said. "He's really going to drop a bomb." My seven-year-old daughter grew wide-eyed as I recounted this conversation to the family. "He's going to drop a bomb? Here?" she quavered, as she scuttled under the kitchen table.

The president's announcement of August 15 didn't kill anyone, but its impact was explosive. The New Economic Policy he laid out that night included an immediate suspension of gold payments, which effectively caused the value of the dollar to float, as well as a temporary 10 percent surcharge on imports and a 10 percent reduction in foreign aid. Measures on the domestic side included a ninety-day price freeze, to be followed by a Phase 2 wage-price control program to restrain inflation and maintain our credibility with foreign holders of dollars, along with various tax-cutting measures to stimulate output and employment.

Why did the situation justify such drastic policy moves on the domestic, as well as the international, front? Inflation was running at a rate of about 5 percent annually in 1969–71, higher than it had been since the early 1950s, and the depreciation of the dollar needed to improve our payments imbalance was sure to increase the upward push on prices. At the same time, the unemployment rate had risen to almost 6 percent. Together these developments had produced a "misery index" (the combined value of the inflation and unemployment rates) of about 10 percent, and the president was eager to see it come down before the 1972 election. But the measures aimed at stimulating output and employment would exert a further upward push on inflation. The political imperative to make progress on both parts of the misery index at once led the president, against the advice of his senior economists, to put his stamp of approval on Connally's proposal for wage-price controls, a system that, backed up by rationing of many essential household items, had worked reasonably successfully during World War II.

I knew instantly that these measures would have resounding effects on both the national and the global economies, as well as on our political relations with other countries. A day or two before I left the CEA at the end of August, I wrote a long, detailed memo to McCracken laying out some of the implications of them and various alternatives regarding the future of the international monetary system.

"Now that the future shape of the international monetary system has been opened up far wider than before by the President's actions of August 15," I wrote, "the United States faces two sets of fundamental questions: the short-range ones focused on how (as well as when) to terminate the present state of suspended animation, and the long-range ones involved in defining the characteristics of the new world monetary order we would like to see take shape and, secondarily, in figuring out what course of action will maximize the probabilities of achieving it."[7]

As I ruminated on these cosmic issues, I had no inkling that the drastic measures announced by the president on August 15 would have an equally dramatic impact on my own life and the lives of my family, as I found myself thrust into the forefront of efforts to answer the questions my memo had posed.

My speedy return from a brief stint of academic life back in Pittsburgh to the heady world of Washington policy making began with a press conference where, for the first time in my life, I was at center stage rather than in the audience. I blinked nervously in front of blinding spotlights, the only woman among the seven people that Donald Rumsfeld, the young and aggressive former congressman from Illinois who had been appointed executive director of the Cost of Living Council—the umbrella organization the president and Secretary Connally had placed at the apex of the pyramidal structure created to succeed the wage-price freeze—had just introduced as members of the nation's Price Commission. My male colleagues, all strangers to me, were two business school deans, a prominent African American lawyer, the retired heads of a leading business-information company and one of the Big Six accounting firms, and a former governor of Pennsylvania.

We were hardly a cross section of America, but a group whose collective wisdom and experience would, hopefully, command public respect and support. In his own retrospective book on the Price Commission, its chairman, Jack Grayson, gave a short, pithy description of each commissioner. Here, in its entirety, is his view of me: "Searcher for levers. Newspaper devourer. Economic Portia. Full employment of mind."[8] I took this summary as a compliment.

A few weeks before Don Rumsfeld's public introduction of the Price Commission, as Bob and I were returning to our classes and our children to their old schools and friends, the wage-price freeze was proving enormously popular with the American public, and political pundits hailed it as the opening shot in the 1972 presidential campaign. Strict adherence to the freeze was regarded as every citizen's patriotic duty; accounts of violators being brought to heel and forced to rescind illegal increases by means of the reports of irate fellow citizens provided grist for the media mill. New York City was forced to readjust its parking meters to pre-August 15 prices after it tried to reduce the parking time a dime would buy from two hours to one, and an inmate at the Stateville Penitentiary in Joliet, Illinois, filed suit in federal district court asking that the relevant authorities be held liable for the $125,000 "that prisoners . . . paid in unlawfully inflated prices" during the freeze.[9]

Despite the popularity of the freeze, those in charge of administering it knew that it could not be extended beyond the original ninety days without causing severe distortions and disruptions in an economy as complex and dynamic as ours. The public was acutely aware of the scheduled expiration date of November 13, and concern about what was to follow mounted as the weeks went by. Finally, in a speech on October

7, the president outlined the Phase 2 program he had mentioned but left undefined in his blockbuster announcement on August 15.

The two bodies charged with implementing the controls were a Price Commission, which "will develop yardsticks and will be empowered to restrain price and rent increases to the necessary minimum and to prevent windfall profits," and a Pay Board "to stop inflationary wage and salary increases—the kind of increases that do not really benefit the workingman."

The president stressed that these boards would have small staffs, unlike the huge Office of Price Administration during World War II. "Stabilization must be made to work," he said, "not by an army of bureaucrats, but by an army of patriotic citizens in every walk of life."[10] This tension between the desire to avoid government micromanagement of the economy and the political imperative of meeting the announced goal of getting inflation down to a range of 2 to 3 percent by the end of 1972 was to bedevil the controls program throughout its life.

Late in October, just I was settling back into my teaching routine, I was asked if I would be willing to serve as one of the seven public members of the Price Commission. I was assured that it would be a part-time assignment and wouldn't require me to move back to Washington. Like most American economists, I had a natural antipathy toward direct government controls on the economy, believing that they were bound to cause serious distortions and produce unintended results. On the other hand, this experiment with economywide controls during peacetime would write a new chapter in the recurring tug-of-war between the American commitment to a market-led economy and political pressures for some kind of government intervention, and I was strongly tempted to be part of the action. In the end, I succumbed to a rationale that underpins more decisions than many of us would admit, telling myself that there would be a Price Commission with or without me, and if I was on it I could at least try to reduce the problems it caused for the economy.

The Price Commission first met a scant ten days before the expiration of the wage-price freeze, and we buckled down to designing standards, regulations, and procedures for a program whose ground rules both the president and Secretary Connally had deliberately left vague. We agreed that decisions would have to be made on a case-by-case basis, but it quickly became clear that such reviews would completely swamp a commission composed of part-timers. Bowing to practicality, we soon decided that the full commission would establish rules, definitions, and exceptions but delegate case-by-case decision making to either the senior staff or, in special cases, the commission's chairman.

Despite this delegation of authority, which subjected us to criticism from legislators, who accused us of shirking our responsibilities, we were overwhelmed. We had not anticipated the myriad questions of definition, coverage, exceptions, and adjustments that would arise in making decisions for an economy as complex as ours.

No sooner did we promulgate a decision than the need for exceptions or exemptions arose. And we had to be constantly alert to the law of unintended consequences, like the disappearance of chickens from supermarket shelves when farmers decided that buying chicken feed, a "raw material" whose price was not controlled, to nourish birds that would have to be sold at controlled prices was a losing proposition.

The seven of us struggled with these issues closeted in a small, stuffy, windowless room for long hours at a stretch. Yet we maintained an overall atmosphere of collegiality while wending our way through this thicket of decision making. Only occasionally did things become tense, as when Bob Lanzillotti, a scrappy, assertive economist who was dean of the University of Florida's business school, suggested that I recuse myself from a decision regarding IBM. Knowing that my father had been a consultant to the company and had sold it a couple of minor computer patents (he had insisted that the basic concept of the "von Neumann architecture" that underlay the new generation of computers, developed under the auspices of the US Army, belonged in the public domain), Lanzillotti assumed that I must own IBM stock. In fact, my father, to my later regret, had chosen to take payment in cash rather than stock, and I had never owned a single share of IBM.

Many of the Price Commission's votes were unanimous. Differences soon emerged, though, on how to weight the two sides of a difficult trade-off between making our program strict enough to meet the goal announced for Phase 2 and at the same time flexible enough to avoid severe disruptions. My own belief that the first rule of any government controls program should be to do the economy as little harm as possible put me firmly on the side of flexibility, but the group as a whole often broke three to three on decisions in which this trade-off was particularly crucial. Jack Grayson maintained the impartiality expected of a chairman during these discussions, but he did vote to break a tie when necessary, and almost always threw the decision in the direction I favored.

These arguments over pricing suddenly faded into insignificance in my mind when, soon after Christmas, I got a call from someone in the personnel office of the White House, asking me if I would be willing to be nominated as a member of the Council of Economic Advisers. I would be filling the vacancy created when Paul McCracken resigned at the end of 1971 to return to the University of Michigan and Herb Stein moved into the chairmanship. Without my knowing it, my appointment had been under discussion for several weeks, first suggested by McCracken and then formally put forward by Stein and George Shultz, still director of the Office of Management and Budget but soon to become secretary of the treasury.

Wow! Here I was being offered a chance to leap from the Price Commission's increasingly tedious wrangling over arcane details into a role that was focused on the big issues affecting the United States and even the global economies. Yet that call from the White House threw me into the most painful emotional turmoil of my adult life. Never before had professional opportunity collided so sharply and painfully with my commitment to my family. For someone as personally ambitious and eager to make a difference in the world of policy as I was, being a presidentially appointed member of the CEA charged with advising the president and reporting to the Congress on economic policy was literally my dream job. And its pull was even stronger because decisions on the wage-price control program and negotiations on the reform of the international monetary system, the two areas where I had the greatest interest and expertise, were sure to be front and center during 1972.

I returned to earth with a thud as I thought about the practical obstacles to my taking the job. Bob and I had just returned to the University of Pittsburgh from sabbatical leaves—normally granted once every seven years—and Malcolm and Laura had just returned to the schools and lives we had disrupted by taking them to Washington the year before. Although I would probably be granted another year off because of the prominence of the position I would fill, Bob was chairman of the English department, not a job from which he could take a leave of uncertain duration. After having expressed so volubly my anxieties about the progress of his career during the early years of our marriage, how could I now ask him to relinquish the chairmanship of a large department for an unpaid leave of absence? And, with children aged twelve and eight, the idea of being a commuting mother away from them most of the time was unthinkable.

No amount of agonizing resulted in a solution to my dilemma. So after crying into my pillow for several nights, beset by the fear that my father's dire predictions about the penalties I would pay for early marriage might be coming true, I told Bob one Friday that I would call the White House personnel office on Monday morning to express my regret at being unable to let my name be put forward. He was as torn as I was; he shared fully my delight at this tailor-made opportunity, and he knew how much I would be sacrificing if I turned it down. I would be giving up not only a year or two of full involvement in issues of national policy about which I cared deeply but also a stepping-stone to who knew what future career opportunities.

Years later Bob told me that he had already decided in his own mind that my career should take precedence over his in family decision making, and I'm still touched to the core by the depth of unselfishness this courageous decision entailed. But his efforts to find a workable compromise had so far come up as empty-handed as mine, and our discussion was cut short when he had to go off to chair the monthly Friday afternoon meeting of the English Department.

The resolution of our dilemma came from an unexpected source. Bob came home from the lengthy departmental meeting spluttering with anger and frustration. There was one particular professor in the department, an Australian named Jim Simmons, with greasy hair, bad teeth, and a strong body odor, who took pride in matching his behavior to his appearance, being as contrarian and unpleasant as possible in every situation. Apparently his talents had been in full swing that afternoon, turning the meeting into a shambles. After muttering imprecations against Simmons for several minutes, Bob said, "To hell with the chairmanship! Let's go to Washington." Filled with gratitude and relief, I accepted the offer.

The White House logs preserved on the infamous Nixon audiotapes, which I read thirty-five years after the fact, summarize several discussions between him and his chief of staff, H. R. Haldeman, regarding my appointment.[11] My appearance, my age (I was thirty-six, which would make me, at that time, the youngest person ever appointed to the council), my intelligence, my academic qualifications, my performance on the staff of the CEA and the Price Commission, and the breakthrough importance of appointing the first woman to this high position were all reviewed.[12] There were also several references to my father, his brilliance as a mathematician, the comparison of him to Einstein, and his relationship with me.[13]

Someone on the White House staff had done a thorough job of research. Not only my father and me but also my husband and our children had come under scrutiny. Bob's first book, on a seventeenth-century playwright, was mentioned, in connection with the possibility of offering him a grant from the National Endowment for the Humanities (NEH), so that he could work on his current book (on George Bernard Shaw) while I was working at the council.[14] Our children's intelligence was also up for discussion,[15] as I had expressed an interest in their attending the highly regarded Sidwell Friends School in Washington. Haldeman voiced some misgivings about the "liberal intellectualism" he had observed at the school, where his son was a student, but said that he would nonetheless ask either Secretary of State William Rogers or his wife to call the school and put in a good word for the Whitman children's admission at midyear.[16] No stone was left unturned, either with regard to what advantages I might bring to the administration or what wheels might have to be greased to enable me to come.

The NEH did indeed offer Bob a research grant, and either secretary Rogers or his wife called Sidwell Friends, which invited Malcolm to come in for an interview. But, as it turned out, the seventh grade was already a couple of pupils over the maximum, and the teachers were adamant in their refusal to add yet another. The headmaster was profusely apologetic, but the decision stood. When I later returned to teaching, my many foreign students were incredulous that a school head would have refused a request from the secretary of state at the behest of the teachers. My response, delivered with some pride, was "welcome to America."

The president and Haldeman also discussed the public relations aspects of my appointment, with which they clearly intended to make as much hay as possible. Arrangements were being made for a press conference, along with a photo session, at which the president would announce my appointment, mentioning its significance and calling attention to the presence of other women at high levels in his administration.[17] Details such as the timing of the announcement, who would be invited to attend, and the potential press coverage were all discussed.[18] One of Haldeman's assistants even gave the president a cute story to tell about my father's response to a small boy who asked him a question about mathematics—Nixon the micromanager left nothing to chance.[19]

The upshot of this planning was that I was called on the afternoon of January 27 and asked to come to the White House at 10:00 a.m. the following morning for an announcement in the Oval Office. With almost no time to get ready, I planned to take a very early morning plane from Pittsburgh. But in the late afternoon snow began to fall more and more heavily, and by evening the airport was alternately open and closed. Bob and I grew increasingly worried as the evening wore on, until finally I said, "Why don't I take a Greyhound bus? They always get through, whatever the weather."

A city long-distance bus terminal at 11:00 p.m. is never a prepossessing sight, but at least I felt secure that the four-hour trip to Washington would leave me plenty of time to spare, if not to catch much sleep. As it turned out, the bus to Washington was late pulling in; a woman traveling alone with her small child had just had an epileptic seizure. By the time an ambulance had been called and the woman and child taken away, the bus was even later, but there was still a comfortable cushion of time.

There was time, that is, until the bus broke down in the Allegheny Mountains, just halfway between Pittsburgh and Washington. None of the driver's ministrations, aided by would-be helpful passengers, could get it going again. At one point, a state policeman stopped by, lights flashing, to see what was happening. I thought about telling him of my predicament and asking for his help. But then, looking around at my fellow passengers, the soldiers in various stages of inebriation and the little old ladies with string bags, it occurred to me that if I tried to explain to the officer how important it was that I be on time for my meeting with the president of the United States in the Oval Office at ten o'clock that morning, he might well call another ambulance to haul me off to the nearest psychiatric ward. Eventually the bus sputtered to life and finished the trip. I arrived just in time to rush into the CEA offices to change from jeans into a dress and repair my disheveled hair and makeup. I was in the midst of these preparations when Herb Stein knocked on the door to tell me that the president had postponed the event until the next day. Oh, well, at least I could get some sleep.

When my meeting with the president did take place, he began a rather awkward conversation by commenting on my father, his genius, and his contributions to the nation. He added that, of course, what my father thought and wrote about was way over his head. I replied that he and I certainly had that in common. Only after this stilted little colloquy did the conversation turn to my own prospective appointment and my qualifications for it.

Although I knew nothing at that time about the White House planning that had preceded the president's announcement of my nomination, the fact that the press's interest was focused more on my gender than my qualifications became immediately apparent. Almost every article that came out of the press conference had the words "woman" or "first woman" in the headline. The president did have the grace to say that I had been chosen due to my "intellectual ability of the first magnitude,"[20] and I was grateful for an editorial in the *Detroit News,* which opined that it was my qualifications, rather than my gender, that made me "an outstanding selection."[21]

More typical, though, was the article in the *Wall Street Journal,* which began by stating, "President Nixon is trying another surprise weapon in his effort to enliven the economy—feminine charm," and went on to describe me as "wearing an emerald-green, deeply slit skirt."[22] This condescending tone infuriated me, and soon after I joined the CEA I invited the reporter, Richard Janssen, to lunch to chide him for his handling of the story. He insisted he had only been trying to introduce a little levity but said ruefully that he had already been chastened by the angry reactions of several of his female colleagues in the Washington press corps. Janssen was an excellent reporter, and we ultimately became friends, but I never let him forget his sexist introduction of me to the *Journal's* readers.

I did get a chance during the press conference to make a few points of my own, although I was cautioned not to discuss my views on the wage-price controls or international economic policy before I went through the Senate hearings required for confirmation. I said pointedly that, although I was registered as a Republican, I regarded myself as "highly independent" in political matters, guided in voting by my views of individuals and/or the policies they espoused rather than by party affiliation. Asked for my views on the "women's lib" movement, I answered that I shared its goals but preferred to pursue them in less spectacular ways than did some of its leaders.[23] "I don't want to contribute to the characterization of men as our enemies," I explained. "I'm a strong proponent of the monogamous or nuclear family."[24]

The note of ambivalence that crept into my expression of support was real. I've always chosen to be a reformer from inside the establishment rather than outside, to try to bring about change by means of persuasion and example rather than confrontation, an attitude that from time to time has exposed me to criticism and even, occasionally, my own later regret, as when I look back on my passivity during the civil rights movement. As I saw it, we were all trying to get to the same place, but by different paths.

One reporter commented accurately that I described myself as an economic problem solver rather than an intellectual bomb tosser, and that I was ambivalent about my sudden emergence into the spotlight: "On the one hand, she is delighted at the chance to move from the kitchen of the council into the living room, to become a policy maker rather than a staffer. But counterbalancing that joy is the fear that she is increasingly being pried apart from her family." Then came the punch line: "She bridles at the thought of becoming the sex symbol of the Nixon Administration and, in fact, her tall good looks are more a cross between country wholesome and middle European than Hollywood-style sexy."[25]

That description must have been a first for any presidential appointee, and I didn't know whether to be flattered or outraged. But I mused that my mother, whose expectations for her daughter's success had rested heavily on her efforts to imbue me with her own attractiveness and charm, at times without much hope of success, would see it as confirmation that her efforts had not been in vain.

Back in Pittsburgh there was another press conference, this one arranged by the university. The main local paper, the *Pittsburgh Post-Gazette,* sent a reporter from its women's page, rather than its economics section, to cover the event, and her interest appeared to be mainly in how I thought Laura's pet gerbils would survive the trip. I was furious at the insult, and Pitt's director of public relations later angrily told the paper's executive editor that if he ever again committed such a gaffe his reporters would no longer be invited to the university's news conferences.

Now that Bob, God bless him, had made it possible for me to join the CEA without tearing the family apart, settling the logistical details was a snap, freeing me to focus my attention on boning up for hearings before the Senate Banking Committee, the first and most crucial step in the Senate confirmation required for appointment to the CEA. William Proxmire, the Democratic senator from Wisconsin, began the session by asking my opinion about the progress of the Price Commission, from which I had resigned only two days before. Proxmire, a lean runner before jogging became fashionable, was famous for his annual list of Golden Fleece awards, bestowed on those research projects with the silliest-sounding titles that had received grants from the National Science Foundation (the sheep shorn of its golden fleece was presumably the American taxpayer), and I was afraid that he might exercise his sharp and sometimes unfair wit on me. I replied cautiously that the commission had "gotten off to a far better start than we dared to hope."

Proxmire scolded me about the commission's lack of transparency and asked pointedly whether the other commissioners were ceding too much decision-making power to Chairman Grayson. I stoutly denied his allegation, insisting that I had been anything but "silently acquiescent" and explaining the rationale for some of my votes. He also pressed hard on whether I regarded 5 percent unemployment as "full employment," making it clear that he certainly didn't. Neither did I, I replied; an unemployment rate of 5 percent and inflation in the 2 to 3 percent range stipulated in the guidelines for Phase 2 were merely interim goals; we expected to do better over the long term.

I enjoyed this interchange with a politician who had seriously educated himself on macroeconomics.[26] But, to my chagrin, the gender issue reared its head again. Proxmire and Republican Edward Brooke of Massachusetts, the first black member of the Senate since Reconstruction days, got into a wrangle over whether the fact that I was a woman and a "housewife," as well as an economist, was relevant to my appointment to the CEA. Aside from this perhaps inevitable but rather pointless argument, the hearing seemed like a brief PhD oral exam, serious and substantive but conducted with a civility that disappeared from the scene in the post-Watergate era and has yet to be recaptured.

The next step, after the full Senate had approved my appointment without discussion, was my swearing in, which, again, the president decided had enough public relations value to be worth attending personally. His presence was rewarded by a photograph that ran in several newspapers. showing me flanked by Nixon and my husband holding the Bible on which I had just taken the oath of office, with the president telling me in both voice and body language to "get those meat prices down."

For once, I wasn't fazed by a remark that seemed to highlight my housewifely role. I was much too intent on wishing with all my heart and soul that my father could see me now. There I stood in the White House surrounded by the family that he had feared would obliterate my chances for professional success. And in the middle, with an arm around each of our children, was the president of the United States, who had just announced my appointment as one of his advisers on economic issues. As souvenirs, Bob, the children, and I each received signed copies of a photo of the four of us standing with the president, all staring into the camera, stiff and serious and a bit awed by our surroundings. Our children, long since grown, have hung this photo on their walls to amuse their friends. But to me it is a memento of the joyous occasion when my father's expectations and my own, which had clashed and come between us as he was dying, had finally converged.

When I walked into the familiar Old EOB on my first day back at the CEA, I had to shake myself to make sure this was real. Even though my new office was a scant dozen yards from the one I had vacated just seven months earlier, it was a new world. It wasn't exactly a corner office, but the intricate construction of the Old EOB gave it enormous windows on two sides, one looking out on 17th Street and the other on Pennsylvania Avenue. The eighteen-foot ceilings, handsome furnishings, and decorator touches created an impression of gracious elegance. Even the brass doorknobs on the heavy wooden doors were works of art, heavily embossed with designs of American eagles, with hinges embossed to complement them. I took a deep breath as it hit me: this unfamiliar grandeur was a symbol of my move from the "back office" to the "front office" of the CEA. My brief time on the Price Commission had been a dress rehearsal; now I would be squarely in the public eye representing the Nixon administration.

My office was only one of the perquisites that went along with my new job. These included the right to park on the narrow strip of concrete, gated at both ends, that ran between the White House and the Old EOB and a pass that allowed me to rush unchallenged by guards through the inner sanctum, the red-carpeted labyrinthian corridors of the White House itself, on numerous trips between my home base on its west side and the Treasury building on the east. I also had lunch privileges in the White House Mess (so-called because it was staffed by navy stewards), which provided gourmet meals at subsidized prices and also offered the opportunity for informal conversation with other members of the Executive Office of the President.

I really liked the camaraderie and sense of belonging these lunches gave me, but they also caused me embarrassment. Because I was one of two or three women with Mess privileges, I was recognized immediately by my fellow diners, who thereafter called me by name. But I have always been terrible at names, and after a couple of weeks I was too embarrassed to ask theirs. In several cases, it wasn't until I saw some of them on television, as participants in the unfolding Watergate scandal, that I was able to connect names with faces.

I took on my new role during a rare honeymoon period for the Nixon administration. Not only was Phase 2 of the price controls program both popular and apparently effective but the President was winning widespread plaudits for his overtures to our two main communist adversaries, China and the Soviet Union. In late February, between his announcement that he intended to appoint me to the CEA and my swearing in, he had made a historic trip to China, visiting three major cities and holding an unprecedented meeting with Chairman Mao Zedong and Premier Zhou Enlai. He followed this with a trip to Moscow in May, where he and General Secretary Leonid Breznhev signed both the SALT 1 (Strategic Arms Limitation) and ABM (Anti-Ballistic Missile) treaties.

Nixon's Moscow agreements represented a major step in restraining the two nations' rivalry in both offensive and defensive nuclear weapons, a competition in which the Russians had been gaining ground. The significance of his opening gesture toward China was less obvious but also critical in the long run. Had China become part of Russia's closed economic community rather than entering into trade and investment relationships with the West, the economic pressures that figured so prominently in the collapse of the Soviet Union might not have had the same impact. I dared to hope that "tricky Dick" was becoming a global statesman.

My CEA colleagues also made me feel comfortable in my new role. Herb Stein had become chairman and Henk Houthakker had been replaced by Ezra Solomon, a well-known professor of finance at the Stanford business school. Born in Burma to parents who endowed him with an exotic Burmese British Jewish heritage, Ezra had snapping black eyes, a round head, and a small, taut body. Physically, Herb and Ezra were in sharp contrast, the one as ponderous as the other was delicate, the one as drawling in speech as the other was staccato. But they had in common wise intelligence, dry wit, and a generosity of heart that made them ideal colleagues. I was also a fan of George Shultz, who became both secretary of the treasury and the president's "economic czar" soon after I joined the CEA. I did get annoyed with him, though, when he hatched a plan to have me visit a supermarket with the president and cast baleful eyes on a package of hamburger, a photo op designed to symbolize the president's sympathy for the difficulties rising food prices were causing the American housewife. "If you put me in that position, George, I'll quit," I said, only half in jest, and the idea went no further.

Because I had so recently left the Price Commission, I quite naturally became a spokesperson for the administration on the wage-price control program as soon as I joined the CEA. In my early months there, it wasn't hard to take some pride in the way things were going. The price bulge that had immediately followed the end of the ninety-day freeze in November appeared to be slowing by March and April. In our testimony before the Joint Economic Committee in mid-April, Herb and I could truthfully list signs of progress, pointing out that the Phase I and Phase II programs had significantly reduced the rate of inflation, contributed to a more rapid rise of real (inflation-adjusted) wages, and led to an increase of over 1.8 million in the number of employed workers. We were careful to insert a note of cautions—"We cannot say we are sure that the system *as it now exists* will achieve our goal"—but our overall tone was both optimistic and determined.[27]

Even Walter Heller, the "dean" of Democratic economists who had chaired the CEA under presidents Kennedy and Johnson, acknowledged that he and I "were in substantial agreement that the economy would improve measurably during 1972." Furthermore, he added, Phase II "is nudging wage and price increases down a little faster than natural forces would . . . After a very wobbly start, Phase II is shaping up."[28]

While I was focused on restraining domestic prices as a member of the Price Commission, the international aspects of the president's New Economic Policy had set off a flurry of activity. The other industrialized countries had been caught off guard by his declaration of August 15, 1971, that the United States would simultaneously abrogate its commitment to convert foreign governments' dollar holdings into gold at thirty-five dollars an ounce and impose a temporary surcharge of 10 percent on imports until there was a positive shift of some thirteen billion dollars in the US basic balance of payments.[29] Foreign leaders expressed outrage at these unilateral declarations. Privately, they acknowledged that their reactions were aggravated by the timing of the president's announcement, which had forced high government officials in Europe to cut short their cherished monthlong August vacations and rush back to their capitals. The stage was set for hard bargaining between Secretary Connally and his counterparts in Europe and Japan.

I had been deeply embroiled in the events that led up to the president's dramatic abrogation of the dollar's tie to gold when I was on the CEA staff, and I felt strongly about the urgency of moving to an international monetary system more responsive to the signals from foreign exchange markets than the one negotiated twenty-five years earlier at Bretton Woods. Now I was a full-fledged member of the Volcker Group, which was struggling to develop an American proposal for restructuring the international system.

The need to move forward on a proposal was urgent. The measures negotiated under the Smithsonian Agreement of December 1971, in which all participants made some adjustment in the value of their currencies—the United States by reducing the value of the dollar in terms of gold—weren't adequate to shrink the US current account deficit, downward pressure on the value of the dollar continued, and restrictions on international currency transactions were proliferating in Europe. I, along with others in the administration, had to defend American policy against accusations of "benign neglect" of the situation, and it was clear that there would be no progress until the United States put a proposal on the table.

The most significant structural changes embedded in the US proposal were to make the balance of payments adjustment process much more symmetrical than it had been under Bretton Woods. It would put as much pressure for adjustment on countries with chronic payments surpluses as on those with chronic deficits, whereas the old system had exerted pressure only on the latter. In the new system, furthermore, the US dollar, rather than serving as the currency whose value adjusted passively to eliminate inconsistencies in other countries' balance of payments goals, would be a currency much more like any other, meaning that the United States could now take active measures affecting its own exchange rate. It also meant, I warned, that with the United States no longer functioning as the shock absorber, payments balances would have to "add up" more rigorously than before, and there would have to be a conscious effort to achieve compatible balance of payments goals.[30]

When the Volcker Group's proposal was presented for international discussion, I cautioned that, although it was flexible, leaving plenty of room for discussion and amendment, it would be a mistake to treat it like a Chinese menu, combining some selections from column A with others from column B. The proposal, I insisted, was comprehensive and its parts highly interdependent, just like one of the elegantly curved staircases in the Old EOB, which would collapse along its entire length if one step were to break or be removed.[31]

The administration was doing battle at home, as well as abroad, to create an open and well-functioning global economy. It had been fighting congressional proposals to restrict imports when I left the CEA staff, and the battle was still in full swing when I returned. Seizing the initiative, the administration took the lead in starting up a seventh round of multilateral trade negotiations under the auspices of the General Agreement on Tariffs and Trade (GATT). Its goals were not only to achieve reductions in both tariffs and nontariff barriers but also, by lowering them, to reduce the discriminatory effects of the European Communities' (EC's) preferential trade agreements with both its new members and its former African colonies. Given a chance to put into practice the classroom lectures I regularly gave on the advantages of both trade liberalization and the GATT principle of nondiscrimination, I dove enthusiastically into the preparations for these negotiations.

My interactions with the Washington representatives of the EC countries and Japan sometimes continued, on a more congenial basis, into our weekday evenings, when we were invited guests at dinners hosted by one of their embassies. These dinners, which always ended promptly by ten so that people could be at work early the following morning, generally featured formal dress and boringly predictable menus. Bob was convinced that there was a huge subterranean central kitchen somewhere under the city, whence filet mignon, roast potatoes, and tiny green peas were sent through a network of pneumatic tubes to various embassies throughout Washington.

Whatever the menu, the conversations at these dinners were always stimulating. Where else could one have the deputy director of the National Security Council on one side and the elegant Count Etienne Davignon—a leading figure in the evolution of both the North Atlantic Treaty Organization (NATO) and the European Economic Community—on the other? Nor were all the gatherings of official Washington so formal. Don and Joyce Rumsfeld, in those days the young, ambitious but not yet affluent parents of three young children, gave parties in the garden of their small Georgetown house at which many of the administration's leading lights could be found drinking beer and munching on increasingly soggy popcorn and potato chips.

I was astonished and angry to discover that the gender issue haunted our social, as well as my professional, life in Washington. Before I joined the CEA, I had encountered the separation of ladies and gentlemen after dinner only in the pages of nineteenth-century novels. But at my first official dinner, hosted by the European Union's ambassador in Washington in honor of the heads of Europe's most important central banks,

I was dumbfounded when, following dessert, the ladies were invited to go upstairs to "powder their noses" while the gentlemen enjoyed brandy, cigars, and serious conversation in the living room. Even though I was one of the Nixon administration's most senior international economists, I found myself making small talk in an upstairs bedroom while my husband, the professor of English, listened to Arthur Burns, my old Columbia professor and now chairman of the Federal Reserve Board, discussing the relationships among the dollar, the mark, the franc, and the pound sterling with his European counterparts. The irony of the situation left me inwardly seething.

It was part of Washington lore that when Katharine Graham—owner of the *Washington Post* and a leading figure on President Nixon's "enemies list" for having stood firm on publishing the Pentagon Papers—found herself in a similar situation she simply rose from the table, called for her limousine, and went home. I knew I would never have the courage to do likewise. But, after that first humiliating experience, I did tell my secretary, when responding to such invitations, to ask directly whether it was the host's custom to separate men from women after dinner. If the answer was yes, she was to refuse the invitation and explain quite candidly why. So I never did get to dine at the British Embassy. Eventually, this antediluvian practice was abandoned. Mrs. Graham had won her battle, and I like to think that I was one of her foot soldiers.

By the time the Republican nominating convention was held in Miami in July of 1972, it was clear that the wage-price controls program, which was approaching the first anniversary of its announcement, would be a significant issue in the upcoming presidential campaign. Those of us in the administration took every opportunity to give the president's program credit for the fact that the economy was expanding and the unemployment rate steadily declining, while overall inflation appeared to be on track to reach the "interim goal" of 2 to 3 percent by the end of the year. The Democrats, on the other hand, could highlight the continuing increase in food prices, which had a particularly powerful impact on family budgets. It was no surprise, therefore, that the three council members were invited to attend the Republican convention and brief various groups there, including state delegations and the party platform's drafting committee.

Because protests against Nixon's escalation of the Vietnam War were in full swing across the country, we expected some heightened security at the convention. But the atmosphere of our Miami Beach hotel was that of an armed camp surrounded by enemy troops. Soon after we arrived, having gone for a swim and a walk on the beach, it took considerable argument to persuade the pistol-packing guards to let us back into our hotel because we had forgotten to wear our identifying dog tags. The next morning our bus to the convention center in Miami, even with a police escort, had to plow through a sea of furious faces, shaking fists, hurled epithets, and worse; one angry young man with an ice pick tried to puncture our tire but was quickly hauled off by the police. The center itself had become a fortress, ringed by two concentric circles of buses ringed end to end, with no space in between (I wondered how Miami's bus commuters were getting to work that day). The anger out there was as palpable as the whiffs of tear gas that seeped into our bus, and later into the convention hall itself.

President Nixon's nomination was unchallenged and therefore a foregone conclusion, so almost the entire convention program consisted of speeches of self-congratulation and discussions of how most effectively to attack the other side. It all culminated in the circuslike atmosphere of a screaming audience of supporters, their voices amplified by the acoustics of an enormous arena, its ceiling covered with thousands of red, white, and blue balloons, which were released onto the heads of the crowd in the evening's finale. The fury of the protesters outside was matched, in words though not in actions, by the scurrilous nature of the remarks made inside by the Republican faithful about Democrats, both individually and collectively.

The tone of these comments was utterly alien to me, and the more I listened the more I squirmed. I was a registered Republican and part of a Republican administration, but my voting patterns had always reflected a fiercely cherished political independence, and there was no way that I could regard a group that included many of my close friends as enemies. Political opponents and adversaries, yes, enemies, no. I vowed that if I were ever again asked to participate in such an ugly partisan event, I would find a polite way to say no.

During the fall of 1972, while the administration's economic policy makers were highlighting progress toward the year-end goals of the Economic Stabilization Program in public, internally we were focused on figuring out what should follow Phase 2. The upshot of intense discussions and a wide range of views on the future of controls was an announcement that they would continue, though in a substantially altered form. Phase 2 would be terminated in January of 1973 and the Pay Board and Price Commission disbanded. The standards for price and pay increases would remain the same as under Phase 2, but, with the exception of a couple of key industries, compliance would now be largely voluntary and self-administered.

In both the 1973 *Economic Report of the President* and subsequent testimony before the Joint Economic Committee, the CEA stressed that the revised system "still . . . sets forth precise standards for wage and price behavior consistent with the goal of a lower rate of inflation, and it maintains the ability of Government to compel compliance where voluntary behavior would be inconsistent with that goal."[32] It soon became clear, though, that the shift from Phase 2 to Phase 3 was widely regarded as effective decontrol; one major newspaper headline read "NIXON SCRAPS CONTROLS." It didn't take long for the inflation suppressed by the freeze and Phase 2 to burst forth, accelerated by the emergence of classic demand-pull inflation as expansionary monetary and fiscal policy propelled the economy toward its capacity limits.

The 1973 *Economic Report* also attracted attention to an issue entirely new to its pages: the economic role of women. The reactions of both the public and the members of the Joint Economic Committee were predictable. On the positive side, the chapter was praised for highlighting the important role women play in the American economy and for emphasizing that women work outside the home for the same reasons as men,[33] thus laying to rest the persistent notion that they work only for "pin money."[34] On the negative side, we were chastised that the tone of the discussion was one of laying out facts rather than explicitly advocating change, and that it did not include policy recommendations. But, despite what it didn't cover, that chapter signified official recognition of American women's growing role outside, as well as inside, the home, making me less of an oddity.

The underlying message of that chapter in the *Economic Report*—that women's work and working women should be taken seriously—was to my mind both welcome and long overdue. The gender issue continued to haunt my own interactions with the press. It was one thing to be called, accurately, "the chief public defender of the [wage-price control] policy" by *Time* magazine;[35] it was quite another to read in *Business Week,* "A Nixon aide admits that the White House has a special reason for assigning the most junior Council of Economic Advisers member, as its spokesman at more and more TV press conferences: 'She's pretty.'"[36] A similar comment came from one of the Nixon administration's bitterest enemies, Nicholas von Hoffman, who in one of his columns called me the "Zsa Zsa Gabor of Economics," thereby casting aspersions on my qualifications, my Hungarian parentage, and my role in the administration, all in a single sentence.[37]

The women of the Washington press corps also saw me as a symbol, both of women's aspirations and of the difficulties they encountered on the road to fulfilling them. At that time, female reporters were excluded from the annual White House correspondents' dinner, a high-profile affair attended by the president and other top-ranking officials. When Eileen Shanahan, an economics reporter for the *New York Times* and a pioneering fighter for equal rights for female newswomen, asked me to send a signal by refusing my invitation to the dinner, I didn't hesitate. Some years later she and her women colleagues were finally invited.

The drumbeat of references to my gender threatened to undermine my right to be taken seriously, a matter about which I had qualms from time to time in any case. It should have been reassuring to read in *Parade* magazine, "This wise young woman probably has more impact on American life than any other woman in or out of government."[38] On the other hand, when an article in *Good Housekeeping* asked the children of well-known women in various fields "What Does Mommy Do?" my eight-year-old daughter Laura replied, "She helps the President decide things—like if prices should go up or down—but I wonder if the President pays attention to her."[39] I often wondered too.

There was no doubt, though, that my job came with all kinds of extracurricular benefits for the four Whitmans, and, as I kept discovering them, I felt like a birthday child opening one surprise package after another. One of the perks was the right to request seats in the president's boxes at the Kennedy Center when they were available. This meant that we could attend concerts and plays at Washington's leading cultural venue not only without paying for tickets but in the very best seats in the house and with champagne always available from a small refrigerator in the anteroom.

Part of the fun was finding out when we arrived who else was sharing the box. Once, when we happened to take Malcolm along, he found himself seated next to Henry Kissinger, who, in his pompous but totally authoritative way, gave the mesmerized thirteen-year-old a glimpse into the world of geopolitics, as seen by its master. Years later I was reminded of Kissinger's monologue when I sat next to his brother Walter, a successful investment banker, at dinner. He and Henry, only a year older, had come to the United States at the same time. Why then, I asked him, did he speak unaccented English, while Henry still sounded as if he had just landed on our shores? "Well," Walter replied, "I'm the Kissinger who listens."

We could also sign up to spend a weekend or a week at one of several resort areas, originally built by various presidents as retreats where they could get away from the pressures of Washington but no longer used that way. One of these was Camp Hoover, the precursor of the current and more famous presidential retreat, Camp David. The camp in Virginia's Blue Ridge Mountains included miles of hiking trails amid magnificent scenery and was bifurcated by the clear, fast-flowing Rapidan River, famed for its abundance of trout. Neither Bob nor I had any interest in fishing, but we and the children reveled in the simple but comfortable lodgings, the deep woods, and the clear mountain air. The kids, who saw little enough of me during the work week in Washington, could have the undivided attention of both their parents as we spent uninterrupted weekends together.

The other government-owned facility available for our rare family vacations was a cottage high above Trunk Bay on the island of St. John in the American Virgin Islands. The cottage was simple enough, with two bedrooms, a living-dining room, and a large screened porch, But Trunk Bay, a two-minute walk down the hill, is possibly the most beautiful body of water surrounding the islands—a clear blue-green, bordered by a sparkling sand beach and with no other human beings visible where we sunned and swam. St. John could be reached only by small boat from neighboring St. Thomas, where we had to do our marketing for the week, since the only provisions available once we reached the cottage were the rudimentary offerings of a tiny store serving a nearby campground. We kept meals as simple as possible but delighted in an environment where the rum cost less than the Coca-Cola, and anyway tasted best when sipped from a coconut into which an entry hole had been pounded by a hammer and a large nail.

Sadly, neither the Trunk Bay cottage nor Camp Hoover is any longer available as a retreat for government officials or anyone else; both have been permanently closed, although Camp Hoover has been designated a National Historic Landmark and can be visited on day trips by tourists.

Bob, Malcolm, and Laura thoroughly enjoyed sharing in these once in a lifetime experiences that went along with my job. We all saw them for just what they were, though, experiences to be savored and remembered but never confused with our normal way of life, the one we would return to once my stint at the CEA was over. And these interludes could never completely overcome the nagging pangs of guilt I felt because the routine of everyday life in Washington posed more difficulties than glamour for the three of them.

Cut off from daily interaction with his colleagues, Bob had to contend with intellectual isolation as he worked on the draft of his book on Shaw, and I was too tired by the time I came home to serve as his educated layman critic, a role each of us normally served by reading and commenting on the other's writings. He also had to put up with silly questions at parties. "People are always asking Bob and me if we've exchanged doctorates," I once said in exasperation, "as if God had decreed that women be interested exclusively in literature and men in economics."[40] At least I recognized and appreciated the strength of character that underlay our lifetime partnership. Obviously you have to be a strong person with a strong sense of yourself to put up with me, I told people curious about our relationship.[41]

Bob never expressed any concern about my behavior with any of the many men I worked and traveled with. His faith in my fidelity, which I took as another demonstration of his confidence in himself and our relationship, was entirely justified, but I did occasionally have to extri-

cate myself from a potentially sticky situation. I remember in particular
a wrestling match in the back of a Paris taxicab with a brilliant, usually
delightful but thoroughly inebriated older man, a high official of the
International Monetary Fund and a respected colleague in many international meetings. I never felt any threat to my personal safety, and the
episode ended uneventfully. But I was thoroughly annoyed when, as inevitably occurred after such encounters, I ran into him the next morning,
sober, embarrassed, and contrite, and it fell to me to reassure him that his
behavior wouldn't stand in the way of our continuing to work together.

Because I was at work during most of their waking hours, Bob had to
take on most of the responsibility for Malcolm and Laura's physical and
emotional well-being; my half of our parenting partnership was definitely
not pulling her oar. Bob had always been an engaged father, but now his
efforts to go the extra mile sometimes took amusing turns. One hot July
9, his birthday, I was at a meeting in Paris and Malcolm was off at summer camp. Alone with Laura, he told her she could choose the location
for his birthday dinner. I wonder how many fathers have celebrated their
birthdays eating hamburgers with their eight-year-olds at Roy Rogers? I
tried to make it up to him by bringing back a particularly elegant and
outrageously expensive bottle of cognac from Paris as a birthday present.

Both of the children had to contend with having been uprooted more
or less at a moment's notice and adjusting to a new school and new
friends in the middle of the school year. For Laura, whose sunny dis-
position inclined her toward a generally cheerful view of the world, settling into her new school wasn't hard. She was, in fact, delighted with
her child-friendly fourth-grade teacher and the inviting classroom, filled
with lofts and nooks for reading or collaborating on projects, which he
had built himself.

But for Malcolm, a serious, somewhat withdrawn loner who was
wrestling with the stresses of early adolescence, having to adjust to a sudden shift from one environment to a totally different one for the third
time in eighteen months was traumatic, much as my unexpected transfer
from my mother's household to my father's, as stipulated by my parents'
divorce agreement, had been when I was his age. We should have sensed
what he was going through when his grades dropped from A to C and
he came home from school nearly every afternoon gray in the face from

a pounding headache. But, although we had him thoroughly checked for any physical cause of his symptoms, the notion that he might be suffering from what would now be called childhood depression never occurred to us. Many years later he told us that had been the unhappiest year of his life, and I still kick myself that we did not alleviate his misery by at least understanding what he was going through. From Malcolm's perspective, the balance between work and family life had been badly upset.

My second year at the council began promisingly enough. On January 27, the peace agreement that Henry Kissinger and Le Duc Tho, the representative of North Vietnam, had hammered out in Paris the preceding October was finally signed by all parties to the conflict. Although it did not bring about the "peace with honor" that Nixon had promised when he was first elected, it did end the United States' active participation in a war that by then had become almost universally unpopular.

On matters closer to home, the 1973 *Economic Report of the President* could still strike hopeful notes on the progress of the Economic Stabilization Program, the discussions of US proposals for international monetary reform, and the preparations for a new round of multilateral trade negotiations scheduled to begin in the fall of 1973. We warned, though, that further progress on inflation would require restraint in monetary and fiscal policy, in order to keep the nation's rapid economic expansion from exploding into a price-raising boom. The overall tone of the report, said *Time*, "could best be characterized as soberly glowing."[42]

Things went downhill rather quickly on the economic front after that. We knew, and said publicly, that inflation control would be harder in 1973 than it was in 1972, because expansion was taking the economy closer to its capacity limits, and inflation did indeed speed up. I continued to explain bravely why we expected it to slow down substantially later in the year, but by the beginning of June, Democrats in Congress were beginning to clamor for the reimposition of a price freeze.[43] The president had been listening to arguments, both pro and con, since mid-March. I had thought that the antifreeze side was winning; on June 4 I earnestly told the *Journal of Commerce*, "I have no doubt a freeze would be popular, at least in the beginning, but possibly it would be counterproductive in the long run . . . a freeze is not being actively considered."

Corroborating Laura's doubts about whether he listened to me, the president announced a renewed price freeze on June 13. As Herb Stein recounted it, he and the president were discussing the pros and cons of a renewed freeze when Herb commented dubiously, "You can't step in the same river twice." "Yes you can, if it's frozen," the president shot back.[44] The freeze was to last for sixty days, until new controls—Phase 4—could be put in place.

By mid-1973, inflationary pressures arising from a worldwide boom, a second devaluation of the dollar, and expansionary monetary and fiscal policies at home, along with weather-related crop failures abroad, combined to prevent the second price freeze from being as effective, even temporarily, as the first. In an interview shortly before I left the government in August, I gave my honest appraisal of the controls experiment, displaying "a highly ambivalent attitude toward the controls program." The reporter wrote, "She makes no claim they have succeeded . . . in reducing the rate of inflation from what it would have been without any controls. But her 'tentative' judgment is that in a broader sense, the controls 'have been helpful' in fostering 'a more favorable combination of inflation and real growth' . . . than would have occurred otherwise."[45]

Along with the fading effectiveness of the wage-price controls, things were continuing to deteriorate on the international economic front, as the currency adjustments that had been implemented under the Smithsonian Agreement failed to have their desired effects. Although international discussions on the US proposals for international monetary reform were ongoing, little progress had been made when they were effectively overtaken by the economic turmoil created by the oil crisis instigated by the Organization of Petroleum Exporting Countries (OPEC) in 1973. Instead, several agreements formalized what had already occurred in practice: the legitimization of floating and a major reduction in the role of gold. The world's major currencies have been operating under a system—or what many observers have called a nonsystem—of "managed floating" ever since.

On the trade side, US policy was heavily influenced by the urgency of curbing domestic inflation, particularly for food and farm products. But when the measures taken to restrain these prices included embargoes on exports of soybeans and several other commodities, our anti-inflation policies worked at cross-purposes to efforts to reduce our payments deficit by expanding exports. I summed up the complexities of the situation we faced: when you're trying to keep prices up at the farm and down at the supermarket, while holding down the burden on the taxpayer and encouraging farm exports, it's a tall order with built-in conflicts.[46]

Problems were also building in an entirely different trade policy arena, namely, our relations with Japan. Partly in response to the 1971 "Peterson Report" (the one in which my marginal comments brought Peterson and me face-to-face for the first time), which highlighted the decline of the United States' competitive position and the rise of Japan's, twice-yearly consultations between the CEA and our counterparts in Japan's Economic Planning Agency (EPA) had begun in the spring of 1972.

Although the bilateral discussions were invariably well mannered (and lightened by visits to the theater and other entertainments paid for out of our own pockets because the CEA didn't have an entertainment budget), an ongoing wrangle over the appropriate value for the yen dominated the discussions. The Japanese insistence on keeping it ridiculously low, along with their reluctance to open their economy to increased imports, was a major contributor, we argued, to the large and persistent imbalances in trade between our two countries: their surpluses and our deficits. When I led the US delegation to the third CEA-EPA meeting, in Tokyo, we continued to insist that the Japanese should allow the yen to rise further, while they countered that they had already permitted "more than enough" in that respect.

The lines were hardening. Herb Stein ended a memo to the president at about the time of the CEA-EPA meetings by saying "This developing animosity . . . is dangerous" and urging that we "describe our international economic policies in terms which emphasize our basic common interests and not in terms of a horse race where if we win they lose."[47] But a horse race it was, to the American public. When pollsters asked Americans whether they would prefer to see 4 percent annual growth in the United States and 6 percent in Japan or 3 percent in each country, a majority chose the latter, in defiance of economic logic.

Once, finding myself on a plane next to Congressman John Dingell—a personal friend and a strong supporter of the US auto industry—I protested to him that a restriction he was backing on imports of double-sided galvanized steel from Japan would be hard on American car makers, who couldn't get it at home. His reply was basically, "I don't care if it causes us some pain, as long as it hurts those so-and-sos more." The United States was finding the adjustment from being the world's sole economic superpower to being in a competitive race with a rising challenger hard to swallow.

If the presence of a female high-level government official occasionally created awkwardness at home, that was nothing compared to the discomfort it caused our Japanese hosts. Having a woman as head of a delegation was unsettling enough, but the fact that from time to time my subordinates would openly argue a point with me was more than the strictly hierarchical Japanese could fathom.

While interacting with our group in discussions was difficult, entertaining us within their rigid protocols was well-nigh impossible. Courtesy required that the chief of a delegation be entertained more extravagantly than the other members, but the elaborate rituals of the geisha house hardly seemed appropriate in my case. So, while my male colleagues were being plied with drink and entertained by beautiful young women, I was struggling to stay awake through interminable hours of Kabuki theater, whose language and gestures were both unintelligible to me. Our hosts rounded up several female professors so I wouldn't be the only woman at official dinners, but the culture gap was epitomized by an elderly vice minister who, unable to contain himself, blurted out, "But what does your husband think of all this?"

The Japanese attitude toward women in high places had changed very little when, some twenty years later, I attended a meeting of Japan's Keidanren, the nation's most prestigious business association. My fellow guest was Sylvia Ostry, a high-level Canadian civil servant who had been her prime minister's "Sherpa," or senior adviser, in the protracted Uruguay Round of multilateral trade negotiations. Sylvia's brilliant mind and acid tongue were incongruously housed in a petite body, always swathed in the latest designer fashions. When we both had the temerity to argue with one of our hosts, he privately called us "pushy broads." It was a label we repeated with smiles. With my mother's example always before me, I saw no contradiction in "pushy" and "feminine."

Despite the fact that the performance of the American economy and our efforts to implement the administration's economic policy goals during the first half of 1973 gave me and my CEA colleagues plenty to be modest about, I managed to hang on to my optimism that I might help to promote a return of the United States to a position of world leadership, presenting a coherent view of an open world economy with maximum reliance on market forces. To me, such leadership was essential in the ongoing struggle for hearts and minds against Soviet communism; promoting it was my own way of carrying on the battle that my father had fought through his contributions to America's military supremacy. But I would soon be forced to face the fragility of these expectations, and my preoccupation with economic problems would seem more and more beside the point as I could no longer ignore the increasingly ominous rumblings of the earthquake that, when it exploded, would shake Washington, and the nation, to their very foundations.

· 7 ·

The End of Innocence

My eyes opened wide as Bob and I, along with my two CEA colleagues
and their spouses, walked into the elegant dining room tucked away in
the northwest corner of the main floor of the White House and stood
waiting to be joined for breakfast by the president and Mrs. Nixon. The
state rooms of the White House were old hat to me by now, but I had
never before been inside the Family Dining Room, which was off limits
to the public. With its silk draperies, crystal chandelier, Louis XVI green
marble mantelpiece, and polished period furniture, the room looked
far too formal for ordinary family meals (the Nixons generally ate in a
smaller, more informal room in the second-floor family quarters) and
was in fact used by the president for working lunches and small dinners.

The ostensible reason for the president's invitation was to bid farewell
to Ezra Solomon, who was about to leave the CEA to return to Stanford. We all assumed that this would be a rather perfunctory affair and
had mentally penciled it into our schedules for about forty-five minutes.
Instead, we sat glued to our chairs for a full two hours; only Mrs. Nixon
left earlier to keep another appointment. After some social pleasantries—it was Mrs. Nixon's birthday, and Bob and I presented her with the
birthday cards our children had made for her, decorated with shamrocks
in honor of St. Patrick's Day—the president asked the members of the
council for their views on what steps the administration should take on

the wage-price control program in view of the rapid increases in food prices that were occurring in the early months of 1973.

He quickly discovered the truth of the old adage "Ask a question of three economists, even three Republican economists, and you'll get three different answers." Ezra favored another across-the-board freeze on wages and prices until at least the end of the year. Herb argued strongly that we should hold with Phase III. I was even more emphatic, insisting that there were serious dangers in a return to a freeze or similarly rigid controls program, which could cut off expansion and increase the chances of recession in 1974.[1]

Having exhausted that topic, the president embarked on one of the most remarkable monologues I have ever heard. For the better part of an hour, he expounded on the intricacies of global geopolitics, the position of the United States as the world's power balancer and peacekeeper, and the part his vision and policies would play in leading our country to fulfill that role. The brilliance and subtlety of his wide-ranging disquisition was as breathtaking as the arrogance that underpinned it. As the six of us listened spellbound, Nixon broke off and, switching gears, turned suddenly to my husband, the professor of English literature. "But as a teacher who deals with students, Professor Whitman," he said, "you must know that you can't tell the American people the truth about what you're doing or they won't support you. You have to give them stories that will make them feel positive about what you're doing."

There, right in front of our eyes, Dr. Jekyll turned into Mr. Hyde; the brilliant master of geopolitics became the secretive, suspicious, paranoid Richard Nixon we came to know during the Watergate hearings and who ultimately brought about his own downfall and disgrace. Then the spell was broken, and the breakfast ended with the same sort of small talk with which it had begun.

The earthquake that ultimately buried the Nixon presidency had begun a year earlier, deep underground, with an apparently obscure burglary. At 2:30 in the morning of June 17, 1972, five men were arrested for breaking into and attempting to bug the offices of the Democratic National Committee (DNC) at the Watergate, a hotel and office complex a mile or so from the White House. Two days later the *Washington Post* reported that one of the five was in charge of security for the Committee to Re-elect the President (CRP, but often referred to, sarcastically, as CREEP). On that same day, John Mitchell, formerly President Nixon's attorney general, resigned as head of the CRP while denying any connection to the foiled effort of the so-called Watergate burglars.

I had followed these developments on the front pages of the *Post,* but, preoccupied with the challenges of the renewed price freeze and the pressures the members of the Volcker Group were feeling to come up with a proposal for international monetary reform, with giving speeches in New York and holding a press briefing on the Consumer Price Index in Washington, I paid them little attention—maybe I didn't want to think about the possible implications. In the months that followed, the *Post* reported that a check for twenty-five thousand dollars apparently intended for the Nixon campaign had turned up in the bank account of one of the Watergate burglars, that John Mitchell had controlled a secret fund used to finance widespread intelligence-gathering operations against the Democrats while serving as attorney general, and that the FBI had identified the Watergate break-in as part of a massive campaign of political spying and sabotage associated with the Nixon reelection campaign.

Although, in hindsight, the pattern of malfeasance these developments pointed to seems painfully clear, at the time the possibility that they might affect my relationship with the president and my role in his administration didn't occur to me. When a journalist confronted me, much later, asking "Weren't you in denial?" I had to say that I honestly didn't know. Doesn't denial mean pushing something down from the conscious part of the brain to the subconscious? Apparently the American public didn't focus on those front page stories any more than I did; in November 1972, Richard Nixon was reelected with more than 60 percent of the vote, one of the largest landslides in American political history.

I felt the first vague, queasy pangs of discomfort sometime early in 1973. I was listening to John Ehrlichman, one of the president's two most senior aides, briefing newly elected Republican members of Congress. Among other things, these rookies asked for advice on how to respond to the awkward questions they were beginning to be asked about Watergate and some of the people around the president. The gist of Ehrlichman's answer was, "If you're asked, for example, about what Dwight Chapin (the president's appointments secretary) was doing during the early months of 1972, explain that he was very busy making preparations for the president's pathbreaking trip to China."

This seemed to me like a weaselly answer, but none of the new legislators pursued it further. There were other comments of Ehrlichman's that sounded less than forthright, but I couldn't put my finger on anything specifically wrong. A year or so later I talked with Don Rumsfeld, who had become the US ambassador to NATO, about that Ehrlichman briefing, which both of us had attended. When I mentioned that it had made me vaguely uncomfortable, Don replied, "I had exactly the same reaction." A few months after that briefing, Rumsfeld had been given the NATO appointment, which took him and his family to Brussels, far away from Washington and its swirling rumors.

Circumstantial evidence linking people close to the president to the Watergate break-in kept cropping up during the first few months of 1973. At the end of January, two former White House aides, G. Gordon Liddy and James McCord, were among the seven who pled guilty and were convicted of conspiracy, burglary, and wiretapping. All seven, it turned out, were directly or indirectly employees of the CRP.

Although rumors abounded, and the *Washington Post* and *New York Times* continued to shine a spotlight on the mysteries surrounding the Watergate break-in, all of those involved, with the exception of Mitchell, appeared to be fairly low-level operatives, involved with the campaign committee rather than with the administration itself. The discomfiture created by the Ehrlichman briefing had retreated to the back of my mind when another attack on my comfort level as a member of the Nixon administration came, not from rumors or press stories but from the president himself, at the breakfast in the Family Dining Room.

By that time, investigative stories on the Watergate break-in, written by the team of Bob Woodward and Carl Bernstein, had been appearing with increasing frequency in the *Washington Post* for several months. Gradually, through news and television photos, I began to recognize some of the handsome young faces I'd never been able to attach names to when we had lunch at the round "singles" table in the White House Mess: John Dean, Egil (Bud) Krogh, Jeb Stuart Magruder, Dwight Chapin. All had been high-level assistants or counsels to the president when we ate together, although by early 1973 Krogh had become undersecretary of transportation and Magruder had long since moved to the CRP as John Mitchell's deputy in the 1972 presidential campaign.

As the inexorable drumbeat of evidence linking the White House to the CRP, and through it to the Watergate break-in, grew louder, it began to penetrate my resistant brain. One night in April, I sat bolt upright in bed and woke my husband, saying, "But what if the *Washington Post* is right?" "Well," he replied sleepily, "if you really are having such treasonous thoughts, there's nothing for it but to resign." With that, he returned to his interrupted dream, but I didn't get much sleep that night.

At about the same time, my secretary took a call from the office of H. R. Haldeman, Nixon's chief of staff and one of the two men—the other being John Ehrlichman—closest to the president. The call was to scold me for a minor infraction of the rules: I had used a White House car and driver, which I was authorized to do only on work-related trips, to drive me some five blocks from the beauty shop to my office in the midst of a downpour—proving, once again, that "vanity, thy name is woman." When the message was relayed to me, I grumbled to myself, "He's a fine one to talk; he's going to be in jail one of these days."

On April 30, the president astounded the nation, or at least the world inside the Beltway, by announcing that he had reluctantly accepted the resignations of Haldeman and Ehrlichman and had fired John Dean, the counsel to the president who, we learned later, had talked to the president about "the cancer on the presidency" only a few days after the CEA members and their spouses had breakfasted with the Nixons.

The fact that the two men closest to the president were clearly implicated in the scandal finally did it; I just couldn't believe any longer that the president could have remained ignorant of what was going on. Developments during the weeks that followed made clear that many members of Congress had reached the same conclusion. A Senate Watergate Committee was formed, former solicitor general Archibald Cox was appointed by Attorney General Elliot Richardson as the Justice Department's special prosecutor, and the Senate committee began nationally televised hearings on May 18.

It was then that the country began to learn the concrete details of Richard Nixon's dark side. Bud Krogh, who had resigned his position as undersecretary of transportation a few days earlier, revealed his previous role as head of the White House "plumbers' unit." This was the group that, after White House efforts to stop publication of the top-secret Pentagon Papers through the courts failed in 1971, had broken into the office of the author's psychiatrist, looking for material that might discredit him. John Dean told investigators, according to the *Post,* that he had discussed the Watergate cover-up with the president "at least 35 times."[2] In an allegation that has never been confirmed, Jeb Stuart Magruder stated that the president had known of and authorized the Watergate break-in in advance. All of these men, along with Haldeman, Ehrlichman, and many others, eventually were convicted and served jail time for their roles in the two break-ins and/or the cover-ups that followed.

As I listened to or read about these admissions, I asked myself what on earth could have motivated men like these—all of them highly intelligent, all on brilliant career trajectories, and many of them lawyers themselves—to engage in what they must have known were illegal activities. What were they thinking? Was it personal loyalty to the president? Had the president's own arrogance, his apparent belief that he was above the law and would never be caught, spread over those close to him as well? Did they believe that the "end," so brilliantly articulated by their leader, justified the means? Were they so dazzled by the power and perquisites of their White House jobs that they couldn't stand the thought of having them cut short by scandal, leading them to create the much greater scandal of the cover-up?

Personal ambition didn't surprise or offend me. My father had described himself in a letter to me as "an ambitious bastard," and that trait had been implanted in my own genes and upbringing both. And his passion for being close to power had been crucial in shaping the last half of his career. But honesty and moral courage were just as important a part of his makeup. He displayed these traits most conspicuously in his public defense of Robert Oppenheimer when the latter was wrongly accused of disloyalty and deprived of his security clearance. This was despite the fact that my father's political patron was the wealthy investment banker Lewis Strauss, who had masterminded the proceedings against Oppenheimer and was the chairman of both the Atomic Energy Commission and the Institute for Advanced Study's Board of Trustees.

With this example before me as I was growing up, and my own efforts throughout my life to emulate my father's honesty and fair dealing, despite all the books many of the men (and they were all men) involved in Watergate wrote later, their total loss of any moral compass remains a puzzle to me. I promised myself never to forget for a minute that all the trappings that went with life in the Executive Office of the President— closeness to the seat of power, the sense of actually influencing important decisions, a broad array of special perks—were ephemeral, belonged to the job and not the individual, and were no excuse for breaking the rules of decent behavior.

The most astounding revelation to emerge from the Watergate hearings was the July 13 statement to the committee by Alexander Butterfield, a former presidential appointments secretary. Under oath, Butterfield testified that the president had ordered a taping system installed in his office in 1971 and every conversation and telephone call since had been recorded. The president lost his battle to keep these tapes secret, and they provided much of the evidence that led, after a year of Chinese water torture revelations, to his resignation under the imminent threat of impeachment.

Well before Butterfield's mind-boggling revelation, sometime during the month of April, I finally decided I couldn't wait any longer to take a first step toward leaving the CEA, now that I suspected the president of being at the center of an enormous and expanding web of lies. I told Herb Stein that I was no longer comfortable as a member of the Nixon administration and intended to resign. Herb, a man of unimpeachable personal integrity but also a staunch Nixon loyalist, simply refused to believe that I was serious.

For months, I had been torn between my respect for the institution of the presidency, the enjoyment of my job, and my admiration for the administration officials who had put me there—CEA chairman Herb Stein and treasury secretary and economics czar George Shultz—and the mounting evidence of a cancer growing in the Oval Office that was destroying the credibility and dignity associated with it. Those of us who were part of George Shultz's domain, we learned later, were apparently walled off from the machinations and dirty tricks that were widespread elsewhere in the Executive Office of the President.

One of the things that came to light in the course of the Watergate investigation was the existence of an enemies' list of high-profile people the president regarded as either hostile or untrustworthy. He ordered that people on the list were under no circumstances to be invited to the White House and, more ominously, tried to persuade Treasury Secretary Shultz to turn over to the White House confidential information from the Internal Revenue Service (IRS) about their individual tax returns. When Shultz courageously stonewalled this request, the president reputedly told his aides to keep "Shultz's people," who included the members of the CEA, in ignorance of the darker side of activities originating in the White House. If I hadn't been shielded from what was going on, I would surely have decided to quit, and translated that decision into action, more quickly.

Once I'd made up my mind to resign, I still hesitated to make the decision irrevocable by putting it in writing. This was partly because, between Ezra Solomon's return to Stanford in March and the time when his vacancy was filled in June, Herb and I were the only members of the council. My departure would have left Herb to carry out the duties of the three-member council alone, which would have been an enormous burden, particularly with the high level of activity in the two areas that were my major responsibility: the wage-price controls program and the international monetary system. Furthermore, Herb had recently suffered a hemorrhage that left him permanently blind in one eye. That he had lost half his eyesight but none of his sense of humor was demonstrated when the president called him in the hospital to commiserate with his misfortune. "That's okay, Mr. President," Herb told us he'd replied, "half of what I see isn't worth reading anyway."

I'd also hoped to be able to discuss with Herb the implications of my leaving for the functioning of the CEA. But once the nomination of agricultural economist Gary Seevers, then the special assistant to the chairman, to fill the vacant member's slot had been made public, and my repeated efforts to engage Herb in a serious discussion had failed, I knew the time had come to make my intentions official. On June 14, I wrote a letter of resignation to the president and left a copy on Herb's desk. Then he not only believed me but took my decision as an act of personal betrayal.

I might have had reason to feel morally superior if my letter to the president had been a bold, courageous statement along the lines of "I believe you are a crook, Mr. President, and I can't work for a crook." In fact, though, I wrote:

Dear Mr. President:

When I was offered and accepted appointment to the Council of Economic Advisers in February of 1972, it was with the understanding that, subject to your pleasure, I would remain until the end of the 1972–73 academic year. That time has now run out, and I am writing to tender my resignation from the Council on or about August 1, 1973, in order to return to my teaching post at the University of Pittsburgh for the 1973–74 academic year.

I take this step with the greatest personal difficulty and regret, knowing it will bring to an end a most exciting and rewarding period in my life. Few economists indeed have the privilege of practicing their profession in the service of their country and their President, and to have been able to observe and participate in decisions fundamentally affecting the economic welfare of our nation is an opportunity for which I shall always be grateful. I shall leave with the knowledge that I received far more than I could give, and learned far more than I could teach, and yet with the hope that I was able to make a useful contribution. I shall leave also with the hope that this will not be my last opportunity for government service.

These are difficult times. But when history gives its appraisal of the fundamental achievements of the Nixon Administrations, which have given our children—and children everywhere—a far greater chance to live out their lives in peace, I shall be proud to have been a part of them. It has been an honor and a privilege to serve my government in the position to which you appointed me and I shall always be grateful to you, Mr. President, for having given me the opportunity to do so.

Yours sincerely,[3]
Marina v. N. Whitman

The first paragraph of my letter wasn't entirely true. I had never, either to the president or anyone else, set a time limit on my tenure at the CEA. I reveled in my role there and would, I'm convinced, have found a way to stay on for another year had not the unraveling Watergate saga intervened. But, given my views about the moral culpability of Nixon's sycophants, why was the tone of my letter so polite, even friendly?

The language was partly a result of my determination to make the public announcement of my resignation a nonevent, even if the letter should leak to the press, as many such documents did. But it also reflected a genuine admiration for the Dr. Jekyll side of Nixon's actions as president. I was very much in tune with the progressive aspects of his domestic policies. More important, I genuinely believed, and still do today, that he had taken some major steps forward in foreign policy. He ended our participation in the Vietnam War—though after too much time had passed and too much blood had been shed—and his overtures to China and the Soviet Union were important first moves in bringing stability to a precariously unstable world.

The expressions of admiration and gratitude that filled my letter to the president were returned in his letter accepting my resignation.

Dear Marina:

Although I had known of your intention to return eventually to the academic world, I had not realized that the time was so near. Thus, while I will accept your resignation as a Member of the Council of Economic Advisers, effective August 1, I do so with the deepest reluctance. Your work here has been a source of high satisfaction, not only to me and to your associates on the Council but, also, to all your colleagues throughout government, and you will be greatly missed.

Keynes is reputed to have said that economists have not yet earned the right to be listened to attentively. I disagree, and your distinguished service on the Council more than justifies my position! The brilliance of your contributions to our economic policies cannot be overestimated, and the unprecedented growth our Nation has enjoyed during the past two years is a great tribute to the Council and to its Members. You have every good reason to be proud of the part you played, just as I have been proud and honored to have you as a key member of our Administration team.

Needless to say, you leave public life with my heartfelt thanks and warmest good wishes for continued success in the years ahead. And on behalf of our fellow citizens, I do indeed share your hope that at some future time we may prevail upon you to return once again to government service.

Sincerely,
Richard Nixon[4]

The president may have been distracted by Watergate, but his gracious letter gave no hint of it. In contrast to the nefarious actions against personal and political adversaries that were being conducted in secret, the civility that characterized verbal and written exchanges in official Washington, even among people on opposite sides of the political aisle, seems unimaginable today, when shrill partisanship and universal mistrust dominate public discourse. Ironically, Watergate itself did a lot to create this poisonous atmosphere.

Only once, in the many times I testified before one congressional committee or another, did a member of the committee address me with anything other than the utmost politeness. That was when Herb and I were scheduled to testify before the Joint Economic Committee (JEC) on the Economic Problems of Women. At the last minute, Herb was called to the White House to talk to the president, and I was left to face an angry Martha Griffiths, a Democrat from Michigan, who was presiding. Representative Griffiths was annoyed partly because Herb had chosen to respond to the president's summons rather than hers and partly because she objected to the fact that our testimony, in the form of chapter 4 of the 1973 *Economic Report of the President on the Economic Role of Women,* was descriptive rather than prescriptive and failed to recommend specific policies to alleviate discrimination against women in the workplace. Venting her spleen on the council member who sat before her, she said bluntly that I was in no way an adequate substitute for the chairman of the CEA. I knew better than to take her remarks personally, but they still stung.

More typical was the behavior of the chairman of the JEC, Senator William Proxmire, Democrat of Wisconsin. Even when he was castigating the administration for the performance of the US economy, he was careful to point out his respect for the reputations and expertise of the individual members of the CEA. But the acme of graciousness was reached during my last appearance before the JEC on August 1, 1973, shortly before my resignation from the CEA became effective. Another Democrat, Representative Henry Reuss, took note of my imminent departure.

> I . . . say farewell to Mrs. Whitman, who is leaving for the university in a few days, I understand. You will remain forever green in my mind

for the great job you did in helping close the gold window on August 15, 1971; a good piece of work. You are Mrs. Phase II as far as I am concerned.

That was one time when controls were well administered, so may the angels sing when you go back. We really appreciated you and your work so much.[5]

Senator Jacob Javits added, "To which we all say amen."[6] And the courtly Senator John Sparkman of Alabama chimed in: "May the angels sing while we are weeping."[7] Senator Proxmire ended this remarkable exchange by noting wryly, "We may not have economists on this committee, but we have poets."[8]

I accepted these plaudits with a gracious smile, but inwardly I felt they were not entirely deserved. The relative success of Phase II had owed more to the amount of slack that existed in the US economy at the time than to the brilliance of our execution. As the country moved back toward full employment, Phases III and IV were progressively less effective and the program gradually faded away, ending entirely in mid-1974 without having made a dent in the long-term trend of price increases. I could take solace in the fact that my original skepticism about controls had been justified, and that my CEA colleagues and I had done our best to minimize the harm they did to the American economy. But I couldn't escape the reality that for nearly two years I had been the public face of a failed program.

The push for trade liberalization and changes in the international monetary system that I had worked so hard for at the CEA, on the other hand, were both important and essential, underpinning twenty-five years of healthy growth in international trade and investment. The so-called Tokyo Round of multilateral trade negotiations, which the administration was preparing for when I left the CEA, ended six years later, having spawned significant tariff reductions and new regulations restricting a variety of nontariff barriers to trade. Building on this success, the high-water mark of trade liberalization was reached in 1993, when both the Uruguay Round, the most ambitious round of multilateral trade negotiations to date, and the North American Free Trade Agreement (NAFTA) were completed and the World Trade Organization (WTO) was established.

At the time, the US proposals for a new international monetary architecture developed by Paul Volcker and advanced by many of us in the administration appeared doomed to failure. They were overtaken by events, and the world has been operating ever since with an ad hoc mixture of pegged, freely floating, and managed floating exchange rates, very different from the orderly system we had tried to bring into being. But the two main ideas of the Volcker Group proposal rose from the dead in September of 2009, becoming the focus of intensive discussion at a meeting of the leaders of the Group of 20, the leading industrialized and developing countries. One was the need for countries with the biggest surpluses, as well as those with the largest deficits in their payments balances, to adopt policies that would reduce the imbalances on both sides. The other was the desirability of gradually reducing the dominance of the US dollar as the primary currency in surplus countries' international reserves, by increasing the acceptability of other assets in this role.[9] There has been little progress so far on implementing these proposals, but the need to move forward on them is widely recognized.

Balancing my successes and my failures, I left the CEA feeling that I had used my economic expertise as best I could to promote policy choices that would enhance the nation's economic welfare. Once again, I wished that my father could know not simply that I had become a professional success but that, like him, I had to the best of my ability put my mind and my training to use in helping shape our nation's policies, and that my contributions had been recognized in a glowing letter from the president himself. The goals John von Neumann and I supported—the military might of the United States in his case and the effectiveness of the country's economic policies in mine—were controversial, attracting both admiration and criticism. But his commitment to American leadership in global affairs, combined with the ambition to be personally involved, had both been passed on to his only child.

A more direct link with my father's past came from a totally unexpected source. A month after I had left the CEA, the president announced the appointment of my successor, William Fellner, recently retired from the Sterling Professorship of Economics at Yale. According to *The Economist*, "Mr. Fellner . . . would not claim to be as pretty or as young (he is 68) as Mrs. Marina Whitman, who has gone back to the

University of Pittsburgh and whose place he takes. But he is an academic economist of such distinction . . . [that] [o]bservers of the Council, who have feared that it was becoming too involved in the political hurly-burly welcome Mr. Fellner's willingness to serve."[10]

The same article noted, "Mr. Fellner, who was born in Hungary, has a belief in free markets which accords with President Nixon's philosophy, if not his practice." What it did not mention, and was doubtless unaware of, was that Willi Fellner had been a close friend of my father's during their high-school days in Budapest, a friendship that ended only with my father's death. That my father's lifelong friend should become his daughter's successor at the CEA gave me, once again, a strong sense of continuity with my family's history.

The angel voices that Senator Sparkman had heard so clearly on my departure from the CEA were muted by the time I returned to Pittsburgh. "Sure enough, there behind the dirty windows of room 416 sits the only woman ever to have served on the President's Council of Economic Advisers,"[11] wrote a surprised reporter shortly after I had traded in the spacious elegance of my EOB office for my cramped, dingy academic quarters back in Pittsburgh. Some things had changed, though: I now had a fancy title and higher salary, and the Whitmans had a new house, the old one having been so trashed by tenants that I said to Bob, "It'll be easier to sell it than to clean it up."

Above all, the high visibility I had acquired in Washington followed me home. I was in constant demand for interviews and speeches and became the poster girl for a *New York Times* article on a new phenomenon: husbands who were willing to become "trailing spouses," moving temporarily or permanently away from their own jobs in the interest of their wives' careers.[12] But old customs weren't quite keeping up with the realities of change. When the Pittsburgh Jaycees chose me as one of their fifteen outstanding citizens for 1976, I was hailed as "Man of the Year" in the finance category.[13]

While I was settling into my new role as a local celebrity, the slow torture of Watergate's unraveling was eclipsing everything else that was going on in Washington and the country. Along with millions of my fellow citizens, I followed the drama day by day, on television and in the press: the windup of the televised Senate hearings; the appointment of a special prosecutor for Watergate, Archibald Cox; and his refusal to obey the president's order, which cited executive privilege, to drop the subpoena for the Watergate tapes. Cox's refusal was followed by the "Saturday Night Massacre," when Nixon forced Attorney General Elliot Richardson and his deputy, William Ruckelshaus, to resign because they refused to fire Cox. After Cox was finally dismissed by Solicitor General Robert Bork, demands for the president's impeachment became widespread, and he felt compelled to declare publicly, "I am not a crook." A new special prosecutor, Leon Jaworski, was appointed, and the struggle to obtain the tapes continued.

Meanwhile, seven individuals, including the president's highest-ranking aides, had been indicted by a grand jury that secretly named Nixon as an unindicted coconspirator. Finally, on July 24, 1974, the Supreme Court unanimously ordered the president to hand over the tapes to Jaworski; he complied a few days later. Back in Pittsburgh, I thanked heaven that I was there and not still at the center of the maelstrom.

By the time Richard Nixon, under imminent threat of impeachment by the House and removal from office by the Senate, announced his resignation on August 8, the four Whitmans were on a family vacation in Europe. My mother, who had been appalled that we would go abroad when our own country was in such a state of turmoil, nevertheless put us in touch with a courtly, Old World, Viennese friend from her youth. As he was showing us around his enchanting city, he expressed considerable puzzlement at the Nixon resignation. Why, he asked, hadn't the president simply called out the National Guard and thrown the legislators in jail?

I despaired of explaining the workings of the American democratic process to a monarchist who longed for the restoration of the Austro-Hungarian Empire. His view of the world, I realized, like that of my parents, had been formed by the turbulence that Europe had endured during and between two world wars. Their response had been a wholehearted embrace of the United States and its form of government, whereas he saw a return to monarchy as the best path to peace and order. I tried to persuade him that the very orderliness of the transition from Nixon to Gerald Ford had shown democracy at its best.

From Vienna, we braved the Iron Curtain to get to Budapest, so we could introduce our children to the birthplace of their maternal grand-parents. Even though it was blanketed with the grayness of Soviet communism, Budapest was a beautiful city, and the Hungarians we met were impressively entrepreneurial; the ladies managed to afford their Chanel knockoff suits by working two or three jobs. Again, I wondered how my father, the anticommunist superhawk, would have reacted to what his birthplace had become. Would he have nodded with grim recognition at the restricted existence he had predicted would befall those who came under communist rule? Or would he have been heartened that, as he once put it, the Hungarian ability to go through a revolving door behind you but come out first had managed to survive?

While I was in Budapest, I learned that the new president, Gerald Ford, had chosen Nelson Rockefeller as his vice president. I had gotten to know Rockefeller the previous November when, as governor of New York and at the president's request, he had established a National Commission on Critical Choices for Americans and appointed me as one of its members. Assigned to the panel on Energy and Its Relationship to Ecology, Economics, and World Stability, I had found myself in continuous disagreement with Edward Teller, another of my father's childhood friends and famous, or infamous, as the father of the hydrogen bomb. Teller had argued strongly for making nuclear energy the focus of a national energy program; I had held out just as strongly against putting all our eggs in that particular basket. In the end, it made no difference; the commission's work was halted in midstream when its founder became vice president, and its conclusions were relegated to oblivion, as so often happens, by the changing of the guard in Washington.

With the departure of President Nixon and the inauguration of President Ford, the Watergate drama appeared to have come to a close. But of course it hadn't. Gerald Ford's pardon of Richard Nixon was widely believed to have cost him election to a full term in 1976, Nixon spent the rest of his life trying to rehabilitate himself as an elder statesman, and the men who went to jail for their roles in the Watergate burglary or its cover-up had their lives forever changed. And a hardening of the lines that began with Watergate, in the attitudes of the public toward government, of members of the three branches of government toward each other, and of decision makers on one side of the political aisle toward those on the opposite side, still shapes the policy-making environment, more brutally today than ever before.

For me personally, the denouement came nearly twenty years later. The two rookie investigative reporters who blew the Watergate cover-up wide open, Carl Bernstein and Bob Woodward, reported to the young deputy metropolitan editor of the *Washington Post* (the *Post* initially treated Watergate as a local rather than a national story), whose job it was to try to make sure that their reports were accurate. By 1992 that young editor, Leonard Downie, had become the executive editor of the *Post* and, of much greater importance to Bob and me, the father of the groom at our daughter's wedding. Laura Whitman and David Downie had met as undergraduates at Duke University and, totally unaware of this history, fell in love and married. The result is that we share with Len Downie two absolutely perfect grandchildren.

The change in my own status carried no such drama. It did give me, though, a very different perspective on my professional role; I could now talk about the Nixon administration's economic policies without the constraints on expressing doubts or disagreements imposed by being a member of that team. I believe firmly that you can be an inside adviser or an outside critic, but you can't be both at the same time. This truth is hard for academics to accept, especially in light of the special license that society has given us to speak out freely on any subject without being concerned about the impact on the institution of which we are a part. But academic freedom is only for academics. I had seen several of my colleagues, people of great intelligence and personal integrity, ignore this trade-off when they went into business or government and then be surprised when their internal effectiveness was drastically undermined— generally to the point that they either quit or were fired.

My thoughts along these lines made me recognize a contradiction inherent in the very existence of the CEA, a hard truth that had lain buried under the frenzy of day-to-day activity. It was spelled out in a comment by Professor Carl Christ, one of several well-known economists who had written critical reviews of the CEA's 1973 *Economic Report of the President* in the *American Economic Review:* "[T]he report is inherently 'a somewhat schizoid document.'" It is intended to serve two purposes that are not entirely compatible—first to function as an apology for or celebration of the President's economic program, and second, to constitute a professional job of economic analysis and policy recommendation."[14] Every CEA, both before and since the one I served on, has been confronted with this dilemma without fully resolving it. And I wasn't the only member of that body, I'm sure, who felt twinges of discomfort when the two purposes came into conflict with each other.

Now that I was an outsider, I was filled with a missionary's zeal to explain to as many people as possible the realities of economic policy making as I had come to know them in the trenches. I pushed my audiences to understand the complexities of these issues, and to think about them from the perspective of the nation's long-run economic welfare, rather than focusing only on particular interests and immediate effects. I also used these speaking and writing opportunities as a way of forcing myself to reflect on what contributions I had made to the formation of good economic policy, and what I had learned from the experience.

I had taken away a hard-won realism about economic policies and those who formulate them, lessons I boiled down to three points. One was that you don't bring about enormous changes in policy. If you move things two degrees in one direction or another, that's a pretty big accomplishment. Also, in a job like mine, where your only output is advice and analysis, when a decision goes your way you can never be sure how heavily your input was weighted. And, finally, you discover that a lot of your achievements are negative. You go home at night feeling really great that you prevented something bad from happening.[15] The young girl who had dreamed of changing the world had become a woman who recognized both the opportunities and the limitations of the profession she had chosen.

Underpinning this modest assessment was my core belief about how decisions are made in a democracy: there is no such thing as a free lunch, and there are no easy answers to hard questions. And, in a society striving to achieve multiple and often mutually contradictory targets, the role of the economist is to spell out the choices available and the nature of the trade-offs, leaving it to the political process to select among them and determine what the ultimate compromise is to be.[16]

One offshoot of my high visibility at the CEA was that I began to be offered honorary degrees by colleges and universities, eventually becoming an honoree at more than twenty commencement ceremonies. These events held a special significance for me. Never having anticipated this sort of recognition, I wore with pride my father's plain, black, moth-eaten wool academic robe, until Bob gave me for my birthday the more colorful, less sweltering, sky-blue gown that identified my Columbia PhD. But, whatever the color of the gown, each of these occasions brought back memories of the many times my father had worn the one I had inherited from him at some of the world's most prestigious universities on several continents. When I was asked to give the commencement address, along with receiving an honorary degree, I tried especially hard to make the messages that I delivered, along with the fact that I was being so honored, worthy of his approval—an approbation I craved even long after he was dead.

The opportunity to air economic issues before an audience larger than I'd ever dreamed of came in 1978, some five years after I left the CEA, when I was invited to host a series of hour-long television programs to be distributed through the Public Broadcasting Service (PBS) network. My first reaction was one of open-mouthed astonishment: "you're asking me to become a TV personality?" I replied in disbelief. Despite the incongruity of the idea, I was instantly enthusiastic about the challenge of making economics more accessible and less intimidating to the general public or, as Bob teased me, "Wonder Woman wants to bring enlightenment to the ignorant masses and convince them that they can enjoy the process." Once again, my youthful enthusiasm for new experiences, along with a heavy dose of naïveté about what it took to be a successful TV host, led me to say yes.

I'd expected that the hardest part of getting the show together would be choosing topics that would appeal to a PBS audience and persuading high-profile experts to come on as guests. On the contrary, our biggest obstacle turned out to be snowstorms. Bob Chitester, the entrepreneurial president/manager of WQLN in Erie, Pennsylvania, had insisted that the show's pilot be made at his station. On the day scheduled for the taping, a blizzard shut down the Erie airport, and our producer couldn't find a limousine—he even tried funeral homes—willing to drive us there. In the end, Pittsburgh Yellow Cab came to the rescue, and our new program's first guest, the president of the United Steelworkers Union, shared with me a three-plus-hour ride from Pittsburgh to Erie, being tossed about in the backseat while an old taxi with busted springs negotiated slippery, snow-covered roads.

I had a strong sense of déjà vu when, on the day Ralph Nader was to tape a program with me in Washington, much of the East Coast was shut down by a massive blizzard. I managed to fly to New York from a meeting in Bermuda, but getting from there to Washington was no mean feat. It involved a postmidnight ride on a deserted New York subway, lugging a heavy suitcase, three consecutive shifts from one unheated railroad train to another, and a ride hitched on a snowplow before I reached the Washington television studio, exhausted and bedraggled, but triumphant. The staff and production crew managed to trickle in as well, but Nader, who lived a few blocks from the studio and prided himself on not having a telephone, was a no-show. When we finally made contact several days later, he said breezily, "Oh, the weather was so terrible, I figured no one would show up."

Despite human and logistical problems, we covered a vast array of economic topics over the twenty-six weeks that *Economically Speaking* was on the air. The format, a panel show with a host and two guests, one on each side of a current economic controversy, was a natural framework for my conviction that there are no simple answers to complicated questions. My guests aired opposing views on issues that included the declining dollar, agricultural subsidies, airline deregulation, the future of American unionism, the breakup of the AT&T monopoly, affirmative action (where the negative side was argued by a conservative African American economist, Walter Williams), and the financing of health care. Many of those programs could be rerun today with little change; in some cases, even the participants might be the same.

For the finale of the series, we staged an hour-long airing of the running debate on "Why Economists Disagree" with the icons of the two leading schools of economics in the country at the time, Walter Heller and Milton Friedman. Heller, the nation's leading proponent of Keynesianism, had been chairman of the CEA under President Kennedy and the top economic adviser to both Kennedy and his successor, Lyndon Johnson, whom he persuaded to undertake the War on Poverty. Friedman, who refused ever to accept a position in government, was the country's best-known proponent of free-market economics.

Friedman got the discussion off to a rousing start by declaring that the major basis for disagreement among economists was not a matter of Keynesian versus monetarist or liberal versus conservative, but rather that his perspective focused on long-run results, while Heller's emphasized short-run outcomes. Heller strongly if politely disagreed, insisting that differences in values, or at least in priorities, underlay their opposing views of economic analysis and policies. The give-and-take between the experts and the audience that made up the second half of the program not only underscored the differences between the two leading lights of American economics but also gave audience and listeners alike a quick, intense version of Economics 101. Our experiment, we felt, had gone out with a bang. Overall, the series had fulfilled my goal of demonstrating not only that "there are two sides to every question" but also the truth of Oscar Wilde's quip, "The truth is rarely plain and never simple."

The program's originator and its financial sponsor disagreed with me. There were several reasons why they failed to extend *Economically Speaking* after the original series ended, including the fact that it had not attracted a large enough audience. But they decided against giving it another chance to establish itself mainly because they felt that the program had been too neutral, too balanced, for the free-market position they both espoused to emerge a clear winner. This experience drove home a hard truth that I have encountered again and again, that people prefer to see the world in black and white, rather than in the shades of gray that I see as a true reflection of reality.

Meanwhile, I had been keeping my finger in Washington's policy pie by serving as an adviser to several offices and agencies of government on issues related to trade, the US balance of payments, and the international monetary system. We had just come home from our trip to Europe in the summer of 1974 when I was invited as one of twenty-eight "leading economists" to participate in a Summit Conference on Inflation called by President Ford to advise him on the economic conundrum that confronted his new administration.

The postwar economic mainstream in the United States had been grounded in the Keynesian belief that skillful management of monetary and fiscal policy could keep an economy in balance, growing at a healthy rate without dangerous inflation. The rules were simple: in recession, the government should reduce taxes and/or increase spending and the Federal Reserve should lower interest rates; in an inflationary boom, both fiscal and monetary policy should move in the direction of restraint. But there was no prescription for what to do about the "stagflation" that emerged in the 1970s, when excess unemployment and high or accelerating inflation occurred simultaneously.

Inflation had reached double digits when the kickoff meeting of the conference was convened in the East Room of the White House, and the misery index faced by President Ford was far more severe than the one that had provoked President Nixon into instituting wage-price controls a few years before. Explaining his insistence on a meeting open to the press and the public, the president joked, "Some skeptics have warned me that putting 28 of our most distinguished economists and eight members of Congress, both Democrat and Republican, on public display with live microphones would produce a spectacle something like professional wrestlers playing ice hockey." But his charge was breathtakingly ambitious: "Our purpose is to find ways by which we, the American people, can come to grips with our economic difficulties and surmount them."[17]

The emergence of stagflation had laid to rest the Keyensian belief in demand management as a macroeconomic shortcut to nirvana, and the resort to controls had, if anything, made the situation worse. That meant that the hunt for solutions now had to focus on microeconomic or structural changes, supply-side measures that would enhance efficiency and lower costs in the US economy. Both the conference participants themselves and the reporters who wrote about the session were pleasantly surprised by the degree of unanimity among economists across the political spectrum and optimistic that a good start had been made on attacking inflation. And many shared the concern I had often expressed for avoiding a battle over income shares among business, labor, and other groups in the economy.[18]

At a follow-up meeting on September 23, we economists tried to convert the suggestions for structural change we had offered at our earlier meeting into specific proposals to slaughter a variety of political "sacred cows," primarily regulatory restrictions on competition. The aim was to tame inflation by reducing costs and increasing the availability of goods.[19] During the weeks that followed, the administration held meetings with different interest groups in cities around the country. As reports of the outcomes of these meetings emerged, some of the optimism about the president's anti-inflation initiative began to evaporate. Each group explained why the economy would benefit if price increases (or, for labor, wage increases) were limited in every sector except its own. As one reporter noted wryly, "Interest groups, representing various sectors of the economy, have said not what they would do for their country, but instead what their country should do for them."[20]

By the time of the final summit conference, where each of these groups summarized its self-interested position in a circuslike atmosphere, complete with cheering, waving signs, and balloons, disillusionment was setting in. And once the Congress, yielding to interest group pressures, had finished consigning most of the president's structural proposals to the scrap heap, little was left of the highly touted effort other than the large red, white, and blue WIN (Whip Inflation Now) buttons that every participant received.

Two years later, with stagflation's misery index still in unacceptable double digits, it was the turn of Jimmy Carter, who had just been nominated as the Democrats' presidential candidate, to invite groups of economists to his home in Plains, Georgia, to give a series of seminars on economic policy with a student body of one. As the token Republican in the group, I joined "a distinguished bipartisan group of experts on international economic policy."[21] In his remarks to the press, Governor Carter found plenty to criticize in the design and implementation of economic policies during the Nixon and Ford administrations. But he agreed with them that floating exchange rates were here to stay and that he supported lower trade barriers at home and abroad. The reporter for the *New York Times* tried to give color to his article: "'United States international economic policy,' said Marina Whitman the other day, standing beneath some tall pine trees in Plains, Georgia, 'is not an area of great partisan division—there is a very wide range of consensus.'" And, he concluded, "Mrs. Whitman was right."[22]

Ironically, Jimmy Carter, the Democratic victor in the 1976 election, presided over many of the pro-competitive structural changes that the defeated Republican, Gerald Ford, had been unable to bring about.[23] But, despite the deregulation of a variety of important industries—including airlines and trucking—that began during the Carter administration, it took the tight-money policies of Federal Reserve chairman Paul Volcker, accompanied by some five years of painfully high unemployment (1979–83), to break the back of stagflation and set the nation on a path of noninflationary growth.

Demand-side macroeconomic policies and supply-side structural measures both played important roles in making possible the twenty-five years of sustained economic growth that began during the Reagan presidency—the period that has come to be called the "Great Moderation." As I once quipped, it takes both halves of a pair of scissors to make them work. A more difficult lesson was that there is no such thing as a painless cure for stagflation. It required individuals who stuck to their economic principles—presidents Carter and Reagan to pro-competitive measures and Federal Reserve chairman Paul Volcker to drastically tight monetary conditions—even in the face of mounting criticism, to make the country take its medicine.

Having returned from the CEA to private life determined to spread the gospel of facing economic realities head-on, I now realized how much personal determination and political clout were required to move in that direction. The collapse of President Ford's effort, after a promising beginning, to conquer stagflation by eliminating many of the economic inefficiencies created and fought for by particular interest groups had taught me my own hard lesson about the vagaries of the political process in a democracy. I had been proud of my country as I described to my mother's old friend in Vienna the virtues of democracy at its best. Now I was frustrated and disappointed as I watched democracy's downside in action: the ability of special interests and partisan politics to gut policies that would benefit the nation as a whole. Was business, I wondered, with its typically hierarchical structure, better than the democratic processes of government at getting things done?

· 8 ·

A Lady in the Boardroom

My first glimpse of the boardroom of the Manufacturers Hanover Bank, a world no woman had ever penetrated before, was dazzling. Although the scene was gracious rather than forbidding, I had again the sense of entering the halls of power that had come over me when I passed through the guarded gate of the Old EOB. The bank's board of directors met around a long, highly polished mahogany table, lit by crystal chandeliers, in a room high above New York's Park Avenue. This elegant, rarified environment gave no hint of the upheavals that would reshape the organization several times during the years I was associated with it. All the appurtenances were in a matching formal style, and each director's name was permanently embossed on a brass nameplate in front of his seat. As I went around the room to shake hands with my new colleagues, most of whom were the chief executives of leading companies, I could see that some of them were not entirely at ease with this strange creature in their midst. We were only a few minutes into the meeting when short, portly Richards Reynolds, heir to the tobacco fortune, followed up an emphatic "Damn sure" with a hasty "Pardon me ma'am; we're not used to having a lady in here" in his Virginia drawl.

I had joined this exalted group as the result of a luncheon invitation a couple of months earlier, just as I was about to leave the CEA, from Gabriel Hauge, chairman of Manufacturers Hanover. Mr. Hauge turned out to be a courtly silver-haired gentleman with a piratical black patch over his left eye (he had lost the eye, I learned later, to the cancer that would eventually kill him). I was vaguely aware that Manny Hanny, as it was invariably called, was one of a handful of large so-called money center banks, with headquarters in New York but a presence all over the world. That's about all I knew when, somewhere between the salad and the coffee, Mr. Hauge asked me if I would consider joining the bank's board of directors.

I was so taken by surprise that I didn't have the wit to inquire about what the duties and responsibilities of an "outside" or "independent" board member (one who is not part of the company's management) were, even though I was totally ignorant about what I might be getting into. Like most newspaper-reading Americans, it was always the chief executives I had read about; their boards of directors were generally shadowy figures in the background. It was only many years later, when the Enron scandal of 2001 and the financial crisis of 2008–9 clobbered the US economy and wiped out many families' financial security, that the American public became aware that the failure of many boards of directors to discharge their responsibilities effectively was a key to these disasters. Nor did it occur to me to ask about the compensation that came with such directorships, although I soon discovered that it was large enough to have a significant impact on our lifestyle, and eventually to raise serious questions from the same American public about whether the performance of company directors really made them worth their pay.

I was excited by the opportunity to penetrate a sanctum few academic economists had ever entered, even though for-profit companies were major players in the issues and events we studied, analyzed, and taught. I had no illusions, though, about why this opportunity had opened up. Part of it was that my training as an economist had made me comfortable with the mysteries of profit and loss and the bottom line. And my stints in the administration, with both the Price Commission and the CEA, had given me an insider's view of the US regulatory environment, as well as a priceless network of acquaintances in government. But these qualifications paled in importance before the fact that I wore a skirt. By the mid-1970s, companies were feeling strong social pressures to elect women and minorities to their white male boards, and a few of the more forward thinking were beginning to search for and recruit viable candidates.

How much influence women would gain by joining corporate boards was a question that hung in the air. In a 1974 article entitled "New Voices in Business: Ladies of the Boardroom,"[1] most of the other women quoted there agreed with my comment that the CEOs who had approached me about directorships—there had been several—had made it clear that the fact that I was a woman was relevant. They weren't playing games. In less than a year, I said, I had discovered that 95 percent of the time we directors are rubber stamps; women will get significant leverage in the economy when they accede to responsible positions inside corporations, rather than serving only as outside directors. Significantly, none of the women directors interviewed, except for a couple who headed family-owned companies, was the CEO of a major corporation, the usual route to a directorship. Their leadership experience, like mine, was in government, universities, or nonprofit organizations.

Despite such doubts, I accepted Gabe Hauge's invitation with the comment "I realize I'm a token, but please don't expect me to be *just* a token." Manny Hanny's Board already had its token minority member, Jerome "Brud" Holland, who had won fame as the first black football player at Cornell. A sociologist and former president of two historically black colleges, he had been appointed by Richard Nixon as the US ambassador to Sweden, the first African American to attain such a high diplomatic position. During the two years he spent at that post, he had endured having eggs and tomatoes hurled at him as the anti-Americanism engendered by the Vietnam War reached its height.

Eventually, either my fellow directors' discomfiture at having a woman in their fraternity dissipated or they learned to hide it better. But it wasn't long before the gender issue came up explicitly during the planning of one of the board's trips to the bank's facilities in other countries. The established pattern was that while the directors were receiving all-day briefings on the economic and political environment, as well as the bank's own operations wherever they were visiting, their ladies were entertained with fashion shows or luncheons with the wives of government leaders.

These outings held no appeal for Bob, who would have much preferred to sit in on the briefings. When I passed his request on to Gabe Hauge, the chairman responded with an immediate invitation for Bob to attend. But when Laura Holland, Brud's wife, expressed the same preference, she was at first refused, which embarrassed and infuriated Bob and me. Eventually, a choice between attending these briefings or participating in the programs planned for them was extended to all the spouses and, though almost all of them continued to choose the ladies' outings, I felt gratified that we had won one more small victory over male chauvinism.

At my first Manny Hanny board meeting, I had tried to stay alert in a haze of cigar smoke, listening to a series of boilerplate reports required by banking laws and wondering how long it would take me to understand, let alone make intelligent judgments about, the performance of the bank's loan portfolio and the economic and competitive conditions that affected its financial results. How in the world, I asked myself, did new board members acquire the knowledge needed to do their job? I realized gradually that new members were expected to acquire expertise about the company by osmosis, keeping quiet for the first year or so until they felt enough on top of the situation to ask a pertinent question or make an intelligent comment. Naturally impatient and congenitally incapable of remaining silent for so long, I was determined to accelerate the process. Besides, I felt pressure to come up to speed as fast as possible—wasn't my performance a test of whether women were up to holding such important positions?

After a couple of meetings did little to reduce my befuddlement, I asked the corporate secretary to set up private sessions with the heads of the bank's business units and major staff functions, so that I could learn more about what a money center bank does and what distinguishes a profitable operation from an unprofitable one. My request was met with an immediate offer to set up such sessions before or after each board meeting. But it was also greeted with surprise, as if no one had ever asked before.

Even after I had been given these tutorials, I was frustrated by the fact that neither the board meetings nor those of board committees seemed well designed to elicit useful questions or comments from the outside directors. In meetings of the Loan Committee, for example, the time was spent reviewing sample credit analyses for a cross section of borrowers, many of them in the "rag trade," the insiders' name for the New York garment industry. I couldn't for the life of me figure out what value I or my fellow directors could add in these discussions; surely we couldn't outguess the professionals' judgments about the creditworthiness of individual borrowers.

Looking back, I realize that the purpose of these carefully packaged presentations may have been to increase the directors' confidence in the bank's lending decisions and so discourage penetrating questions that might make the management uncomfortable. Even so, because there was no follow-up to connect the specific cases we saw to their ultimate outcomes, there wasn't any opportunity for us to learn by doing.

Learning to speak up, to ask challenging questions in board meetings, didn't come easily, even to someone as naturally outspoken as I am. One number that Manny Hanny's directors were expected to keep a watchful eye on was the bank's capital-to-asset ratio, an important measure of the institution's safety or soundness, its cushion against disaster. The management assured us that our bank's ratio was comfortably in the middle compared to those of its competitors. But what, I wondered silently, if *all* those banks' ratios are too low to protect against a sudden increase in bad loans; what if each of the huge edifices that money center banks had become was balanced on the head of a pin? Since the other directors seemed satisfied, I kept my worries to myself.

As bank failures increased during the 1980s in the wake of worldwide recession, US regulators decided that banks' capital ratios, which had been falling for many years, were indeed too low, and they established higher minimum requirements. My gut reaction was vindicated, but I felt like an idiot for not having followed my instincts and spoken up at that earlier board meeting; I had certainly muffed one chance to try to make a difference. The new, higher capital requirements in turn proved badly inadequate when large banks' headlong increase in risk taking propelled them into the center of the worldwide financial crisis of 2008–9. So why had banks' boards of directors been so easily reassured? Why hadn't we all learned to ask harder questions?

My education in banking, and in the responsibilities of directors, took another leap forward in the 1980s when Manufacturers Hanover had a near-death experience caused by a severe debt crisis and spreading loan defaults in several Latin American countries where the bank was a major lender. Things were shaky enough to bring on quarterly visits to board meetings by the president of the New York Federal Reserve Bank, our main regulatory supervisor. Despite that gentleman's low-key style, these visits were an ominous signal, a sharp reminder of the directors' responsibility for overseeing and guiding improvement in the bank's condition. We got the message that our job was not to be simply rubber stamps for management, and, under our polite but persistent prodding, the painful but necessary changes were made. Most significantly, we prevailed on the CEO to fire the executive in charge of the bank's international lending, sending a sharp message about personal accountability.

Over the years that I spent on the board, the bank I had joined as Manufacturers Hanover provided a crash course in mergers and acquisitions. The bank, itself the creation of a major merger in 1961 and numerous smaller ones since, merged with the Chemical Bank and adopted the latter's name in 1992; the process was repeated when Chemical became Chase Manhattan in 1996, which in turn became JPMorgan Chase in 2000. The days and weeks leading up to these decisions involved difficult meetings, intense discussions, and the knowledge that any slip of the tongue could put a director at risk for violating strict regulations against trading on inside information, with the possibility of a serious fine or even jail time.

This exposure was brought home to me when I was suddenly called to a meeting in New York in connection with one of the mergers and had to make apologies to the hosts of a dinner party we had promised to attend, saying simply that I "had to go out of town." The host, an active and knowledgeable investor, asked casually, "Oh, by the way, are you still a director of Chemical Bank?" I realized immediately that he had guessed the reason for my trip, and my heart sank as I contemplated the potential fallout if he took advantage of his knowledge to trade in the stock. When I returned, just after the merger between Chemical and Chase had been announced, he called to tell me that he had indeed guessed that the merger was about to occur, but, he added, "I didn't trade."

Our vote authorizing a merger was just the beginning. Actually merging previously distinct executive ranks, workforces, branch systems, information technology systems, and, above all, cultures was a complex and often painful process, as employees from the top to the bottom of the organization were squeezed out in order to avoid redundancy and achieve the cost savings from consolidation that were the whole point of the merger. Many of the surviving employees also felt extreme stress, as their job descriptions changed or, at the least, they had to adapt to new ways of doing things. The one-on-one competitions to be the survivor in a particular job slot were fierce, and persuading old Manny Hanny and old Chemical survivors to regard themselves as part of one team often seemed like a Sisyphean task. My heart ached for Manny Hanny's CEO, John McGillicuddy, a warm and public-spirited man, as well as an outstanding banker, as he was gradually but inevitably marginalized during his brief time as head of the merged entity by the former CEO of Chemical, who, by mutual agreement, had been designated as McGillicuddy's successor.

When I joined the board of Manufacturers Hanover in 1973, banks, even sophisticated money center banks, generated earnings primarily by taking in deposits, using those funds to make loans, and deriving profits by charging higher interest rates on the loans they made than they paid out on their deposits. By the time I retired from the board of JPMorgan Chase in 2002, the activities that produced the earnings of money center banks had changed dramatically. Of the loans originally made by the bank, less than 25 percent remained on its own books. The rest were either sold outright or "securitized"—that is, packaged into groups of loans with differing characteristics and sold to a variety of investors.[2] The bank's profits now came mainly from the fees it charged for these and many other financial services, and from trading in currencies or securities for its own account.

Understanding the risks these varied activities carried was a complex business. As a member of the bank's Risk Policy Committee, I was actively involved in discussions about the sophisticated statistical techniques used to estimate various types of risk to which the bank was exposed. Yet no one from management ever mentioned to us that the structured transactions it had entered into with Enron before the latter's collapse in 2001 might entail financial risk, as well as risk to its reputation. The bank's leadership apparently believed that it was fully hedged against financial losses, although these transactions eventually cost the bank several hundreds of millions of dollars. As the world of banking changed, we directors struggled to keep up, but we weren't fast enough up the learning curve and neither, it turned out, were the managers. Neither group seemed to learn from experience either; the same sort of failure by banks, on a vastly larger scale, to understand or estimate accurately the risks they were taking culminated in the financial crisis of 2008–9. By then I had retired from all corporate directorships and could only join my fellow citizens in shocked disbelief as I watched the financial sector's house of cards collapse into a global disaster.

With one notable exception, every one of the large, successful firms whose boards of directors I joined soon found themselves threatened, as Manny Hanny was, by challenges they hadn't prepared for, challenges that forced on them wrenching changes in form or function or, often, both. One of those companies was Westinghouse Electric, long established and highly respected as one of the premier firms headquartered in our hometown of Pittsburgh, but with operations in many countries. Its major business, nuclear power, was one of special interest to me—after all, my father had been a major figure in the Manhattan Project; my mother had been a founding employee of Brookhaven Laboratory, one of the national labs created to explore the peacetime uses of atomic energy; and I had argued with Edward Teller over the role of nuclear energy as a member of Nelson Rockefeller's Commission on Critical Choices for Americans. As the clincher, my brother George had spoken admiringly of its CEO, Don Burnham, whom he had gotten to know while he, George, was director of the National Productivity Commission.

About the time Bob Kirby succeeded Burnham as chairman and CEO of Westinghouse, soon after I joined its board, the price of uranium began to shoot up, reaching forty dollars per pound by 1975. This escalation meant that the company would have gone broke trying to fulfill contracts it had signed when the price was five to six dollars per pound, promising to deliver the uranium they needed to the owners of the nuclear power plants it had built. Instead, it reneged on the contracts. The twenty-seven utility customers promptly sued, exposing Westinghouse to a potential two billion dollars in liabilities and setting off a round of suits, countersuits, and associated suits that would occupy the firm for the next five years, tie up many of the nation's major law firms, and set the company on a path of diversification that would ultimately end in its transformation into an entertainment company, CBS.

The situation created a great deal of tension for the directors personally. At one point, we were advised that the board as a whole should hire its own lawyer to protect itself against the numerous lawsuits in which we were named as defendants, quite separate from those who were defending the company itself. Our choice was John McCloy, the elderly but still canny establishment lawyer, banker, and adviser to presidents who had been US high commissioner for Germany just after World War II, the president of the World Bank, chairman of Chase Manhattan Bank and the Ford Foundation, and president of the Council on Foreign Relations. Despite his awe-inspiring pedigree, McCloy's advice to the members of the board was down to earth and practical, always cautioning us to keep our heads and not panic, however much our personal assets and reputations might appear to be threatened. "The worst thing you can do," he told us, "is let your opponents see that you feel threatened by their accusations." We swallowed hard and tried to remain calm in the face of the huge sums for which the other side tried—ultimately unsuccessfully—to hold us personally accountable.

Although my six years on the board had been dominated by those lawsuits and the tensions they created, both inside and outside the company, I had actually felt more comfortable on that board than I did during my early years at Manufacturers Hanover. Even though I was, once again, the first and only woman, I didn't stand out as an oddball nearly as much in Pittsburgh as I did in New York. Perhaps it was because we were all too busy concentrating on the company's problems; there's nothing like a crisis to create team spirit.

Neither the Westinghouse management nor any of my fellow directors was directly responsible for the gender-related restriction that separated me from the rest of the pack. All of Westinghouse's senior executives, along with the top executives of every major corporation headquartered in Pittsburgh, belonged to the Duquesne Club. The companies generally paid their executives' membership fees and deducted them from taxes as a business expense. It was illegal, though, for any club that served a business purpose to discriminate in its membership policies, and, during the late 1970s, feminist and minority activists were beginning to bring lawsuits against these firms, arguing that they could not deduct the dining club and country club fees they paid and at the same time insist that the clubs were purely social.

I had been freed from the humiliation of being relegated to the Duquesne Club's ladies' entrance when the club tightened its security, by closing that door, after it was briefly stormed by a group that included some of my more radical faculty colleagues. Now, I figured, I ought to strike my own blow for equality by joining any such lawsuit, if the opportunity came up. This would have been highly embarrassing to Westinghouse, and when I told Bob Kirby of my intention, he replied, "I hope there will be enough time for me to get the club to shape up before that happens." Kirby was as good as his word, and the Duquesne Club soon took in its first minority member, the African American dean of the Duquesne University Law School. He and I had made a bet as to which of us would be invited first; he was, so I won the bet. It wasn't long before the first woman joined as well, but it wasn't me; by that time I no longer lived in Pittsburgh.

McCloy's wisdom stood me in good stead on a very different issue from the one he had been engaged for. While I was still on the Westinghouse board, Ben Stein, Herb Stein's son, coauthored with his father a novel about the chaos created by runaway global inflation and an attempt by the Chinese to secretly acquire the world's supply of gold. It was a suspense story and also a roman à clef, featuring thinly disguised individuals who had served in the Nixon administration along with Herb. My fictional counterpart was the heroine, who rescued civilization by figuring out where the gold was disappearing to and getting it back, enabling the United States to go back to a gold standard, stopping the worldwide inflation in its tracks.

No one could object to being cast as the savior of Western civilization. But the authors also enmeshed my character in a torrid love affair with one Peter Hanrahan, who would be immediately recognizable by any journalist or Washington insider as Peter Flanigan, who had succeeded Pete Peterson as director of the Council on International Economic Policy while I was at the CEA. I was amused but also ticked off by this linkage, not least because Flanigan was on my personal blacklist. I had been annoyed and embarrassed at a dinner party given by him and his wife, when I was sent off with "the ladies" after dinner. "How pretentious can you get," I had thought to myself, "emulating a custom still practiced only by the stuffiest of embassies?"

When Mark Perlman, my rigidly moralistic friend and chairman of the Pitt economics department, learned about this story line shortly before the book's publication, he insisted that I should be prepared to sue the authors to protect my good name. "Come on, Mark," I responded, "how Victorian can you get?" But I decided to ride Westinghouse's coattails by seeking some free advice from McCloy. After he had skimmed a prepublication copy of the book, he advised me that my best chance of winning a suit would be to sue not for libel, which is very hard to win under US law, but for calumny. "What on earth," I asked, "is calumny?" "The false imputation of unchastity," he replied with a straight face.

"Are you suggesting that I do that?" I asked. "Well," McCloy said, "let me put it this way: it's a perfectly dreadful novel, and I'm sure it will sink like a stone. The one thing that might save it is the publicity that would result if you sued." I took his advice, and the novel did sink, although that didn't prevent Ben Stein from later gaining fame as an actor, columnist, and television personality.

I really began to flex my muscles as a director at Marcor, a Chicago company that, among other things, owned the catalog retailer Montgomery Ward. Just after I joined that board in 1974, Mobil Oil Company announced its intention to buy 51 percent of the company's stock, in addition to the 4.5 percent it already owned. Despite objections from Marcor's management and the Department of Justice, Mobil persevered and won.

Mobil's representative in discussions with Marcor's board about the price that Mobil would offer for the remaining shares of Marcor stock was its president, William Tavoulareas. A tough-talking lawyer and accountant, Tavoulareas was already famous as the canniest of all the Western oil companies' negotiators with Middle Eastern governments. He used every one of his negotiating tricks to keep the price offered for those Marcor shares as low as possible. He would challenge us with statements such as "What do you mean I can't be part of the discussion about the price that's paid for the remaining shares? We now own a controlling interest in Marcor, dammit." We reminded him that it was the Marcor board's fiduciary duty to represent the interests of the remaining minority shareholders by getting the best possible deal for them, and he wasn't yet a member of the board.

The more Tavoulareas tried to manipulate us, the angrier I got. My pent-up frustration boiled over during the board's discussion of Mobil's "absolutely final offer," and I found the courage to pipe up. "That doesn't seem fair," I objected. "Let's tell him no and see what happens." I was the youngest, newest, and most inexperienced director, and my more seasoned colleagues were dubious—after all, Mobil held all the cards—but they agreed to try. Tavoulareas, caught off guard by our unexpected stubbornness, raised his offer. So the last act of Marcor's board of directors before it was dissolved was to get a slightly better deal for the company's remaining minority shareholders. Among all the boards I sat on, my tenure on Marcor's was the briefest, but it was also the one on which my input most immediately affected the outcome, and I felt a flush of satisfaction as we shook hands at the end of our farewell dinner.

With the Marcor board dissolved, I was free of any potential conflict of interest in joining the board of Procter and Gamble (P&G), one of the world's largest consumer products companies. That firm had won its way into my heart even before I attended my first board meeting. Just after my appointment was announced, two young women who were on the first rung of the its famed process for grooming future executives came to visit me in my office. They wore blue suits and matching pumps, then the regulation uniform for aspiring females in the business world, but their manner was open and friendly. They said they had come simply to introduce themselves and welcome me to the company. I asked them what it was like to be female pioneers in P&G's highly sought after and competitive program. "Lonely," was their answer.

I had assured the CEO, and I meant it, that I had no intention of using my board seat to be an advocate for women as a special-interest group. But I did bring a different and therefore useful perspective on some issues important to the company. Soon after I joined the board, I met and talked informally with a large group of women employees; quite a few of them told me later how much such interaction with a director of the company had meant to them. When I was shown some of the advertising department's favorite ads as part of my introductory training program, I commented that several of them, featuring a male authority figure and a smiling housewife, struck me as sexist. Although their initial reaction was open-mouthed astonishment, gradually P&G's ads came around to recognizing that women are not obedient automatons but capable decision makers, able to evaluate detergents and diapers without male guidance.

I had to wait a long time, though, before my hope of no longer being the only woman on every board I sat on was fulfilled. When Lynn Martin joined the P&G board in 1993, I greeted her by saying, "Welcome, Lynn; I've waited seventeen years for you!" A former Republican congresswoman from Illinois, Lynn had also been the secretary of labor who coined the term *glass ceiling* in her efforts to reduce or eliminate the barriers that confronted women in the workplace. Once she had joined, Lynn distinguished herself by being the only member of the board who tried out every new P&G household product herself and gave her opinion at the next meeting. "The Swiffer did a really terrific job on my floors," she reported when the innovative sweeper was introduced, but she didn't see much use for Fit, a rinse tailored for fruits and vegetables, which never did catch on with the American public.

Of the four firms whose boards I joined in the 1970s, only P&G was still an independent company, with the same name, when I stepped down. There was continuity in management there as well; every CEO had been either president or its equivalent before he succeeded to the top job, consistent with the company's commitment to promotion from within. At first, coming from an academic environment where the most effective way to get a promotion was to brandish outside job offers, I had been appalled by such insularity. As I saw the results over time, though, I had to admit that the powerful culture and unwavering loyalty to the company and its principles that this process produced was a major strength. This emerged not only in the consistency—with one notable exception—of P&G's financial results and successful global expansion but in its impressively high level of social responsibility.

This last was attested to by the awards, prizes, and public recognition it garnered every year for its achievements as a "most admired company" that offered a welcoming workplace to women, working mothers, minorities, and people with disabilities. It also received accolades for its environmental progress, its use of advanced technologies to improve consumers' quality of life worldwide, and its work on finding alternatives to animal testing—this last in the same year that its annual meeting was picketed by animal-rights activists for not having eliminated such testing entirely.

Cautiously and gradually, P&G's strong culture became less insular, opening up to the outside world. In its research and development, this process took off in the late 1990s. For decades, the company had a closed innovation process, centered around its own secretive research and development operations. Then, in less than a decade, P&G increased the proportion of new product ideas originating from outside the firm from less than a fifth to around half.[3] Nor did their conservatism and insularity prevent P&G executives from taking forward-looking positions on local issues. When a group tried to close down an exhibit of Robert Mapplethorpe's controversial photographs by bringing obscenity charges, several of these executives said publicly that this misguided effort would only subject the city to national ridicule, a stance the board roundly applauded.

The chief executives at P&G may all have been "proctoids," as they were sometimes derisively dubbed, but that's not to say that their personalities didn't vary widely, requiring the directors to adjust to a new style with each change of leadership. A particularly sharp style change occurred when quiet, courteous, consensus-building John Pepper succeeded autocratic, sharp-tongued CEO Edwin Artzt, whose nickname both inside the company and in the press was the "Prince of Darkness."

The one time I saw Artzt act with ruthless decisiveness was when a senior executive failed to alert him to a potential crisis, a wrangle over the allegedly deceptive labeling of P&G's pasteurized orange juice as *Fresh Choice,* which led the Food and Drug Administration to order the product to be immediately pulled from supermarket shelves. Artzt, who had not been told about the situation, was blindsided and, as he told the board, "mad as hell." The executive vice president responsible, who had been regarded as a possible heir apparent to the top job, suddenly resigned.

In another embarrassing situation, though, Artzt showed that he did not hold himself excused from accountability. He turned down a hundred thousand dollars of his annual bonus in 1994 in the wake of losses on complicated derivative securities transactions the company's treasury department had entered into with Bankers Trust, without his knowledge and against guidelines authorized by the board of directors only a month or so before. Even though P&G eventually recouped almost its entire loss in the settlement of a lawsuit against Bankers Trust, heads rolled again, including that of the company's treasurer, because these executives had explicitly violated the board's guidelines on using derivatives. By turning down his bonus, Artzt signaled that, as the captain of the ship, he, too, had to bear some responsibility.

Artzt's biggest public relations stumble occurred when he discovered that somebody on the inside was leaking proprietary information—company secrets—to the *Wall Street Journal.* In his eagerness to locate the culprit, he asked the Cincinnati police department to comb through hundreds of thousands of phone calls to the *Journal* reporter who wrote the stories. When he told this to the board, my heart sank as I thought to myself, "Don't do it, Ed," remembering the pithy advice Jack McNulty, the vice president of public relations at General Motors (GM) had given me: "Never get into a fight with someone who buys ink by the barrel." I said as much, and others chimed in, but it was too late; the search of telephone records was already under way.

Whether the inside leaker was located and punished or not, it wasn't worth the widespread negative publicity; the furious journalist published a book about the company that was as negative as she could possible make it. Artzt had to admit publicly to "an error in judgment," and the whole episode at least temporarily tarnished the company's image in the eyes of the public. But the board had spoken its displeasure out loud, and Artzt took the lesson to heart, behaving much more circumspectly after that.

One of the primary responsibilities of any board of directors of a publicly held company is to hire and, if necessary, fire the company's chief executive. All of us on the P&G board knew that, of course, but we never thought it would happen to us, or anticipated how painful it would be.

When John Pepper announced his intention to retire as P&G's chairman and CEO, there was no doubt as to who the top executives had agreed his successor should be: Dirk Jager, the second in command. In fact, Jager had been Artzt's choice as his own immediate successor, but the board had persuaded him that Pepper should become CEO and Jager president. As Jager's mentor, we had argued, Pepper could smooth off some of his rough edges. Jager was a total product of the P&G system; he had joined the company straight from university and worked his way up through successively more responsible positions. He was a large, blond Dutchman with steel-rimmed glasses and a stern visage. This appearance, along with his clipped speech, made him seem cold and distant. But he was admired for his well-honed analytical mind and his hands-on approach to his job. Even as president, he never missed an opportunity to visit grocery stores to see for himself whether P&G products were properly displayed and how they were selling.

The directors were less certain than the top executives about Jager's suitability; we had a lively discussion chewing over the pros and cons. "He's absolutely brilliant, totally customer oriented, and has a fabulous track record," argued his supporters. "But he's got lousy people skills and is quick to blame others for problems," countered those who had their doubts. In the end, though, we agreed that he should succeed Pepper in the top job. The first signal that the doubters might have had the better argument came quickly. Jager's first board meeting as chairman and CEO had been preceded by a dinner the night before in honor of a recently retired P&G executive vice president who was also a member of the board. Jager, who made no secret of his dislike for this man, remarked loudly at the luncheon following the board meeting that he had skipped the dinner in favor of staying home to watch TV with his wife. With that pointed comment, he shattered the sense of team spirit so important among top executives and boards of directors alike. I knew right then that we had made a mistake in appointing Jager. So, from the looks on their faces, did my fellow directors. But it was too late for us to do anything about it.

Less than eighteen months later, after three successive negative earnings "surprises" and a 50 percent drop in the price of P&G stock, Jager was gone. Despite his obvious strengths, his inability to set appropriate goals or exercise effective leadership had proven too costly to the company and its shareholders, including nearly all of its employees, who had chosen to put their retirement nest eggs entirely into P&G's profit-sharing plan and now saw their value cut in half. The episode was most painful for Jager, who, I believe, never did understand where he had gone wrong. But it was also painful for the board members, who had to admit to a serious error in judgment; we should have been more alert to the warning signs that had come up in our discussions of the CEO succession.

In light of the fact that Jager had spent his entire career at P&G and been responsible for many of its successes during his climb to the top, the board regarded three years' compensation as a reasonable severance payment. But when the amount he received, which totaled about nine million dollars, became public, we were heavily criticized for giving an outrageous "reward for failure." The American public was beginning to be resentful of the sums that were bestowed as parting gifts on chief executives as they were being shown the door by disappointed boards of directors. In the first few years of the current century such severance payments, often made to CEOs with very brief tenures at their companies who had built guarantees of such compensation into their employment contracts, became truly outrageous, often amounting to more than ten or even twenty times what we had decided on as Jager's payment.

By then I had joined one or two outspoken directors of other large firms in insisting, both privately in meetings of board committees and in public speeches, that the total compensation of many top executives was exceeding the bounds of reason and decency, and that self-policing by companies' compensation committees was urgent. If we don't fix it, I warned, others will, and you executives won't like their fix one bit. My friend Ann McLaughlin, who was also a member of the board at several leading companies—including GM—put the warning even more tersely: adapt or Congress will adopt. I had no trouble getting other directors, many of whom were CEOs themselves, to agree with me in compensation committee meetings, but none of them was willing to step forward and say so publicly, each insisting that he would be verbally lynched by the community of fellow executives if he did that.

With the financial industry meltdown of 2008, the American public's building anger against executives who grew unimaginably rich while the activities that ballooned their paychecks created economic disaster for many ordinary Americans exploded in a demand for government action. Congress and the administration have responded by making Ann McLaughlin's and my warnings a reality. Firms that have received government assistance are subject to a variety of restrictions on executive compensation, and, at one point, legislation was proposed to claw back bonuses, through retroactive taxation at confiscatory rates, from executives who have already received them. Board compensation committees are beginning to be held more strictly to account by both shareholders and the public, and at least some of them show signs of acting more independently of management.

Gradually but continuously over the more than three decades (1973–2005) I spent as an outside director on corporate boards, they were evolving from the rubber stamps of management I found when I first entered these august boardrooms to monitors who tried to look out for the interests of both the shareholders and the organization itself. In Manny Hanny's case, the initial impetus was primarily external, as when the president of the New York Fed put the board on notice that it was responsible for making sure that the bank's fragile condition improved with all deliberate speed. At P&G the embarrassing fallout from Dirk Jager's failures and subsequent removal played a role.

Above and beyond developments at individual companies, though, those years had been ones of upheaval and change in the governance of all public corporations that swept their directors along. We had been subject to increasing pressure from several landmark lawsuits and a dramatic shift in the ownership of corporate shares from individuals to activist institutional investors, mainly pension funds and mutual funds. This new class of owners was capable of turning the glare of unfavorable publicity on firms whose governance didn't meet its requirements. In response, the standards by which a board's performance was judged rose dramatically, affecting the makeup and processes of every board on which I sat.

Boards became better suited to fulfilling their monitoring role as they both shrank in size and became more diverse, and the number of directors who were also members of management fell, often to the CEO alone. Directors spent more time studying their homework in advance of meetings, and the training sessions for new directors that had been a novelty when I joined the board of Manufacturers Hanover have become routine at most large public firms, supported by a cottage industry of training programs for directors at law and business schools eagerly embracing a new cash cow. As someone who had often questioned just how much I was contributing to a company's performance by sitting on its board, I welcomed this more intense engagement, even though it increased both the hours I spent preparing for meetings and the personal exposure, both financial and reputational, that I risked.

At P&G, these developments were accelerated by the recruitment of an increasingly diverse, sophisticated, cosmopolitan, and strong-minded group of outside directors. These included not only younger CEO's from companies in industries newly relevant to P&G's success, such as software and Web services, but also outstanding people from outside the business world, like Joshua Lederberg, who won the Nobel Prize for Medicine at the age of thirty-three, and Ernesto Zedillo, the former president of Mexico, who brought an international perspective. As a group, we exerted polite but constant pressure to cut down on the carefully scripted presentations by management, allowing the meetings to become more informal, better focused, and with more opportunity for spontaneous give-and-take.

Meetings of the outside directors, without management present, which used to occur only at times of crisis, became regularly scheduled events, and we developed processes for annually evaluating the performance of the CEO, as well as the effectiveness of the board's own functioning. A growing minority of US firms has instituted the separation of the roles of chairman and CEO, which is usual in many European countries; in those that haven't, the role of lead director has developed as a partial substitute. This nonmanagement director works with the chairman to set the agenda for board meetings and presides over meetings of the outside directors without management.

At P&G, towering, deep-voiced Norman Augustine was chosen for this role by the universal acclaim of his board colleagues. Augustine, the CEO of Lockheed Martin, had held several important positions in our government's defense establishment and gained fame as the author of *Augustine's Laws,* a book about government and business bureaucracies as wise as it is hilarious. He applied this wisdom by putting his stamp on both the structure and the content of P&G board meetings.

In the wake of the Enron and other corporate scandals, most of these changes were codified into requirements by means of legislation and regulation. I was closest to these developments at P&G, where I chaired the

Governance and Nominating Committee for several years. In that role, I worked closely with CEO John Pepper to make sure the board's membership and procedures met the highest standards of corporate governance, a steadily moving target. The result was that, when the Sarbanes-Oxley legislation and its implementing regulations were passed in 2002, I was proud to discover that P&G already met almost all its requirements relating to boards of directors.

The one exception was that certain committee assignments had to be changed for two directors the board had categorized as independent but who did not meet the tightened criteria for director independence mandated by the new legislation. Ironically, one of the two was Lynn Martin, far and away the most candidly critical and outspoken of all the directors. The issue arose because she was associated with the consulting arm of Deloitte and Touche, P&G's main accounting firm; her role was to advise companies on how to eliminate practices that could be regarded as sexual harassment. "Legal requirements have trumped common sense, Lynn," I grumbled when P&G's lawyers told us that she could no longer be a member of the Governance and Nominating Committee that I chaired.

One change in governance that the P&G Board made on its own initiative was to establish term limits for directors. As successful younger people, some in their early forties, were elected to the board, the possibility that tenures of thirty years or more would make it harder to bring new faces and ideas onboard led to the decision to limit directors to four three-year terms. As the chair of the committee that proposed this change and the longest-serving director, with twenty-seven years on the board, I immediately told my colleagues that I wouldn't stand for reelection at the next shareholders' meeting.

I had no doubt that this was the right move for the board and P&G, but it gave me a sharp pang of loss. I still miss the P&G board meetings, the thrill of being involved with a superbly managed and successful company, and the interactions with my outstanding colleagues there. Despite its reputation for conformity and its commitment to promotion from within, P&G has risen to the competitive challenges of a globalizing world through a process of continuous change, without the wrenching distortions that have made most of the other companies I've been associated with either disappear as independent entities or alter so drastically as to be virtually unrecognizable.

Years later, with the experience of thirteen years as a senior executive at one of the country's largest multinational companies, General Motors, under my belt, I had a much better understanding of what makes big companies tick when I joined the boards of Browning Ferris Industries (BFI), a Texas-based waste management company, and Unocal, the old Union Oil Company of California, in the 1990s. I had worked with and come to admire BFI's chief executive, Bill Ruckelshaus, during the Nixon administration. As deputy attorney general in 1973, Bill had resigned rather than follow Nixon's orders to fire the Watergate special prosecutor, Archibald Cox, in what came to be known as the Saturday Night Massacre.

It's hard to imagine what could make a garbage company exciting. But there was plenty of excitement when Bill told the astounded board that he and the company's general counsel had been working secretly for months with the Manhattan district attorney to end the Mafia's stranglehold on commercial waste disposal in New York City. The Mafia had fought back with tactics we had all watched goggle-eyed in *The Godfather*: the wife of BFI's New York district manager, greeting some women guests, had found a severed dog's head on her doorstep. But BFI had the last laugh when the Mafia refuse collectors were rounded up, tried, and convicted. In his Texas drawl, with an unlit cigar clamped in the corner of his mouth, our lead lawyer explained: "I took the papers that would complete BFI's purchase of his company to the jail where one of the Mafia owners was locked up and watched while he signed them, cussing all the way. I had to bob and weave to duck his spit."

Despite its success in this bit of heroic derring-do, BFI was struggling in an industry where the accounting practices of at least one of its largest competitors skirted the edge of legality. In 1997 the board decided that selling the firm to another company (not the one with the dubious accounting) was in the best interest of the shareholders. We didn't come to the decision easily; when BFI's young president first broached the idea, several of the directors said to Ruckelshaus, "You should fire him for disloyalty." The evidence was ultimately persuasive, though, and we voted the company, along with ourselves as a board, out of existence.

Given the roughneck nature of the petroleum industry, it's not surprising that, when I joined the board of Unocal, I was nonplussed by the "cowboy culture" I found there. At one of my first meetings, the chairman reported on a leak that had allowed a toxic substance capable of causing skin irritation and flulike symptoms to escape from the firm's San Francisco refinery. The refinery's managers, he told us, had known about the leak but decided to do nothing about it until the time came for a scheduled overhaul of the plant. "And how," we asked, "had those managers been punished for their irresponsible decision," a misjudgment that ultimately cost the company some hundred million dollars in fines and penalties? "Oh, they were reprimanded and temporarily suspended," came the bland reply. "You mean they weren't fired or at least transferred?" I sputtered.

Speechless with indignation, I couldn't manage even a sputter when Unocal's president, John Imle, reported that he had entertained several members of the Taliban at his home for dinner to discuss the possibility of Unocal getting involved in business in Taliban-ruled Afghanistan. It wasn't long before Unocal recognized the impossibility of working with the Taliban, and Imle was pushed out of the presidency not long afterward, but other elements of the company's traditional culture took longer to uproot.

Soon after I joined the board, the outside directors, acting through the various committees of the board, started putting steady, persistent pressure on Unocal's top management to change the firm's behavior from top to bottom, which in some cases involved ousting or reassigning some of its senior managers. Many of these initiatives originated with the Corporate Responsibility Committee, which I chaired during much of my time on the board. The directors themselves wrote a charter for each Board committee, and conducted an audit every year to check whether its commitments had been met and whether any revision or updating was required.

Beginning in 1994, Unocal started to issue an annual report to stockholders, separate from the required one focused on financial performance, in which it discussed candidly its problems in the areas of corporate social responsibility—health, safety, and the environment—and what it was doing to correct them. And it adopted as its motto "To improve the lives of people wherever we work." The process was a gradual one, but, over time and with the directors pushing and prodding every inch of the way, Unocal took steps to match its actions to its words. It became more forthcoming in admitting to and aggressive in cleaning up underground leaks that had persisted for many decades, and in compensating the communities that had suffered as a result. It strengthened the language in its code of conduct for both employees and directors, which was then cited by several activists as one of the most progressive in the industry. And it's Operations Management System, introduced in 1999 to identify, evaluate, and mitigate the various safety risks in its operations, was so cutting edge that Unocal received requests from other companies for help in implementing such a system in their own operations.

The most inflammatory issue Unocal's directors had to confront was the company's participation in building a gas pipeline through Myanmar (Burma), a country then ruled by one of the most thuggish regimes on the planet. The company was under constant, highly emotional pressure to get out of the country by selling its share in operations there. How, our angry critics demanded, could we partner with the state oil and gas company of such a reprehensible regime? My fellow directors in corporate jobs could shield themselves from hostile calls, but, as a member of a university faculty whose telephone and office door were open to anyone who called or knocked, I was confronted face-to-face by groups of students who told me bluntly that doing business in such a country was immoral.

We argued intensely over the relative merits of selling our interest in the project, what I dubbed the Pontius Pilate choice—washing our hands of responsibility for a situation by placing it in the hands of others—versus "constructive engagement." Neither side persuaded the other, of course; some of the students prayed for my soul, while others burned me in effigy on the Diag, the center of the University of Michigan campus, where I had become a professor.

The Unocal directors chewed over the Myanmar issue frequently and at length. We quizzed the top management intensively on the nature of operations in that country, sending the CEO there in person to see the situation for himself. When he returned, we demanded and got from him personal assurances that, contrary to widespread allegations, the actual operator of the facilities in which Unocal held part ownership (a French firm called Total) had never cooperated with the Myanmar government, either in using forced labor or in relocating villages to make room for the petroleum pipeline. On the contrary, he described to us in detail Unocal's active program of providing schools, clinics, and training (as, for example, in fish farming) to the people in villages along the pipeline route.

Our CEO's replies to our probing were corroborated by four field reports, covering the period 2002–5, based on extensive interviews with a broad range of stakeholders inside Myanmar, including villagers in most of the communities along the pipeline. These interviews were conducted by a small American nonprofit focused on working with companies to help them ensure that they have positive rather than negative impacts on the communities where they operate. The final report concluded, "[T]he overwhelming majority of [those interviewed] argue that Total [and its partners] should neither leave the country nor limit its interaction with the military regime in Myanmar/Burma."[4]

We recognized that when revenues began to accrue from the pipeline, some would go into the coffers of the despised and cruel autocracy that held—and continues to hold—the country in an iron grip. Weighing all these considerations, we concluded that the benefits we could bring to at least a small part of Myanmar's population by staying in the consortium there was preferable to a forced sale to another company, probably Chinese, that would almost certainly not continue investing in socioeconomic projects that benefited the local population.

Because of this decision to stay, Unocal was sued in 1996 by activist groups under a centuries-old law originally directed at curbing the operations of pirates on the high seas. The case dragged on inconclusively for nearly a decade. Meanwhile, the directors had gradually come to the conclusion that Unocal was too small to reap full economies of scale, implying that it would be in the shareholders' best interest to sell the company to a larger firm. This decision meant disposing of the lawsuit that was hanging over its head, and the case was settled out of court in 2005. Chevron, the company that ultimately bought Unocal, has continued to support economic and social initiatives in Myanmar and has continued to come under pressure for disinvestment.

Most of my years on the Unocal board were characterized by slow, steady progress in the effectiveness of board oversight; the final year, in contrast, was one of high drama. After the company had been in play, or up for sale, for several months, it entered into negotiations with the only bidder that had met the announced deadline, Chevron, America's second-largest oil company. Terms had been agreed to and the transaction appeared well on its way to a shareholder vote when the Chinese National Overseas Oil Corporation (CNOOC), a firm 70 percent owned by the Chinese government, tendered an all-cash bid with a significantly higher value than Chevron's combined stock and cash offer.

With two contenders now in the game, the Unocal board, whose fiduciary duty was to get the highest possible price for Unocal's shareholders, successfully elicited a higher offer from Chevron. But in the meantime, all hell was breaking loose in Washington. Several legislators, egged on by Chevron's lobbyists, were raising objections to a sale to a state-owned Chinese firm on grounds of national security. They were threatening, at the very least, to complicate and stretch out the required approval process, to the point that CNOOC withdrew its bid. Chevron's was accepted, and Unocal was merged into Chevron.

How much the buildup of both congressional and public hostility to the CNOOC bid was actually based on national security concerns, in the military or strategic sense, and how much on a belief that a company owned and possibly subsidized by the Chinese government would provide unfair competition to privately owned American firms is impossible to tell. In any case, CNOOC's withdrawal rendered moot what would have been an interesting but difficult discussion by Unocal's board, centered on two questions. First, how should we have weighed our fiduciary obligations to the shareholders against our obligations as citizens to our country's best interests? Second, if we had concluded that the latter should dominate, would we have decided that the United States would be better off if CNOOC were allowed to buy Unocal or if it were prevented from doing so?

That conversation never took place in the Unocal boardroom, but I have played it over in my own mind every time a proposed investment in the United States by a foreign entity has attracted controversy. No general rule can cover all cases, but my own belief is that, if the United States is to continue to be regarded as a hospitable host to foreign investment, such transactions should be prohibited only when national security, in the conventional meaning of the term, is at issue. Given that CNOOC had undertaken to sell all of Unocal's US assets—its interest was in the ones in Southeast Asia—it's hard to believe that our national security would have been threatened if the Chinese company had been the winning bidder.

Reflecting on the more than three decades I spent as an independent director of multinational companies, I ask myself how much value-added I had contributed to changes in corporate governance, beyond my symbolic role as a pioneering woman. In most cases, I'm confident that I did have some impact on the board's deliberations and the company's behavior. The one situation about which I feel no such reassurance is my performance as a director of Alcoa, the worldwide aluminum company. I had been asked to join that board by its chairman and CEO, Paul O'Neill, another acquaintance from my days on the CEA, when he was a rising young deputy director of the Office of Management and Budget (OMB). Paul liked to anchor Alcoa's strategic decisions firmly in the current global political and economic picture. As part of that approach, he relied on Ken Dam—who had been Paul's colleague at OMB and, at later points in his career, became deputy secretary of both the state and treasury departments—to give periodic reports on political developments and trends around the world, not only to the board but to business unit managers as well; Paul relied on me to do the same on the economic side.

For very different reasons, both Paul and I struck out after he resigned, in 2000, to become secretary of the treasury and took Ken Dam with him as his deputy. Paul's successor at Alcoa, Alain Belda, had a very different management style, which did not include our global briefings. Apparently that difference made me superfluous in Alain's eyes; one day he invited me into his office a few minutes before a meeting of Alcoa's nominating committee and asked me to resign to make room for a new director. I was hurt and angry at the grade of F he had implicitly given me and thunderstruck by the brusque way in which it was delivered, allowing me almost no time to make up my mind. But, privately, I had to admit to myself that I hadn't found a way to have much impact on the board's deliberations or decisions once Paul O'Neill had departed. Paul's dismissal from his cabinet post was far more public. It came from Presi-

204 · THE MARTIAN'S DAUGHTER

dent George W. Bush, after Paul disagreed with the President and his other economic advisers on their proposed tax cuts and insisted repeatedly that there was no evidence of weapons of mass destruction in Iraq.

Whatever progress "my" boards made in corporate governance, it wasn't enough. Of the seven firms, only two—P&G and Alcoa—preserved their identities in the face of the upheavals that were reshaping American business during the last quarter of the twentieth century. Marcor, BFI, and Unocal were acquired by and merged into larger firms; Manny Hanny had been involved in three major mergers and name changes; and Westinghouse, known as a leader in the nuclear power industry, had sold off its birthright and transformed itself into the entertainment company CBS. And the financial scandals, crimes, and disasters that marked the first decade of the twenty-first century revealed how far corporate boards of directors still have to go to fulfill their monitoring role effectively. Women are still in the minority on corporate boards today, but very few of them are feeling the isolation of being the first woman, as I did. Silently, I say to them, "Go girl; be a pushy broad and put some spine into whatever board you're on."

The governing bodies of leading universities were grappling with some of the same social issues as the boards of for-profit corporations, I discovered when I served on two of them. One was Harvard, where I had spent my undergraduate years; the other was Princeton, which had played such an important role at various stages of my life, even though it had refused to admit me as a graduate student. Both institutions were also caught up in questions of effective governance. And, although universities are grounded in a dedication to the principles of openness and the free exchange of ideas, both conducted much of their decision making in sessions closed to outside eyes.

Harvard and Princeton had their own version of the "withdrawal versus constructive engagement" controversy several decades before it erupted at Unocal. There the question was whether to continue to hold stock in companies that did business in South Africa, then under the yoke of a regime firmly committed to apartheid. As was true of many college campuses during the 1970s, Harvard was feeling strong pressures, intensified by student protests in 1972 and again in 1977, to disinvest entirely from such companies.

Like many of its sister institutions, Harvard at first chose a path of compromise, actually selling stocks only in cases where companies failed to adopt the Sullivan Principles. These principles required firms operating in South Africa to treat all employees equally regardless of race, to promote the advancement of blacks and other nonwhites in the workplace, and to take measures to improve the quality of life for these groups outside the workplace as well. This question, which was roiling the Harvard campus when I left its Board of Overseers in 1978, was doing the same at Princeton when I joined its Board of Trustees in 1980. Later, as a director of Unocal, I was to confront the issue once again. In each of these situations, I would have found it more comfortable to come to a decision based on some simple universal principle. But the moral choice is never unambiguous, the empirical evidence is mixed, and the question is not likely to be resolved definitively in my lifetime, if ever.

Like the Harvard and Princeton governing boards at the time, I believed, and still do, that in most situations constructive engagement—maintaining limited political and business links with a country despite its inexcusable policies, while continuing to press for political or social reform—is likely to be more effective than total withdrawal. In hindsight, though, I have become convinced that, under the particular circumstances of apartheid South Africa, disinvestment was the more effective course. By the end of the 1980s, Harvard had almost entirely withdrawn from investment in South Africa; Princeton eventually did the same. And the Reverend Sullivan, a director of General Motors and the author of the principles that bore his name, had himself abandoned his original principles as ineffective and become a champion of disinvestment.

A very public issue, the changing status of women in the corporate world, had its counterpart in the private world of Harvard. Although many of the restrictions on female students' full participation in Harvard life had been eliminated by the time I joined its board, women undergraduates, who were more and more often seeing themselves as Harvard rather than Radcliffe students, had become increasingly vocal about their dissatisfaction with the distinctions that remained. They were particularly unhappy that the men's and women's housing were separated by a mile or more, and that the Harvard Houses offered a range of house-centered intellectual and cultural activities that the Radcliffe dorms lacked.

This gap in the lives of female undergraduates was filled by the creation of a unified house system for undergraduates. Women would be allowed to live in the Harvard freshman dorms and upper-class houses, and men could choose to live in the Radcliffe dormitory quadrangle, which gradually acquired many of the ancillary benefits enjoyed by the Harvard Houses. As a Radcliffe student twenty-five years earlier, I had been denied access to multiple Harvard facilities, including its undergraduate library and its MBA program. Now, as a member of Harvard's governing board, I felt a special thrill of satisfaction in helping to knock the last of these barriers down.

The dramatic changes in the status of Radcliffe undergraduates were formalized in a 1977 agreement between the President and Fellows of Harvard College and the president of Radcliffe, which stated, "Undergraduates admitted to and subsequently enrolled in Radcliffe will thereby be enrolled . . . in Harvard College with all the rights and privileges accorded Harvard College enrollment."[5] No longer would women graduates have to be awarded Harvard degrees retroactively, as my generation was, in order to be able to vote in alumni elections and to serve on either of Harvard's two governing boards.

The status of women faculty at Harvard has not been so easily resolved. The question of why there were so few female faculty members, especially at the senior level, came up again and again in meetings of the board and its committees. Harvard's president at the time, Derek Bok, repeatedly stated his commitment to the recruitment and advancement of women faculty, and I believe he was sincere. At the same time, he clearly believed that women's sense of obligation to family often prevented them from pursuing an academic career with the same single-minded intensity as men.

Bok may have been influenced in this judgment by the experience of his wife, the influential philosopher and ethicist Sissela Bok who, despite her growing eminence, declined to fight her way up the tenure-track ladder. As someone who had only recently completed that climb while raising children, I felt that the president's view was rather patronizing and told him so, but I doubt that I had much effect on his outlook.

Why, I wondered when I was elected to Harvard's Board of Overseers, are we called overseers rather than trustees? Whereas other universities have a single governing board, Harvard has two. The Harvard Corporation, known formally as the President and Fellows of Harvard College, is the university's executive board. This self-perpetuating body meets every other week and effectively runs the institution; in the words of the *Harvard Guide,* "[T]he seven-member board is responsible for the day-to-day management of the University's finances and business affairs."[6] The second governing board, the Board of Overseers, is a larger body elected by the alumni for six-year terms; its role is to "advise and consent."

It didn't take me long after I was elected to discover two things about the Board of Overseers, whose archaic title, the Reverend and Honorable Board of Overseers, goes back to the charter granted to Harvard by the Commonwealth of Massachusetts in 1650. One was that the presence of women was as much of a novelty there as it was on corporate boards. The first one, Helen Gilbert, also chair of the separate Radcliffe Board of Trustees, had become an overseer only two years before Adele Simmons and I were elected. Because only Harvard alumni could vote for overseers, Radcliffe graduates had been awarded Harvard degrees retroactively so they could vote in these elections or serve as overseers.

The male overseers had welcomed Helen Gilbert, a middle-aged Boston grande dame with strong aristocratic features, gray hair befitting her age, and impeccable social credentials, without difficulty; she actually headed the board during my first year there. Adele Simmons was another matter. A history professor at Tufts University and dean of its women's college at the time, she later became a Princeton professor and dean, president of Hampshire College, and president of the MacArthur Foundation. Adele was also beautiful, an outspoken blonde barely into her thirties. I shall never forget the faces of our male colleagues sitting in the basement bar of the Harvard Faculty Club as they watched Adele, earnestly discussing some fine point of Harvard governance as she simultaneously nursed her new baby and drank an old-fashioned through a straw.

The other salient truth that struck me almost from my first moment was that Harvard's bicameral governance structure was a perpetual source of angst and soul-searching to the overseers. Since the Harvard Corporation made or approved all the important decisions, what was our function? As one member put it, the Board of Overseers was an impressive club to belong to, but she didn't see that it had any real responsibilities or influence over Harvard policies. The rationale for the bicameral structure, the functions of its two bodies, and the relationship between them, were the object of a major review as my term as an overseer was coming to an end. Some incremental changes were made in the interest of better defining their respective roles and increasing the interaction between them, but the bicameral structure itself—and the overseers' angst—remained. Not until 2010 was a more drastic overhaul of the composition, structure, and practices of the Harvard Corporation announced;[7] it is too early to tell what effect that will have on the practice of governance of the university.

The makeup of the Board of Overseers itself was also a cause for hand-wringing The 1970s was an era of social ferment and change, when antiestablishment views gained currency and the military-industrial establishment was widely regarded as the axis of evil. The Harvard alumni tended to reflect these views, and they expressed them in their votes for overseers. A candidate who was a woman, a minority, an environmentalist, or a public servant was virtually assured of election, while it was almost impossible for a businessman or banker to be among the chosen. But since one of the responsibilities of the board has traditionally been fund-raising for Harvard, the discovery that the current membership, however worthy, collectively had very shallow pockets and lacked a wide circle of deep-pocketed acquaintances was unsettling. As I quipped, "If you turned all the overseers upside down and shook them, a few nickels would roll out."

The problem was resolved by Andrew Heiskell, himself a successful and wealthy alumnus, when he became the board's president. A man with an overbearing personality to match his towering physical presence, he prevailed upon the Harvard Alumni Association, which was responsible for selecting the slate of nominees, to designate a slate so heavily loaded with CEOs and bankers that some of them would have to be elected.

Because of their restricted role in making policy for the university as a whole, the overseers' most hands-on involvement occurred through their leadership of the visiting committees to each of the university's many schools and departments. The charge of these committees was both to evaluate the effectiveness of the university's schools and institutions and to provide them with encouragement and advice.[8] I chaired two of them, and they stand out in my mind as much for what they were unable to accomplish as for what they did.

The graduate students in the department of economics poured out a litany of complaints to its visiting committee: graduate courses were too large, often they were not well taught, and the senior faculty paid little attention to the students, their concerns, and their progress. Two years later their view was that "Substantial steps have been made towards increasing faculty-student interaction . . . But much more needs to be done."[9] And student complaints about the aloofness of the Harvard faculty, and its members' frequent absences from the campus, have persisted down through the years.

The main recommendation of the visiting committee to the statistics department was to urge greater communication and coordination among statisticians throughout Harvard, many of whom were outside that department and had little or no contact with it. Our committee reported substantial improvement in the two years between reports, but we still expressed frustration at the bureaucratic obstacles to giving statisticians joint appointments in more than one school or department.

This inability to coordinate expertise scattered throughout the university is just one example of the limitations created by Harvard's tradition of departmental autonomy. "Every tub on its own bottom" is not just a motto but a key operating principle, and more than one commentator has observed wryly that the president of the university has less effective decision-making power than the dean of arts and sciences. Twenty years after I served on the Board of Overseers, I was a member of the committee visiting the Kennedy School of Government. At one of our meetings the dean, Joe Nye, commented that both the Kennedy school and the business school were in the process of establishing programs in public management. "Why on earth couldn't the two schools join forces and establish a strong joint program in this new area?" I asked. Joe's only response was to shake his head and say, "Marina, you know Harvard better than that." And I did.

My term as a Harvard overseer had barely ended when Bill Bowen, my late-night library companion in graduate student days, asked me to become a trustee of Princeton, where he was now president. I knew I would like working with Bill, whose crinkly-eyed smile and midwestern twang camouflaged the most intense workaholic I've ever known—I used to tease him that he wrote books faster than I could read them, all the while heading Princeton and, later, the Mellon Foundation. Along with all the positive reasons for saying yes, I felt a touch of sweet revenge at the chance to be at the top of the power structure of an institution that had once refused to admit me.

Some of Princeton's trustees were elected and some appointed by the board itself, which avoided the difficulties Harvard had faced in getting on its board people who had reached the pinnacle of business or financial success and were therefore a promising potential source of gifts to the university. Princeton had also come up with an innovative response to the pressures that had built during the activist 1970s to add students to the board. Each year a graduating senior was elected by the votes of juniors, seniors, and the two most recent classes of alumni to a four-year term on the board. These young alumni trustees could bring the perspective of their age group to bear on the deliberations of a body whose college days were long behind them, without being subject to political pressures from their on-campus peers.

It took only a couple of meetings of the trustees for me to see how sharply decision making at Princeton differed from what I had become used to at Harvard. Whereas Harvard was a decentralized collection of feudal fiefdoms, held together loosely by a lord who depended heavily on persuasion and negotiation to make his limited powers effective, Princeton was a benevolent monarchy, with important decisions centralized in Nassau Hall.

Two of the major changes that marked my term as a Princeton trustee held a special importance for me because of events in the lives of our own two children. When our son, Malcolm, was finishing high school in the late 1970s, Bob and I took him on the obligatory tour of potential colleges. At my urging, he somewhat reluctantly included Princeton. After his visit, I asked him what he thought. He replied that, because he was already committed to a career in the biological sciences, he couldn't possibly consider Princeton, whose biology department wasn't good enough to prepare him for a first-rate PhD program.

Bill Bowen clearly agreed with Malcolm's evaluation, and he was determined to change it. Soon after I joined the board, he began a decadelong discussion with the trustees about making Princeton one of the nation's leading universities in the biological sciences. Starting basically from zero, but with our strong support, he set about raising money for a building with the most modern laboratories and equipment and assembling a world-class faculty. By 1986, the Lewis Thomas Laboratory building was dedicated and two of the country's leading molecular biologists had been recruited to form the core of the faculty that populated it. By the time I left the board in 1990, Princeton was becoming recognized as one of the nation's top-tier institutions in the field. If Malcolm were choosing a college today, Princeton would have to be high on his list.

Another major change that occurred during Bill Bowen's presidency and my time on the board was the creation of residential colleges for freshmen and sophomores. The upperclassmen had their eating clubs to provide a social framework for their lives, but the underclassmen, perhaps the most in need of some community smaller than the university as a whole, had only the beds and desks in their dormitory rooms to call home.

Our daughter Laura had found a similar situation less than a month after she started at Duke as a freshman. The absence of any kind of community living structure became critical for her when her freshman roommate, rendered half unconscious by her first encounter with alcohol, was gang-raped by the pledge class of a fraternity. Because there were no adults to turn to for help, Laura found herself coping alone with the fallout from this tragedy: escorting her roommate to the hospital and the police and searching all over the campus for her when she left notes in their room hinting at suicide.

The first residential colleges at Princeton were simply groupings of existing dormitories, but as they acquired faculty associates who often dined with the residents and participated in house-centered cultural and social activities, a sense of community developed. Later, generous gifts from two billionaire alumni enabled the university to purchase the sprawling Princeton Inn on the edge of campus and convert it into Forbes College, and then to have a building specially designed and built as Whitman College. (Meg Whitman, a Princeton alumna and the former CEO of eBay, is a distant relative of my husband.) Princeton's underclassmen would now have the kind of supportive housing environment that Laura and her roommate had so painfully lacked.

These two transformative changes at Princeton might not have occurred without the conjunction of Bill Bowen's strong personality, his ability to articulate and raise funds for a compelling vision, and a centralized, unicameral governance structure that enabled him to work closely with a supportive Board of Trustees. Such advances had been harder to come by during my term as an overseer at Harvard, where the leadership was less persuasive, responsibility for governance was divided between two bodies, and decision making on academic issues was famously decentralized.

When Bowen told the trustees that he intended to step down from his fifteen-year term as president, I was appointed to the search committee whose task it was to identify the man best suited to replace him. (The notion that a woman might be eligible to become Princeton's president had to wait until 2001, when the university's own renowned molecular biologist Shirley Tilghman was appointed.) The unanimous choice of my search committee, enthusiastically supported by an advisory committee of faculty, staff, and students and approved by the full board, was Harold T. Shapiro, then president of the University of Michigan. I was living in Ann Arbor at the time, and the community was volubly upset when they learned that I was party to luring away their wildly popular president to a much smaller school "out East." "I wonder," I mused to Bob, "whether I'll need a bodyguard to protect me from all of Shapiro's angry admirers."

Shapiro, a noted economist, was one of identical twin sons born to a couple in Montreal who had never graduated from high school but owned and ran the largest kosher Chinese restaurant in Canada. When their father died suddenly during their senior year in college, the twins managed the restaurant successfully for five years before resuming their education. Each went on to earn a PhD and, eventually, to head a major research university, Michigan and then Princeton in Harold's case, McGill in his brother Bernard's.

Shapiro's popularity at Michigan did not immediately carry over to Princeton. Bill Bowen and his provost and close confidante, Neil Rudenstine (who later became the president of Harvard), had run the university like a mom-and-pop shop, involving a lot of personal interaction with the campus community, particularly the faculty. Theirs was an extremely effective partnership, one that shepherded the important advances I've described, along with many others.

When it was time to search for a new president, the trustees recognized that, partly as a result of those successes, Princeton had grown large and complex enough to require a different management style, and we discussed this requirement with the candidates for the presidency. But neither the search committee nor the campus advisory committee that worked with us conveyed the need for such a change to the faculty. The names of candidates had been a carefully guarded secret to avoid embarrassing the ones who weren't chosen. But a more open process would have had the advantage of raising the issue for discussion and understanding by this crucially important constituency.

Harold Shapiro, coming from a university many times the size of Princeton, brought a style of leadership that involved a more complex administrative structure and more delegation of authority than the faculty was used to. Resenting the absence of the hands-on relationship they had had with Bowen and Rudenstine, the professors gave Shapiro a very tough first year. But they gradually recognized that he had his own ways of paying attention and showing respect. Whenever a member of the faculty sent a copy of his or her newly published book to the president, a thank-you note from Bill Bowen had been immediately forthcoming. A response from Harold Shapiro involved a delay of weeks or even months, but when it came, it included detailed comments showing that he had actually read the book, even if it was in a field totally unfamiliar to him.

The faculty eventually came to appreciate Shapiro's more formal, scholarly style, and with their strong support, his was an extremely successful and innovative presidency. Among other achievements, he raised more endowment money than any president before him. Nonetheless, I have always felt a bit guilty that Harold's difficult introduction to Princeton might have been avoided if we trustees had been more effective in conveying our vision for Princeton's future leadership, and the reasons for it, to the campus community. The experience taught me that when decisions are made in secret to ensure timeliness and effectiveness, the decision makers have a special responsibility to explain honestly and persuasively the reasons why they decided as they did.

My fiduciary role at all these institutions, both corporate and academic, taught me that the answers to the important questions confronting many organizations are often neither black nor white but shades of gray. Learning not only to tolerate but to embrace complexity and ambiguity, as uncomfortable as it is, has been important in my own progress toward maturity, although it has often made me the butt of jokes about the economists who so infuriated Harry Truman by saying, "On the one hand . . . but on the other hand." When I tried to bring this conviction to life in my public television series, though, I learned the hard way that it's hard to persuade other people to see the world through the same lens.

Fig. 1. My father, *right*, in Budapest with two of his boyhood friends. The young gentleman on the left is William Fellner, decades later my successor at the Council of Economic Advisers.

Fig. 2. My parents at the wedding breakfast of Johnny's cousin, Catherine (Lily) Pásztory-Alcsuti (later Pedroni). My father is to the bride's left, my mother to the right of the groom.

Fig. 3. Mariette and Johnny living it up at a 1930s Princeton party. My mother is in the lap of Eugene Wigner, who later won a Nobel Prize in physics; my father is reclining in a chair next to Wigner's wife.

Fig. 4. My father in 1952 with his just completed MANIAC computer, which was officially named the IAS (Institute for Advanced Study) Machine. (Photo by Alan Richards.)

Fig. 5. My father and Klari standing in front of the house at 26 Westcott Rd. in 1955, with their dog Inverse between them. (Photo by Yuichi Sakuraba.)

Fig. 6. My father, terminally ill with cancer, receiving the Medal of Freedom from President Eisenhower in 1956.

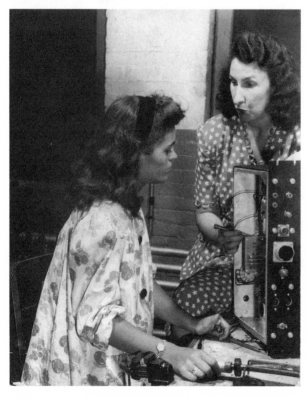

Fig. 7. My mother teaching a young woman how to assemble a radar set in World War II.

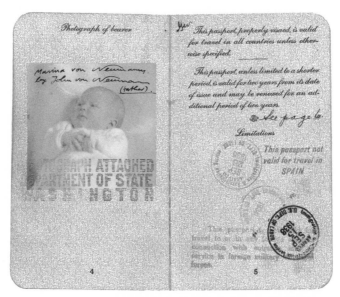

Fig. 8. Passport picture of me, six weeks old, with swastikas on the pages that followed.

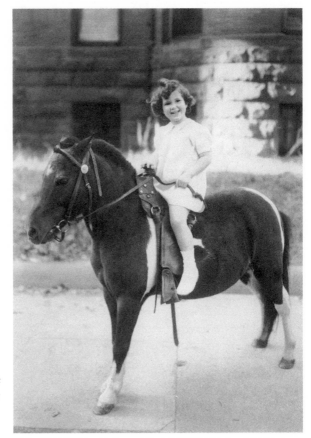

Fig. 9. In Budapest, at age three, I'm trying to follow in mother's equestrian footsteps.

Fig. 10. My father and me, at age eleven, walking down a street in Santa Fe.

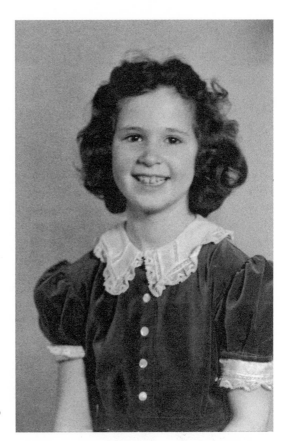

Fig. 11. Dressed for dancing school at age seven; it's hard to tell that there is a war on.

Fig. 12. The Radcliffe freshman relaxes on the lawn after a game of tennis.

Fig. 13. The war was real
for Lt. Robert Whitman,
US Air Force.

Fig. 14. Brides were
expected to look
ethereal for their
portraits in 1956.

Fig. 15. Bob and I grin as we leave Caroline Church on June 23, 1956.

Fig. 16. Bob and I are smiling, but Malcolm (age twelve) and Laura (eight) look serious posed with President Nixon after he announced my appointment to the Council of Economic Advisers.

Fig. 17. I'm caught anything but smiling as I describe the state of the economy to the press in 1973.

Fig. 18. Back behind my desk at the University of Pittsburgh.

Fig. 19. As host of a PBS program, *Economically Speaking,* in 1978–79.

Fig. 20. Receiving an honorary degree at the University of Notre Dame along with Father Ted Hesburgh (*right*), the recently retired president of the school, who was marking his one-hundredth such honor.

Fig. 21. Listening raptly to the young governor of Arkansas, Bill Clinton, speak at a conference in Washington, DC.

Fig. 22. The new vice president and group executive for public affairs at General Motors, 1986.

Fig. 23. Me today at the University of Michigan.

· 9 ·

*R*oger and Me

"Oh, shit!" My husband's language while driving had never been notable for its restraint, but in this case the outburst was entirely justified. Driving along a country road near Palo Alto, on a beautiful California April day in 1979, he had been watching the gasoline gauge drop to empty. We had run out of gas while looking for gas. For the second time in a decade, political turmoil in Iran had combined with misguided US price controls to produce empty pumps and long lines at gasoline stations, particularly in automobile-dependent states like California. If I'd been more savvy about the economics of the American automobile industry, I might have realized what this situation implied for the fortunes of the company I was about to join and wondered if I'd made a mistake in deciding to make a sharp career turn by becoming the chief economist of General Motors. But in my naïveté, I never connected the dots and anticipated the problems that were about to confront GM. Even less did I foresee its total inability to meet these challenges head-on.

We were on the other side of the country from our home in Pittsburgh because I was spending a year on sabbatical leave, free of teaching duties, at the Center for Advanced Study in the Behavioral Sciences in Palo Alto. High on a hill overlooking the campus of Stanford University, the center each year gave some forty to forty-five social scientists the opportunity to think, read, and write in their own specialties, while at the same time promoting interaction among scholars in different fields. To encourage contemplation, the center provided each fellow with a simple study cabin, a single room comfortably furnished but without a telephone. In the days before cell phones and the Internet, this arrangement was very effective in giving us the opportunity to be alone with our thoughts. Above the center's redwood compound were more hills, with pebbled paths up and down, which groups of us would run, breathlessly if not always swiftly, dodging not only cowpatties but the cows themselves, which stared at these huffing creatures with bovine astonishment. When we arrived in summer, the dry season, the hillsides, dotted with pines and live oaks, were a shimmering golden brown.

Late in January, when the California hills had turned from gold to green, Lake Lagunita had reappeared in the dry bed below the center, and we were reveling in outdoor tennis games, I ran across the compound to take a phone call from Paul McCracken, my old boss at the CEA. McCracken, now back at the University of Michigan Business School, was also a consultant to GM. He told me that an executive from GM, Roger Smith, wanted to meet with me while he was in Palo Alto visiting his daughter at the Stanford Business School. I had no idea who Mr. Smith was or why he wanted to see me, but I said fine, I'll treat him to one of the center's excellent lunches. Back in Michigan, it was widely known that Roger Smith was slated to become the next chairman of GM within the year.

The gentleman who appeared at my rustic office was a short man with thinning, wavy blond hair and a squeaky high voice, wearing a business suit that contrasted sharply with the casual jeans and T-shirts that prevailed on the Hill. After a few pleasantries about his daughter's life at Stanford and the contrast between January in Detroit and Palo Alto, Mr. Smith suddenly asked, "Would you be interested in being vice president and chief economist at General Motors?" My first thought was that, with his fair complexion and mottled skin, the man must have had too much sun. But I was curious enough to ask him to tell me more about the job, from which the longtime incumbent was about to retire, as well as why he thought I would be a good fit.

It would have been hard to imagine a more improbable candidate to become a high-level automotive executive than me, who couldn't tell a Chevy from a Ford without a guidebook, left the mysteries of what went on under the hood to my husband, and drove a slightly rusty six-year-old Dodge station wagon as the family car. But Roger Smith wasn't proposing that I design, build, or sell cars. What attracted him, aside from Paul McCracken's apparently enthusiastic recommendation, was my reputation as an academic economist but, even more, my government experience and the visibility it had brought with it.

The Price Commission had made some significant decisions affecting GM, and I suspect that my efforts to minimize the damage to the economy from price controls, both there and then at the CEA, had come to the company's attention. As the largest firm in a heavily regulated industry, GM relied on its chief economist, among other duties, to make its case to the Congress and various regulatory agencies, and the ability to articulate the arguments persuasively was important. On my side, my varied career experiences combined to pique my interest. To an economist whose specialty was international macroeconomics, GM's sheer size and impact on the American economy, as well as its operations on several continents, made it enticing. My work on the Price Commission and at the CEA had given me an insider's view of the importance, and the complexity, of relations between government and business. And membership on the boards of Procter and Gamble, Westinghouse, and Manufacturers Hanover Bank had given me insights into how large multinational firms made critical business decisions.

In the back of my mind was also the thought that I was being offered an opportunity to make my mark in the business world, an arena that no one in my family had entered, at least in living memory. I told Mr. Smith that I would think hard about his offer but, because I didn't know whether we would still have one child at home for the next couple of years, in any case I wouldn't be able to give him a definite positive response for several months. "Okay," said Mr. Smith, "I'd rather have a yes in April than a no in February." Not until I had been at GM for some time did I realize what a remarkable reply that was. Generally, in industry, people are expected to say yes or no to an offer or a promotion within a few days at most.

The key question was whether Laura would return to the school in Pittsburgh she had attended since kindergarten or go off to boarding school the following year. The free and easy California culture that had unexpectedly produced what looked to Bob's and my astonished eyes like a positive orgy of partner swapping up on the Hill, also pervaded the Gunn Senior High School in Palo Alto, where she was spending her sophomore year.

The transition from a small, all-girls private school in Pittsburgh to a large public high school in Palo Alto would have been sharp in any case. But Laura, who was used to demanding teachers and a solid curriculum, found herself, as a latecomer, shut out of all the honors courses except English. Her other classes she dismissed, with adolescent scorn, as "ridiculous." "I do wish Mr. Love wouldn't let kids smoke pot in Algebra," she would say, slamming her books down on the kitchen table, "because then we have to teach it all to ourselves after school." Or "The social studies teachers keep showing films in class because they're too dumb to lecture." I thought she was indulging in teenage hyperbole until I met the teachers in question. And Gunn was reputed to be one of the best public high schools in California.

What Laura did learn during that West Coast year was how to handle social situations involving alcohol, drugs, and casual adolescent sex without either violating her own standards or being shut out of the social whirl. Bob was pulled away from a dinner party more than once by a call from Laura, saying, "Dad, would you come and pick my friend Tammy and me up at so-and-so's house?" which he did promptly, no questions asked.

The nadir of this California culture struck us when I had to find a pediatrician to fill out Laura's health form for Phillips Andover, the boarding school back east where she had been accepted for the following year. She had applied there because her experience at Gunn had made her more and more certain that she didn't want to return to the Ellis School in Pittsburgh where, she said, given the use of drugs that had begun to pervade the social scene, she would have to "choose between being a pothead and a pariah." She knew she would encounter the same issues at Andover, but she felt that in a larger and more varied school environment she would be able to find friends who shared her outlook.

I made an appointment for her with a highly touted pediatrician on the Stanford medical faculty, and she pedaled down to his office on her bike. When I got home that evening, I found her white-faced with fury. When I finally wormed the reason out of her, it turned out that the doctor had asked her if she was sexually active (she had just had her fifteenth birthday) and, when she said no, suggested that some psychiatric sessions might help her overcome her frigidity problem.

A colleague to whom I poured out my indignation asked me if I was considering a malpractice suit. "No," I replied, "I'm much too busy keeping my husband from committing homicide." Even after she had moved beyond the "problem" pinpointed by the doctor, Laura was still angry, and her conviction that women deserved more respect from the medical profession was a factor, I'm convinced, in her decision to become a physician herself.

Once Laura's schooling was settled, Bob and I decided that we could handle the complexities of a commuting marriage, and I finally said yes to Roger Smith. The more I thought about it, the more the notion of this major career change excited me, creating another piece to fit into the jigsaw puzzle of my professional life. My training in economics had given me a set of analytical tools, what I think of as a mental filing cabinet, to work with. As a professor, I had used this tool kit to teach and write for captive audiences, students and professional journals already solidly anchored in the economist's perspective. It was a tempting new challenge to use it instead to persuade the unconverted, business executives and members of Congress who, rather than sharing the unspoken assumptions of economics, tended to be highly skeptical of them. I never dreamed that the real challenge would be a persistent and ultimately unsuccessful battle to change an ingrown, self-satisfied, and self-destructive corporate culture.

The competitive decline of America's Big Three automobile companies had begun during the first oil shock in 1973. The combination of a sudden surge in gasoline prices, caused by OPEC's sharp cuts in petroleum output, and an artificial scarcity created by US government price controls on domestic oil, caused a sudden shift in the preferences of American consumers. Buyers turned away from the large, powerful cars that were the Big Three's specialty toward the smaller, more fuel efficient vehicles in which Japanese producers like Toyota and Honda excelled, and which they were exporting to the United States in increasing numbers.

If only I had read a book with the prescient title *Paradise Lost: The Decline of the Auto-Industrial Age,*[1] published the same year as that first oil shock, I might have been better prepared. In it the author, Emma Roth-schild, argued that a productivity slowdown, skimping on investment, and technological backwardness were bringing about the decline of the US automobile industry. She described a variety of new ventures, many of them showcased at a government-sponsored exposition called Transpo '72, that offered possible sources of revival. General Motors' display included recreational vehicles, mass transport, and experimental "city cars," including a minicar and an electric-gasoline hybrid suitable for rental car fleets that could be picked up and dropped off around town. Many of these new vehicles were eventually introduced in the United States, years later, but GM wasn't in the forefront of building and marketing them. Despite its slogan at Transpo '72—"GM is a total transportation organization"—the company chose to focus on incremental improvements in its cars and trucks. Its gradual but persistent decline in market share was under way, however much those in charge tried to explain it away as just a temporary glitch.

The encroachment of Japanese vehicles on the US market was speeded up by the second oil shock of the 1970s, set off by the Iranian Revolution of 1979. The worldwide decline of a mere 4 percent in petroleum production sparked panic and a sharp rise in oil prices.[2] In the United States, the Carter administration responded by imposing price controls on gasoline, causing severe shortages, which pushed consumers, even more precipitously than in 1973, toward the small, fuel-efficient cars that were a Japanese specialty.

This may have been the reality of the firm I was about to join, but neither the company nor the American public had yet absorbed the impact of what was happening. My friends congratulated me on joining "Generous Motors." And that quip closely matched the company's image of itself: the nation's largest corporation, stable and secure, with a dominant market share, large profits even in bad times, and an iconic role in American society. As the combined pressures of recession and growing Japanese competition made me the frequent bearer of bad news during my first few years on the job, senior executives assured me that the world would soon "get back to normal," by which they meant a world in which GM sold half of all the vehicles purchased in the United States, as it had in its heyday.

Like my appointment to the CEA, my arrival as one of the first female vice presidents in the notoriously macho automobile industry attracted a good deal of press attention. But, unlike that first episode, this time the press mostly played it straight. With the exception of the business editor of a small California newspaper, who referred to me as a "delicious looking dame,"[3] the outpouring of press reports on my new position described my background without coy references to my appearance.

Although GM's official headquarters and the center of its operations were in Detroit, the chairman's and treasurer's offices were in the elegant General Motors Building on the corner of 59th Street and Fifth Avenue in New York City, and that's also where the chief economist's office was located. We chose my old hometown, Princeton, as a reasonably convenient suburb in which to live, with good train service and many old friends from our earlier life there. The house we bought, a large, half-timbered stucco structure with a hedge of magnificent rhododendrons, served as a striking backdrop for a photo of us that accompanied an article in *Fortune* magazine about a new phenomenon: husbands who were willing to become "trailing spouses" as they relocated for their wives' executive jobs.[4]

These living arrangements meant hectic commuting schedules for both of us. Bob drove an hour to Newark to fly to Pittsburgh every Tuesday morning to teach and reversed the trip on Thursday evenings. Meanwhile, I took a 7:00 a.m. train each morning to Penn Station, where a GM driver picked me up in a current model Cadillac to drive me to the GM Building and took me back to catch a train that got me home around 8:00 p.m. And during most weeks, while Bob was in Pittsburgh, I spent a day or two at GM headquarters in Detroit, spending the night in one of the sterile, impersonal bedrooms reserved for visiting executives on the top floor of the stolid granite GM Building there.

I was well aware that the corporate environment I had stepped into was very different from the academic one I was used to. I quickly overhauled my wardrobe and accepted that, for the first time in my professional life, I had a real boss, something no tenured professor would ever admit to. At the same time, I moved rapidly to make an impact on that environment by means of two hiring decisions that could never have occurred without me. I offered a job to a smart, assertive young Greek economist who was being blackballed because she had lodged a harassment complaint against her employer, the United Nations. I did the same for a woman who, seven months pregnant when she applied, said she would like to work part-time after the baby was born and then ease gradually into a full-time position. The personnel department's functionary was appalled. "There's no precedent in this company for the risks you are taking with these hires," she declared, but she couldn't overrule the decisions of a vice president. The first woman didn't last long at GM; the other has spent her entire career there—I had batted .500.

It took me longer to come to terms with more fundamental differences in the way academic and corporate economists functioned, and to adapt to these new demands. At the University of Pittsburgh I, like my colleagues, was judged by my output of basic research, work that developed and tested new theories and models. At General Motors, my success depended on how well my staff and I used both theory and evidence to help resolve pressing problems confronting our employer. As a professor, I could plug away at an article until I felt it was ready for publication, while all the work we did at GM was tied to tight deadlines dictated by the needs of the business. In my academic life, I was a specialist in international economics; GM, like the CEA, required me to apply my skills more broadly, bringing together insights from whichever branches of economics were relevant.[5]

Universities are the last frontier of individualism; my lectures and research output were my own, as were the plaudits or brickbats they attracted. In business, as in government, I soon discovered, achievements are almost invariably collective, and the ability to listen, interact, persuade, and compromise is as important—if not more so—than simply being right. And, while trenchant criticism is an academic tradition, the corporate world requires the softer touch that had been one of my father's hallmarks. I soon learned that I couldn't criticize subordinates in front of other people, or write comments like "bullshit" in the margins of their work.

Perhaps the biggest difference of all was the ambiguity of my perspective, which, I soon discovered, was a mixed blessing. I had a double vision as an insider and an outsider, and that was both my strength and my weakness. Because I was one of the few at GM who wasn't born there, I brought a different perspective from those of employees who had started their careers at the company, but I was also continually being tested. I had to continually prove myself.[6]

Although I didn't realize it at the time, the role changes that accompanied my move from Pitt to GM echoed the much more dramatic shift my father had made in midlife. Up until he became an American citizen and the US military began to ready itself for war, all his brilliance had been focused on various aspects of pure mathematics, and his fundamental contributions to the great scientific issues of the early twentieth century were largely individual achievements.[7] From about 1937 on, his focus shifted to applied mathematical research in the military field and in numerical analysis, computers and automata, as well as the application of game theory to economics, all of which involved working as part of a team.[8] He was sometimes criticized for having abandoned the purity of abstraction for the messy problems of the real world, but, convinced as he was that he was fighting a battle of Armageddon, he expressed no regrets.

My situation was hardly comparable to my father's, but I did decide almost immediately after I arrived at GM to work at changing the role of the chief economist from providing economic data and analysis, as well as material for speeches, to the chairman and the financial staff to producing output that could be useful to the operating units, the profit-making side of the house. My personal focus would be, I told myself, to explain the world to GM and GM to the world. But I quickly discovered, to my dismay, that this shift meant coming to terms with GM's deeply embedded and profoundly dysfunctional culture.

Maryann Keller, an astute observer of the automobile industry, summarized GM's self-destructive attributes as a Goliath complex, a parochial worldview, leadership by the numbers, and contemptuous paternalism.[9] To this list, I would add the incredible isolation of the company's top executives, the inhabitants of the legendary fourteenth floor of the GM Building in Detroit.

General Motors had long been accustomed to being the largest automobile company in the world, and the belief that the economies of scale arising from its size were a fundamental source of competitive advantage ran throughout the company. I heard Roger Smith opine more than once, and in all seriousness, that being CEO of the largest firm in the United States should entitle him the highest compensation of any chief executive, regardless of how the company's profitability stacked up.

The GM I joined in 1979 was proud of being known as a midwestern car company. The Midwest was its world, and its lack of understanding not only of its Japanese competitors' sources of strength but even of its own customers' attitudes was devastating. It did make use of a standard market research tool, focus groups of potential customers, but it did this so late in the design and production cycle of a new model that, as I commented in frustration, practically the only thing that could still be changed on the basis of their comments was the color of the seat covers.

Since the late 1950s GM's chief executive had almost always been drawn from the ranks of the finance staff, whose members were the company's elite: recruited from the best schools, afforded the highest pay scale, and responsible for coordinating information and decision making for top management. Because their primary attention was to the numbers in making product and investment decisions, the concerns of designers and engineers were too often pushed aside. And these financial "hi pots" (high-potential employees whose careers merited special nurturing) were skilled in the art of making the numbers support whatever decision the chairman favored.

Coming from the ruthless up-or-out tenure system that governed faculty appointments at major universities, I was astounded to discover how rarely anyone was fired at GM. The job security enjoyed by blue-collar workers, with generous benefits guaranteed at the end of a lifetime career, extended to salaried staff and even to the executive level. Incompetence in the higher ranks might prevent someone from being promoted, or even lead to being shuffled off into a backwater position, but the company's paternalism was near-certain protection against being shown the door. When Elmer Johnson, newly arrived as an executive vice president, tried to institute a rigorous evaluation system that called for dismissing those who ranked at the bottom of the curve, his effort was short-lived; although the chairman never explicitly overruled Elmer's innovation, the old practices crept back. And the talented African American factory manager Elmer had installed as personnel vice president to execute the new system soon left the company.

Transported by GM drivers (no one used the "foreign" word *chauffeurs*) in late-model GM cars into the private garage under the GM Building, the company's top executives ascended by a private, key-operated elevator to the fourteenth floor, where their area was protected by two sets of heavy, electronically locked doors, a security guard, and a receptionist. They lunched together in their private dining room—actually, there were three levels of executive dining rooms in the building—and could leave at the day's end uncontaminated by contact with the ordinary mortals who ate in the large cafeteria on the first floor.

These executives were isolated not only from the rest of the world but from each other. Their offices were all along the same corridor, but there was no spontaneous popping in and out or casual talk around the water cooler. The door to each executive's office was generally closed; in order to enter, one had to make an appointment and be admitted by the secretary who sat on guard in the outer office. This protocol didn't apply, of course, if the visiting executive stood above the visitee in the corporate hierarchy, and a summons from one's superior always sent the recipient sprinting down the hallway.

This was a culture that provided an effective bulwark against reality. With their heads planted firmly in the sand, the majority of GM's top management clung stubbornly to their belief in a stable, reasonably predictable world. The incursion of new Japanese competitors who happened to be in the right place with the right kinds of cars when the oil shocks hit was seen as a temporary or at least reversible aberration. For most of them, furthermore, the only vehicle market that mattered was the one in the United States, which accounted for some 70 percent of GM's production and sales. The idea that the markets and the competition relevant to the company's fortunes were rapidly becoming global was foreign to their thinking.

The picture of the world I tried to persuade GM's management and directors to accept was very different. I began by shifting my staff's forecasts and analyses away from treating the United States as a basically self-sufficient economy, onto which international trade and investment were tacked almost as an afterthought, to seeing it as fundamentally interdependent with the rest of the world. In the decades immediately after World War II, when exchange rates were fixed, foreign competition had not yet revived, and very little capital moved across international boundaries, a decision by the Fed to push interest rates up had affected GM mainly through a drop in total vehicle sales. Sales fell both because Americans cut back on spending in general and because the cost to automobile dealers of financing their inventories and to customers of financing their car purchases rose.

In the more financially integrated world of the early 1980s, in contrast, the sky-high interest rates that resulted from Paul Volcker's determination to break the back of double-digit inflation brought funds pouring in from abroad. With exchange rates no longer fixed by governments, this capital inflow caused the dollar to appreciate relative to other major currencies, making imports cheaper and exports more expensive and putting GM's products at a competitive disadvantage vis-à-vis imported vehicles. Both the business risks and the appropriate responses were different in an economy that was now far more open to the outside world.

I made these points over and over again in presentations to the top management and Board of Directors before this integrated worldview sank into minds that found it strange and unfamiliar. Some of GM's shareholders took real umbrage at my internationalist perspective, writing angry letters to the company protesting the appointment of Marina Whitman, a member of two "treasonous" organizations, as a vice president of their company. One of these organizations was the Council on Foreign Relations, since its establishment in 1921 the incubator and home base of America's East Coast foreign policy establishment—most secretaries of state, many other cabinet secretaries, and several US presidents have been members. It was a men-only club until the 1970s when, fresh from the CEA, I was one of the first women to join.

The other object of the shareholders' anger was the Trilateral Commission, a group of 150 high-profile members, equally divided among North America, Europe, and Japan. It had been founded in 1975 by David Rockefeller, with the aim of pulling Japan, our former adversary and by then an important ally, solidly into the ambit of the "Western" world. No one could fault the commission's organizers on their ability to select as members the rising political leadership of the United States. The winner of the 1976 presidential election, Jimmy Carter, his two major opponents, John Anderson and George H. W. Bush, and 26 senior appointees in the Carter administration were all members, as were Walter Mondale, Bill Clinton, and numerous high-ranking members of subsequent administrations, both Republicans and Democrats.

The powerful positions occupied by members of both organizations, and especially the fact that David Rockefeller, the multimillionaire head of Chase Manhattan Bank, was a leader in both of them, strengthened the spread of conspiracy theories. On the left, both the council and the commission have been suspected of existing to further global business and banking interests at the expense of ordinary folk. On the right, they have been accused of promoting world government and chipping away at the sovereignty of the United States. Some of the more paranoid opponents of the internationalist outlook they represent have even spread rumors of a secret fleet of black United Nations helicopters poised to invade and take over the United States.

My views about the integration of the global economy didn't shake the complacency of GM's senior executives until I laid out the implications in more detail. In op-ed pieces in the *New York Times,* I hammered home the idea that the trend toward more fuel efficient cars was worldwide, and that the bottom line would almost certainly be a stepped-up pace of innovation and competition in an increasingly global—rather than national—automotive industry.[10] Furthermore, I pointed out, the two oil shocks were producing both an uncomfortable transition from cheap to expensive energy and a diffusion of economic power toward newly industrializing countries.[11]

With these pronouncements, I was striking at the heart of GM management's long-held beliefs. "You're exaggerating," the vice chairman said testily after he'd read these opinion pieces in the predigested selections of newspaper clippings that were handed to the top executives every morning by their drivers as they got into their cars. "You'll see; these changes won't last, and customers will shift back to GM cars." My entire career at GM was marked by growing frustration as my economist colleagues and I were unable to persuade our top decision makers that competition from foreign producers was here to stay and would only intensify. As I, along with a few other brave souls, repeatedly tried to bring the fast-changing competitive dynamic to bear on senior management's thinking, I felt like the princess of Greek myth, Cassandra, whose dire warnings about the true nature of the Trojan horse were fated to be ignored, resulting in the destruction of her father's kingdom. My father's Cassandra-like observations, in the early 1930s, about Europe's coming fate had proved all too accurate; was I fated to be just as prescient, and just as helpless to change the outcome, I wondered?

Ironically, among these would-be changers of the culture was Roger Smith himself, the individual most often blamed for GM's downfall. Although our motives and ways of going about it were very different, we were both among the handful of executives who saw the future and tried to jolt the company into adapting. As I look back on these efforts, I'm reminded of my father's long-running battles with the military bureaucracy as he fought to ensure the United States' military superiority in the Cold War. The big difference was that my father and his allies were successful,[12] whereas Smith and I, along with other would-be reformers, failed to break GM's mold of inertia and complacency.

Roger Smith had started trying to change some aspects of this GM culture even before he became CEO. As early as 1974, as executive vice president, he had formed a small group to develop the broad, long-range strategies for the future that the company lacked and enticed a far-thinking, British-born engineer named Mike Naylor away from another GM division to head it. But old habits die hard. The operating people, focused on building and selling cars, strongly resisted what they saw as the pie-in-the-sky abstractions of strategic planning.

Soon after I started at GM, Mike and I invited several group vice presidents to take part in a standard strategic planning exercise. It consisted of showing the audience a matrix of several strategies and scenarios and then asking them how their ranking of the various strategies would change under different scenarios. How, for example, would their ranking of strategies change if the auto companies were to find themselves in a fully regulated industry, like public utilities? Or how would they react if the price of a gallon of gas, which had just risen above a dollar for the first time, were to rise to three dollars?

But these group vice presidents refused to play ball. Rather than thinking seriously about how they would act in such situations, they nodded in agreement with the colleague who said, martini in hand, "Aw, come on, I'm not going to waste my time thinking about that stuff.

That's never going to happen. If it did, oh hell, I'd retire and move to Florida."[13] Naylor and I tried to come up with different approaches. But we never did find a way to unlock their thinking. And by the time those scenarios turned into unimaginable reality—when gasoline prices spiked above three dollars, vehicle demand imploded and, eventually, government intrusion into all major decisions was the quid pro quo for using taxpayer money to rescue GM and Chrysler from financial collapse—all those executives were long gone to Florida or the great beyond.

Once he became CEO, Roger Smith tried other ways to crack open the inflexible GM culture. Traditionally, the route to the company officer ranks was through promotion from within; Smith took an unprecedented tack by recruiting outsiders who had reached high positions in their own fields to join the company at the level of vice president. Eventually, these would include Betsy Ancker-Johnson, a physicist who had been deputy director of Oak Ridge National Laboratory, to head the Environmental Activities staff; Bob Frosch, another physicist, who had run the National Atmospheric and Space Administration (NASA), as chief of the Research staff; Steve Fuller, a highly regarded professor at the Harvard Business School, to head the Personnel staff; Elmer Johnson, a high-profile corporate lawyer and adviser to leading corporations, as executive vice president and general counsel; and myself as chief economist. Roger's effort to bring in fresh thinking was genuine, but every one of us outsiders in the end retired or left the company frustrated by what he or she saw as a failure to break through the old boys' network and make a significant dent in the way the organization thought and operated.

Smith's attempts to bring the outside world into GM didn't stop with recruiting individuals. In the course of his chairmanship, he brought both Electronic Data Systems (EDS), along with its founder, Ross Perot, and the Hughes Aircraft Company into the GM fold. He had various reasons for making these breathtakingly expensive purchases, but among them was the hope that EDS's aggressive culture and the innovative high-tech atmosphere that prevailed at Hughes would have an impact on GM's bureaucratic style. But although both these acquisitions proved to be huge financial successes for GM when they were sold or spun off as separate entities once again, neither was ever functionally integrated into the parent company or stimulated the cultural change Smith had envisioned.

General Motors' hidebound culture was a many-headed Hydra. During one of my weekly trips to Detroit, I discovered a group of about a dozen economists, entirely separate from the Economics staff, called Legal Economics. Its sole function was to produce a book laying out the arguments against breaking up GM, in case a renewed spate of antitrust suits, such as had occurred during the 1960s, were to raise that possibility. Although the US Senate had held hearings in 1968 on whether GM constituted a monopoly and should be broken up, by the time I arrived on the scene a decade later, the rapid buildup of Japanese competition had made such a threat one of the least of GM's problems.

I managed to persuade my boss, who also had Legal Economics under his wing, that it should be dismantled, and that I couldn't imagine any useful role for its director, whose professional skills were hopelessly outdated. Since our common superior, an amiable Canadian, was clearly unwilling to take on the unpleasant and, at GM, almost unheard-of task of firing someone, I said I would deliver the message. But I hadn't counted on his giving the man a raise just before he sent him down the hall to my office to get the bad news. The unhappy ex-director was both confused and infuriated by this mixed message and took out his anger on me, the bad cop in the farce. When I confronted my boss with the situation he had created, his explanation was "I felt sorry for the guy."

This unnerving episode typified an unwillingness to take individual responsibility that ran throughout the company. I soon discovered that GM headquarters operated through decision making by committees at meetings, which diffused the pinpointing of responsibility, leading me to murmur in exasperation, "Nobody here but us committees." These committee meetings consumed an inordinate share of the workday, particularly because every attendee demanded that his staff brief him beforehand on the issues on the agenda, to avoid any chance of being blindsided. And, in the end, after all the presentations and the discussions, the chairman's view was the one that counted.

Two of the most important committees were the ones on pricing and production scheduling. Although the same top executives belonged to both, the two functioned independently. No one seemed to be concerned with the relationship between the expected demand for particular models, which drove production scheduling, and how they were priced. I had managed to pound the concept of a demand curve into the heads of undergraduates, who knew it would be on the exam, but I had no such success with GM executives. My objection, that the company wouldn't have to lean so heavily on customer incentives to move the merchandise if it made decisions about prices and volumes jointly from the start, fell on deaf ears.

Despite setbacks like this, I was becoming expert in the corporate hand-to-hand combat involved in bringing into my fold several activities key to the goals I had set for myself as chief economist; I hadn't been labeled a pushy broad at Japan's Keidanren for nothing. One was the Corporate Strategic Planning Group; another was GM's European Advisory Council (EAC), another string in my bow aimed at moving GM toward a more global perspective.

The twice-yearly meetings of the EAC were among the highlights of my job. This council, consisting of some of Europe's most prominent citizens from more than half a dozen countries, had been created by Roger Smith to advise on economic and political conditions affecting GM's operations in Europe. My task as chairman was to acquaint them with how things were going there for us, and to lay out the questions on which we especially wanted their wisdom and guidance. Drawing out the views of these leaders on issues affecting GM's business success was stimulating enough. But what I learned from these men—yes, they were all men—at the dinners preceding our meetings ranged far beyond issues germane to GM's European business to encompass almost every aspect of political, economic, and security developments in Europe. It was like once again sitting in on the conversations around the dinner table in Princeton when I was a teenager, except that now I was an engaged and respected participant rather than a sulky and impatient listener.

One of the ways in which I tried to focus GM senior management's attention on the new realities was by sponsoring, in 1982, an intensive analysis by the Economics and Financial staffs of the reasons why the Big Three's production costs averaged fifteen hundred to two thousand dollars more per car than those of the Japanese imports, even after including the costs of transportation across the Pacific. The key message of the study was that the US auto industry was in big trouble and that its problems were long-term structural ones that would not be cured by economic recovery from the ongoing recession of 1981–82.[14] Now that there was a single worldwide auto market, rather than national ones separated by different consumer demands in different countries, we simply had to dramatically reduce the large cost differential. Part of this cost gap was due to external factors like tax systems and exchange rates. But, the study revealed, the vast majority of this disadvantage was attributable to US management and US labor; primarily to the higher per-hour cost of labor and lower labor productivity in the American auto industry.[15]

This analysis of the relative cost disparity got its authors in trouble with almost everyone. Ford and Chrysler had been insisting loudly that the most important causes of the cost differential were differences in the overall tax systems of the two countries and the "artificially" low value of the yen. Since these were disadvantages created by government policies and beyond the control of the automobile producers, they argued, it was up to our government to eliminate them or, if that proved impossible, protect the domestic industry by placing restrictions on imports.

The United Auto Workers (UAW) had a different but equally vehement objection. As part of GM's labor negotiations, I was sitting across a table from the head of the UAW's GM Department, Don Ephlin, discussing with him one-on-one the GM analysis of the US-Japanese cost differential. Ephlin was normally an even-tempered man, known for promoting a cooperative problem-solving relationship with management. But he blew up at my explanation that about half the cost difference was due to our higher labor costs per hour and the other half to differences in labor productivity. "That makes it sound," he spluttered, "as if everything was the workers' fault, that management's failings in the design of both the products and the production process, and its long-standing lousy relationship with our union, had nothing to do with it." Startled and embarrassed, I replied, "But that's not what the study said; it stated clearly that both management and labor bore some responsibility for the cost gap." It had never occurred to me that what I had regarded as a value-neutral piece of accounting would be seen from his perspective as putting the blame exclusively on his members.

Quite a few analysts, journalists, and legislators reacted by insisting that the Japanese advantage was due almost entirely to better management. I responded whenever I was asked that it was "all of the above—

better motivation and productivity, lower wages, new plants, lower materials costs and, well maybe, better management on the Japanese side."[16] An independent study produced jointly by the University of Michigan and the consulting firm Arthur Anderson came to basically the same conclusion.[17]

The differing explanations of the Japanese cost advantage became a huge bone of contention because they provided ammunition to various sides in the ongoing wrangle over US trade policies. In 1980, as the Japanese share of car and truck sales in the United States was moving inexorably upward, and the size of their competitive advantage was becoming clear, Ford and the UAW jointly petitioned the US International Trade Commission (ITC) for a so-called escape clause action, which would impose restrictions on imports of Japanese cars for a minimum of five years. Those of us at GM who opposed import protection managed to hold off strong pressure to join the petitioners by persuading Roger Smith to support our position. The company refused to join the Ford-UAW action, with the result that they lost the case.

Ford and the UAW persisted, though, despite a testy comment from Henry Ford II to Ford CEO Philip Caldwell: "I'm sick and tired of GM sitting back and letting us carry the ball on the Japanese . . . You know, Phil, we're in business to sell cars. I don't feel that this government lobbying has gotten us much so far except for some bad publicity in the mass media and the financial community."[18] The difference of opinion between the two companies surfaced publicly at the 1981 plenary meeting of the Trilateral Commission, to which both Caldwell and I belonged. Caldwell made a vigorous case for protectionism, while I minced no words in voicing my strong doubts about going that route. Our disagreement was highlighted in an article in the *Washington Post*.[19]

At the beginning of his first term, in 1981, Ronald Reagan negotiated with the Japanese government a so-called Voluntary Restraint Agreement, limiting imports of Japanese cars to 1.68 million annually for a three-year period. Just before the president took this action, I sent a strong memo to my superiors, urging them to resist the siren song of protectionism. Although import protection would undoubtedly reduce competitive pressures and increase our profitability in the short run, I argued, it would work to our disadvantage in the long run, by reducing our leverage with the UAW in bargaining for wage concessions and modification of some of its restrictive work rules. It would also subject the United States to retaliation from our trading partners and could easily lead to a breakdown of the trend toward a liberalized trading system, a system that was essential if multinational corporations were to be free to operate on an increasingly global basis, including investing in facilities overseas. "The only reason to sacrifice one's long-run position to short-run advantage," I concluded, "is if you don't think you can survive to enjoy the long-run otherwise. Chrysler is obviously in that position. I hope, and believe, that we are not."[20]

Once the restraints were imposed, I defended this action in public statements and interviews, saying, in effect, "They will give American producers a breathing space in which to adjust to intense foreign competition, and, besides, there is less danger that they will become permanent than some of the protectionist legislation being proposed in Congress, which they have been designed to fend off." Inside GM, though, I warned that this move carried several dangers to our ability to compete. One was that it would encourage Japanese firms to evade the quotas by building auto plants in North America, adding to global car-building capacity, which already greatly exceeded worldwide demand. Another was that, since the Voluntary Export Restraints (VERs) would limit the number of cars sold in the United States rather than their total value, the Japanese would logically move up-market and begin to produce the larger, more expensive, and more profitable vehicles that were the heart of the Big Three's business. And finally, the increase in profits generated by quota-induced artificial scarcity would accrue primarily to the Japanese manufacturers, allowing them to invest more resources in newer, better products and processes.

When the VERs' original three years were up, their extension for a fourth was a foregone conclusion. Ronald Reagan may have been philosophically on the side of liberalized trade, but he knew better than to terminate them in an election year. When it came time to discuss a fifth year, Roger Smith, alone among the CEOs of American car companies, called for them to end. In an op-ed piece in the *Washington Post* headlined "It's Time to End the Auto Quotas," he outlined all the investments GM had made and was making to become more competitive with the Japanese. "So let's drop the restraints," he urged, "and get on with slugging it out in the world marketplace. The discipline of worldwide competition not only can assure that customers have access to the best products at the best prices, it also speeds up the pace of technological innovation and industrialization and industrial modernization, which means more growth and better jobs."[21]

I felt a glow of triumph that my oft-repeated arguments had received the imprimatur of the chairman's byline. I found out the downside when the host of *Automotive Report* on WJR, Detroit's most listened to AM radio station, cast Roger and me as allies opposing most of the other executives at GM on trade policy, saying, "A very important philosophical question on whether General Motors should continue to support total free trade with the Japanese is now going on inside the number one auto company . . . The debate . . . has had chairman Roger Smith and New York based economist Marina Whitman on one side, with GM President F. James McDonald, Vice Chairman Howard Kehrl and numerous vice presidents on the other side."[22]

The allegation of a Smith-Whitman alliance on trade issues did me no good in the eyes of many other GM executives. The heads of GM's divisions, the very operating executives I wanted to persuade that the Economics staff earned its keep, were determined to oppose my antiprotection arguments every chance they got. As one of them put it, "The time has come to rise above abstract principles and do what's best for General Motors." Their hostility to my views on trade, I began to sense, was undermining the credibility of my staff's forecasts and analyses in their eyes.

President Reagan did refuse to extend the VERs for another year, to the consternation of Ford and the UAW. Japan continued to impose such quotas unilaterally, though with a substantial increase in the number of cars allowed, until 1994. By that time, the Japanese producers had made full use of all three of the strategic opportunities created by the VERs that I had warned about. They were setting up manufacturing plants in the United States, building larger and more expensive cars for the US market, and investing their quota profits in new products and processes; these moves became critical factors in the decline of the American auto industry. I had the satisfaction of having been right, but that only heightened the backlash against my well-known opposition to import restrictions, which led UAW president Owen Bieber to refer to me privately as "that free-trade bitch at GM." My colleague who overheard the remark wasted no time in passing it on to me.

Roger Smith did believe, as a general proposition, that an open world trading system would give GM maximum flexibility to plan its sourcing and operations on a global basis. But his first concern was with the company's bottom line, and he had more practical, immediate reasons for favoring an end to the VER program. He had never shared his colleagues' blindness to fast-moving developments in the worldwide auto industry, and he knew that GM would have to compete in the increasingly popular small-car segment of the market. But when he saw the original cost estimates for producing such a vehicle, Smith killed the proposal, saying that there was no way the company was going to ramp up to produce cars it would have to sell at a loss.

Smith had in mind his own radical plans for establishing GM as a player in the market for small cars, but it would take several years to bring them to fruition. To bridge the gap, he admitted on station WJR's *Automotive Report*, "[We] do have programs to bring in from Japan some small, very fuel-efficient, low-priced cars—in limited numbers."[23] A continuation of the VERs at their current levels would have allowed no room for these additional imports; only the substantial expansion of the quotas by the Japanese government when it extended the program unilaterally made his bridge strategy viable.

On the other end of the bridge, Smith had a two-pronged approach to building such vehicles in the United States on a cost-competitive basis. One he described on the same radio program: "Our Saturn Corporation, eventually with assets of $5 billion, will build and operate—*in the United States*—its own new, highly integrated manufacturing and assembly complex. It will use new technologies in product and processing and will have separate franchises and a separate labor agreement, using concepts worked out by a joint GM-UAW task force."[24] This announcement set off a hot bidding war among several states, eventually won by Tennessee, for what would be advertised, when it was up and running, as "A different kind of company, a different kind of car."

The other prong to Smith's strategy emerged from the secret discussions he had been having with Eiji Toyoda, the chairman of Toyota, about a joint venture to manufacture small cars in a shuttered GM plant in Fremont, California, using the Toyota production system and a teamwork-based working environment. The two executives regarded this pioneering idea as a win-win proposition. General Motors would get an inside look at the vaunted Toyota system, and Toyota, which was planning to build its own plants in the United States, would test the waters in working with unionized UAW workers.

The proposal, which had to be approved by US regulators, was challenged by Chrysler on antitrust grounds, and I found myself in front of first a judge and then a congressional committee defending the plan for a New United Motor Manufacturing, Incorporated (immediately and ever after known as NUMMI). The proposal had been structured, I emphasized, to be pro- rather than anticompetitive and imposed no restrictions on either firm's ability to continue its fierce rivalry in the United States and throughout the world. Furthermore, I insisted, the knowledge GM would derive from the proposed joint venture with Toyota was essential to Saturn's success.[25]

Chrysler's general counsel argued that the joint venture would in fact restrict competition. Fortunately for me, the committee's chairman, Congressman John Dingell, a strong supporter of the US auto industry and a fearful opponent in the halls of Congress, shared GM's view. He lobbed such softballs to me and such hard-hitting questions to Chrysler's representative that I caught myself feeling sorry for the guy.

As it turned out, my promise that NUMMI would provide a learning experience for Saturn and GM in general was thwarted by the internal bureaucracy charged with implementing it. Smith had intended that GM midlevel executives would go to NUMMI in teams of four, spend several years learning the secrets of the Toyota production system, and return as a team to incorporate them into company operations. But the GM divisions resisted bringing these bearers of foreign ways of doing things into their fiefdoms, and the returnees were reluctantly reabsorbed into the company one by one, a process guaranteed to thwart the changes that were to have been GM's gain from the joint venture. In yet another example of the company's tendency to stick with or revert to its traditional habits, many of the innovations that had made Saturn a new kind of company were gradually abandoned by Smith's successors. The Saturn line of vehicles was phased out as part of GM's government-mandated restructuring in 2009, and the NUMMI plant closed when neither GM nor Toyota showed any interest in continuing to keep it open.

Roger Smith's strategy for producing small cars competitively in the United States typified the visionary side of his nature, in which he saw highly automated factories and paperless offices as the main instruments for restoring and maintaining GM's competitive position in a global struggle for automotive dominance. During his time as CEO, GM invested heavily in the latest and most automated production processes. Why, then, did his long-range planning ultimately fail to achieve its creator's goal but rather took the company to the edge of bankruptcy?

Like the heroes of Greek tragedy, Smith was a great man with some ultimately fatal flaws. His greatness lay in his intelligence, creative thinking, and ability to make big decisions rapidly. But he misunderstood the sources of the Japanese advantage and couldn't make midcourse corrections when his plans blew up in his face. He failed to see that the heart of Japanese product and process innovation lay not in high-tech automation, which they used sparingly, but in a finely honed integration of product design, process simplification, and human behavior. When the expensive machinery Roger was so proud of became the butt of bad jokes about robots dropping windshields and painting each other, he was unable to get the problem effectively diagnosed and fixed. Instead, all the spending on automation took GM from being a low-cost to a high-cost producer, absolutely the wrong direction at a time of intensifying competition.

He was also thrown off course by men with powerful personalities and overweening ambition, men he admired and had worked hard to bring into the GM fold. He was surprised and furious to discover that he couldn't control them, leading to several high-profile disasters. One such miscalculation was the arrangement he made with Horst-Dieter Esch, the hotshot chief executive of the German firm IBH, which purchased one of GM's subsidiary businesses. Although GM's lawyers had warned him that the proposed relationship might be illegal in Germany, Smith was "too quick to structure transactions to accommodate Esch, IBH's flamboyant founder and chairman . . . Esch ran his company the way Roger would like to run his, out of his vest pocket."[26] Ultimately, Esch was sent to prison for fraud, and Smith dared to set foot in Germany only after GM attorneys checked with a German prosecutor's office to make sure that their chairman wouldn't be arrested.[27]

Another misjudgment was the general counsel that Roger brought to GM in 1983. Elmer Johnson was a tall, handsome, silver-haired lawyer noted not only for his legal triumphs but also for his ruthlessness in business. Roger wooed this man with a larger-than-life reputation with the promise of a rapidly expanding role in the company and a chance at the gold ring of CEO. His responsibilities were broadened several times during the next few years. In 1987, he not only was made an executive vice president and a member of the Board of Directors but was named by Smith as one of four contenders to succeed him as CEO.

Soon after that, relations began to sour. Instead of showing up regularly at the many policy committee meetings in which senior executives were expected to participate, Elmer sat alone in his office, writing long, thoughtful memos on how the company's operations could be improved. The coup de grâce was a twenty-five-page document in which he severely criticized the management of one of the two major car groups into which the company's automotive operations had been divided during the wrenching reorganization of 1984, gave detailed suggestions about how the group should be revamped, and suggested that he be put in charge of the group to implement those recommendations.

Many of his substantive suggestions later proved to be on the money. But they earned the enmity of Roger Smith, who didn't appreciate being told how to do his job. Despite the promises with which he had lured Elmer to GM, he soon had no intention of giving this man, seen as a troublemaker, one of the company's top operating positions. His response to the memos was icy silence, and Johnson felt himself being squeezed out of Smith's inner circle. Frustrated, he resigned in mid-1988 to return to his law practice and later wrote a book criticizing America's dependence on automobiles.

The most explosive incident that arose from Roger's failure to understand human nature was his disastrous relationship with Ross Perot, the charismatic founder and CEO of EDS. General Motors bought the data-processing company in 1985 after a complex negotiation, led by Elmer Johnson, that resembled a mating dance as much as a business transaction.

Roger's attraction to EDS derived partly from his belief that the firm could bring order to GM's inefficient, crazy-quilt, data-processing and business systems. But his hot pursuit also owed a great deal to his admiration for Perot himself, and his hope that some of the EDS founder's scrappy, shoot-from-the-hip decision-making style could be transferred to GM's slow-moving bureaucratic culture. For this reason, Smith promised Perot unprecedented independence within the larger company. It was agreed that EDS would operate as a separate profit center, with a separate class of stock (Class E), whose stock-market value would hang on its performance. Perot also became a member of GM's Board of Directors.

It wasn't long before what had been conceived as a marriage made in heaven moved toward a divorce carried out in a hell of resentment and confusion inside GM and a storm of unfavorable publicity outside. Almost immediately, Perot began a barrage of public criticism of the way GM ran every aspect of its automotive business, refused to allow GM access to EDS's books, and publicly spoke out against the acquisition of Hughes Aircraft. In a famous put-down of the GM culture published in *Business Week,* he chortled, "The first EDSer to see a snake kills it. At GM, the first thing you do is organize a committee on snakes. Then you bring in a consultant who knows a lot about snakes. Third thing you do is talk about it for a year."[28]

By the end of 1986, Perot had resigned from the GM board, and GM had bought back all his shares of GM and EDS (Class E) stock for seven hundred million dollars in a departure also negotiated by Elmer Johnson. The company was widely accused of using "greenmail"—excessive payment as a bribe—to get rid of Perot, and, although EDS's market-capitalization of twenty-seven billion dollars when it was spun off a decade later was of enormous financial benefit to GM, the episode was an extremely painful one for the company's morale inside and its reputation outside.

This pain was due not only to Perot's shenanigans but also to the internal discomfiture created by the failed integration of EDS into GM. The other members of Smith's leadership team were resentful that they hadn't been consulted about the EDS acquisition, and the chief financial officer, whom Smith had put in charge of the operation, was oblivious to the human fallout from such a wrenching change. Company managers rapidly came to the conclusion that EDS's pricing was ripping off its parent company. Data-processing employees at GM were deeply shaken and hurt by their forcible transfer to EDS and the substitution of its much riskier compensation structure for GM's secure pay and benefits. Everyone was taken aback by the gun-toting security guards who controlled access to EDS's secretive Detroit headquarters. Roger Smith, a whiz at mathematics and finance, had once again failed to take an accurate measure of human nature.

Even today, twenty years after Roger Smith's retirement and several years after his death, I feel a twinge of disloyalty in my description of his failings. Roger was unfailingly supportive of my career at GM and, for a man widely reputed to resent criticism, was surprisingly open to whatever candid evaluations I offered of a proposed decision or action. Bob O'Connell, the financially creative and blatantly ambitious chief financial officer who was being touted as one of the possible successors to Smith, cautioned me that being "so rough" with the chairman could be a career buster. Like my father, I put a high value on being close to the center of power, but, also like him, I never shrank from "telling truth to power." I knew I had won this gamble the day Roger called me into his office and said, "I have good news and bad news. The good news is that I'm offering you a promotion; the bad news is that you'll have to move to Detroit."

· 10 ·

$\mathcal{W}$e'll Push 'Em Back into the Sea

For a second time, I sat opposite Roger Smith, trying not to let astonishment show on my face. The first time had been across a wooden picnic table in the California sunshine, when he asked, out of the blue and as if it were the most natural thing in the world, if I would consider becoming a vice president and chief economist at GM. This time it was across the broad mahogany desk that set the stiffly formal, top-executive tone of his fourteenth-floor office in Detroit's GM Building. I was enjoying the challenges of the job Roger had offered at that earlier meeting and had never thought past it, certainly not in terms of moving beyond the responsibilities grounded in my economics background into an entirely new world of general management.

The promotion Roger dangled before me was a significant step up, to vice president and group executive for Public Affairs, a group of four staffs, each with its own vice president. Not only did it send a strong signal that I had performed well so far in my foray into the corporate world, but it would also make me the highest-ranking female in the US automobile industry, a notoriously male preserve at the time. More important, it would give me the chance to influence GM's relationships with some of its increasingly important stakeholders: its headquarters and plant communities; national, state, and local governments; environmentalists; and, at least indirectly through public relations, actual and potential customers.

Roger Smith presented me with this opportunity on a Friday; he told me to think about it over the weekend and let him know my decision on Monday. When I broached the subject with Bob, I immediately started to dither and whine about uprooting the household once again, moving us from our Princeton home to an unfamiliar part of the world—Greater Detroit—about which we'd heard only depressing tales, and sticking him with yet another commute to Pittsburgh. Bob interrupted me in midsentence. "Look," he said, "the kids and I can adapt to any choice you make, but the one thing we can't handle is having you spread your guilt all over us." During the decades since, I have passed that piece of wisdom along to several woman friends agonizing over similar career-family decisions, and every one of them found it as invaluable and reassuring as I had.

Bob did have one nonnegotiable demand, though; we had to live in a community with a university and a good research library. That eliminated the elegant suburbs of Birmingham and Bloomfield Hills, the usual choices of high-level GM executives. It didn't take us long to agree that the natural place for us would be Ann Arbor, some thirty-five miles west of Detroit and home of the University of Michigan. After some intensive house-hunting we found a handsome red brick colonial in a neighborhood not far from the university, ablaze with flowering trees and blooming plants in the brief but lovely Michigan spring. Because I care about the touches generally found in older homes—plaster borders on ceilings, hardwood floors—I had always said that any house we bought had to be at least as old as I was. This one just made it; we had both started life in 1935.

We were totally unprepared for Ann Arbor's midwestern hospitality; within twenty-four hours of the moving truck's departure neighbors appeared on our doorstep with casseroles or bottles of wine, and we quickly began to develop a circle of friends that has grown steadily during the years since. Thus began our love affair with Ann Arbor, which has lasted well beyond my retirement from General Motors and in total contradiction to our long-standing expectation that we would retire either to Bob's hometown, Cambridge, or mine, Princeton.

Although I had been working for GM for six years, and had spent quite a bit of time in Detroit for meetings, I was still in for a new set of culture shocks. Living outside the usual GM orbit was regarded as a bit peculiar. When I told Roger Smith where we would be living, he only remarked, "You'll be driving into the sun both ways, east in the morning and west in the evening." But I could tell that he was surprised and mildly disapproving. And when a public relations executive asked me which country club I would like to join, I mentioned the rather modest tennis and swimming club down the street from our new home. A few days later the man came back, puzzled and embarrassed, to report that there was no way he could move us to the head of the queue. We would just have to wait our turn, a situation that would never have arisen if we had settled in a proper GM community.

The biggest ripple caused by my arrival on the fourteenth floor, in addition to my gender, was my choice of a secretary. These executive secretaries were not only highly paid but wielded considerable power, which flowed through to them from their bosses' positions. In return, they kept even longer hours than the workaholics they served, did whatever they were asked, whether it was work related or not, and maintained absolute discretion regarding their bosses' personal lives. Some of them shopped for Christmas presents for their bosses' wives or typed and edited term papers for their children. Elmer Johnson's secretary managed his household accounts, paid his bills, and even held the key to his safe-deposit box. Alan Smith's made daily trips to his Bloomfield Hills home to tend to the family cats while he was away running GM of Canada, even though she was temporarily assigned to work for someone else.

The GM rule was that executives were not allowed to take their secretaries with them when they were promoted, on the sensible grounds that secretaries' career tracks should be independent of their bosses'. But when I selected the most competent secretary in the Detroit offices of the Economics staff to move upstairs with me, I knew that no one would dare refuse my request, any more than the women who reported to my mother in the shop that built radar sets during World War II would have dared to vote no when they were asked to decide whether they would be willing to have "Negroes" work alongside them. Gloria Pearson, a smart and savvy Detroit native and single mother, would be the first African American secretary on the executive floor. I chose her for her impressive skills; her sharp wit came along for free. When I asked her how a black girl from inner-city Detroit wound up as a student at Brandeis University, a Jewish school on the outskirts of Boston, she instantly replied "white liberal guilt." But she was immensely proud that, between us, we had broken through two hitherto impregnable barriers to the fourteenth floor. Her loyalty to and high expectations of me were downright intimidating.

The other executive secretaries gave Gloria the cold shoulder when she first arrived, as much because she was an outsider to their tightly knit group as because of her color. But they soon came to appreciate her intelligence, competence, and keen sense of humor; she eventually became the recognized leader of the group. She was also an early and enthusiastic adopter of computerized office skills when desktop personal computers became available. Having this buffer between my Luddite backwardness and the brave new world made possible by my father's pioneering work was invaluable, but it also led occasionally to a hilarious blooper. Gloria's faith in the spell-check function made her careless about proofreading. Once, reading over a letter I was about to sign, I called to her, "Gloria, it isn't a good idea to leave the *l* out of *public affairs.*"

If only I could have adjusted to life on the fourteenth floor as readily as Gloria did! While I was based in New York, I had dealt with the GM culture from a safe distance; in Detroit I had to confront it face-to-face as I struggled to define my new role. The main function of the group executive responsible for public affairs, as I saw it, was to identify and articulate a vision for the group and then push in every possible way to help bring that vision alive. The vision I articulated for the Public Affairs Group was to provide "windows on the world" for GM. This included "windows out," counseling management on trends and events in the world outside GM, their likely impact on the company, and how it should respond. It also included "windows in," representing GM's situation, viewpoints, and interests to the rest of the world. "More crudely put," I said, "we're advocates outside and nags inside."

There was a world of difference between this high-flown language and the day-to-day realities I had to deal with, starting with my new boss. As chief economist, I had reported to Alan Smith, although much of my interaction was directly with Roger Smith, with whom Alan shared a last name but no family relationship. Short, compact, and silver haired, Alan possessed not only a first-class financial mind but also a wry sense of humor that occasionally burst through the cautious bureaucratic style honed over a lifelong career at GM. The Public Affairs staffs, though, reported to Vice Chairman Howard Kehrl, a living example of the operation of the Peter Principle, which holds that in a hierarchy every employee tends to rise to the level of his or her incompetence. Howard presumably rose through the ranks on the strength of his engineering talents, but as a top-ranking general executive, he was a disaster. A compulsive micromanager, he demanded that every word or action be checked and rechecked several times by successive layers of management, up to and including himself, with the result that no one who reported to him took full responsibility for anything.

No one had his head more deeply buried in the sand than Howard, hiding from the truth about Japanese competition. When a young member of the Economics staff returned from Japan with firsthand knowledge of the Toyota production system (which came to be called "lean production"), I lobbied hard to have him present his findings to top management. Although some of us had been struggling for several years to alert them to the truth about GM's competitive disadvantage, this would be the first time that they would be hearing such a report "from the front." After the presentation ended, the silence was broken by Howard Kehrl, saying, "We can't have something in GM called the Toyota Production System." To my horrified astonishment, there was no follow-up discussion of what the group had just seen, or its implications for GM.

Howard's refusal to recognize the superiority of Japanese production and labor-management methods was impervious to evidence. When he learned that Toyota and Honda were planning to build plants in the United States, he responded, "Just let them come here and try to work with American labor. We'll push 'em back into the sea." And, when I tried to persuade him that restricting auto imports would ultimately stand in the way of GM's plans to become a more global company, his answer was that it was only US production and sales that really mattered to the company's bottom line. This reflected hindsight but no foresight. In 1985, when Howard made this comment, some 70 percent of GM's vehicle output was produced and sold domestically. But the trend was downward; twenty years later GM was producing and selling more cars and trucks outside the United States than it did at home.[1]

Adjusting to Howard Kehrl's management style was difficult enough, but I was even more rattled that my previous boss, Alan Smith, had deliberately cut off all access after I no longer reported to him. Time and time again, I tried to make an appointment to see him to discuss something that either required his approval or on which I wanted to get his advice. But the appointment never materialized, and his door remained firmly closed to me, even though his office was only around the corner from mine and we passed each other in the hallway at least once a day. This humiliating exclusion underscored once again the extremes to which the GM culture carried the compartmentalization and constricted communications against which I did daily battle.

If the viselike grip of the GM culture made relationships with my superiors difficult, it also complicated my relationships with the Public Affairs vice presidents, formerly my colleagues, who now reported to me. They were all loyal GM stalwarts, committed to supporting the company's success as they saw it. Yet each, in their own way, resisted both change and my leadership in trying to integrate their talents into a coherent and effective group.

Betsy Ancker-Johnson, vice president of the Environmental Activities staff, was a solid-state physicist with several patents to her credit, only the third woman elected to the National Academy of Engineering, and the first female presidential appointee in the Department of Commerce. Petite and blonde, with a stern, schoolmarm expression, she was a woman with guts. When, in the early 1950s, no first-rate physics department in the United States would accept a woman as a doctoral candidate, Betsy learned German and earned her PhD. in physics at the University of Tübingen. Barely five feet tall, she loved to drive GM's huge commercial trucks at the company's proving ground. She used her small stature to lobby GM to install adjustable seat belts that would protect children and small adults without threatening to choke them. And, under her leadership, GM won a number of awards from environmental organizations.

The problem with Betsy, from my point of view, was that the same stubbornness that had enabled her to overcome so many obstacles made her as formidable a defender of her turf as any member of the old boys' network. When downsizing and streamlining became the order of the day throughout GM, every effort to get Betsy to comply was countered with a dire warning about how any reduction in her staff's head count would put GM in serious jeopardy of failing to comply fully with the elaborate network of safety, environmental, and fuel-efficiency regulations that engulfed it. None of my superiors, from the chairman on down, was any more successful in taking her on than I was. It was only after she retired that some much-needed reorganization and streamlining of the activities she supervised could occur.

Jim Johnston, the vice president of Industry-Government Relations, was a former Foreign Service officer who knew just about everyone in the nation's capital of importance to the auto industry and, with his affable personality and remarkable memory for names and personal details, was well liked by people on both sides of the legislative aisle and on different sides of controversial issues. Jim and his wife, Margaret, actively followed through on the commitment to social justice that arose from their deeply held Catholic faith. But, as GM's chief lobbyist, he saw protecting the current GM product plan as his primary obligation. That conviction placed him squarely in the path of a collision between the social and competitive pressures on the US auto industry on the one hand and management's bullheaded response on the other.

Society's expectations of the industry, reflected in countless regulations, were increasing every year. And the influx of Japanese vehicles, in addition to sharpening the competition for customers, brought with it better average fuel efficiency than GM and Ford, with their traditional reliance on larger vehicles for profitability, could match. And, although many of the innovations in safety, pollution control, and fuel efficiency had been developed by General Motors, these features didn't always promise a rapid return on the investment needed to put them into its vehicles. So the company headed by Roger Smith, a finance man in every fiber of his being, dragged its feet on introducing many of these improvements into its cars and trucks.

During a period when cost reduction took primacy over other goals and later, when the company's new president, Lloyd Reuss, announced that GM's policy would be to lag rather than lead in introducing safety and fuel-efficiency advances into vehicles because "that's not what the customers care most about," Jim was forced into an awkward position. He insisted that the company should resist admitting the reality of man-made global warming well after most climate scientists, including his colleague Betsy Ancker-Johnson, were persuaded of its existence. I tried to convince him to acknowledge the growing evidence, but his stubbornness on the matter, combined with the primary role he played in defending the company's interests on a wide variety of policy issues, put him at odds with my efforts to make GM's management see realistically the challenges its future held, and to persuade the outside world that the company was playing a role in environmentally friendly innovation.

The person I brought in to succeed me as chief economist was George Eads, then dean of the School of Public Policy at the University of Maryland and formerly high up in the Antitrust Division of the Justice Department. George had both a superb analytical brain and, it turned out, some creative views on how to streamline the Economics staff while making it more efficient and effective. He also had something I lacked: a lifelong love and expert knowledge of cars. But George's interest in public affairs issues took a backseat to his desire to move to a line job with responsibility for one of GM's business units. His openly critical mind did not fit comfortably with the GM culture, and when he saw that he wasn't going to get the kind of position he craved, he left GM, a disappointed and frustrated man.

Jack McNulty, the vice president of Public Relations, was a very different sort. A hard-drinking, florid-faced man with a hard-edged New York accent, he was outspoken in expressing views that made his listeners shudder. He made no bones about the fact that it didn't sit well with him to report to a woman, although he would do his best. His thoughts on how to reach out to potential African American customers were that they were "a great market for used Cadillacs." He encouraged the three-martini lunch, by example as well as quips, and I discovered that the alcoholism rife in his staff was a subject of crude jokes among the Detroit-based press corps. My efforts to change this destructive environment came to naught, at least partly because I couldn't get support from those above me in the chain of command.

I realized how big a problem I had with trying to integrate the Public Affairs staffs into a meaningful group when I found it almost impossible to call a meeting with the four vice presidents. Basically, each wanted to be left alone to manage his or her own staff in pursuit of the goals outlined in its business plan. My efforts to hold monthly meetings to talk about ways to maximize synergies so as to make the whole group more effective met with fierce bureaucratic resistance. Something more important invariably interfered with any schedule I tried to set, and I had to demand attendance, which flatly contradicted my effort to position myself as a leader and facilitator rather than a command-and-control boss. When downsizing became a companywide exercise, each vice president offered good reasons why the reductions should come from somewhere other than his or her own staff. I managed to keep my composure during these discussions but in the privacy of my office, I pounded the desk and mumbled profanities to vent my frustration.

The GM culture confronted me everywhere I turned. Jack McNulty ostensibly reported to me, but his real role was as Roger Smith's personal publicist. Roger was extremely conscious of his public image and very defensive about anything that might cast him in a negative light. That set the tone for GM public relations. Any journalist who dared to write something critical about GM or its chairman invited the threat that the company would withdraw its advertising from the offending publication, which it often did. Company spokesmen responded to difficult questions with carefully worded boilerplate.

One of Public Relations' toughest challenges was caused by the wide release in 1989 of Michael Moore's first hit film, *Roger and Me*. Moore used a combination of manipulation, caricature, half truths, and brilliant comic timing to contrast Roger Smith's pampered lifestyle with the abject misery into which GM's decision to close several plants had cast the citizens of Flint, Michigan. The movie was a sensational hit, setting Moore and his signature baseball cap on the road to fame and fortune. When a reporter asked for GM's reaction to the film, a spokesman replied haughtily that no one in GM would stoop so low as to buy a ticket!

Another major confrontation with the Public Relations staff arose when it didn't take kindly to my attempts to enforce a GM rule that forbade employees from accepting gifts of significant value from the firm's suppliers. The general knowledge that the company's chairman had enjoyed several excursions on Malcolm Forbes's luxurious yacht and had been a guest at his multi-million-dollar birthday bash in the Arabian desert, despite the fact that GM was a major buyer of advertising space in *Forbes* magazine, undermined my efforts. Things came to a head at the splashy Teamwork and Technology show, a pet project of Roger's, which highlighted GM's innovations and current and future products, held at New York's Waldorf Astoria hotel.

When I arrived in my room, I found an enormous box from Tiffany's and, nestled inside, a very expensive Steuben crystal vase. My first thought was "That will make a fine wedding present for someone." Then came my second: "Good Lord, we're not allowed to accept these from the hotel that's selling us the space and services for our show." A call to the manager elicited the information that every GM executive in the hotel had received the same gift. "Well," I said, "you'll have to figure out how to take them back."

The result was a knock from housekeeping on every executive's door. Where rooms were empty and the gifts still wrapped, they were retrieved. But no one, including me, had the nerve to insist on recapture when it required a face-to-face explanation, so a few vases escaped. When we got back to Detroit, my vice presidents had to listen to yet another explanation from me about the rules forbidding gifts, and, to the best of my knowledge, the practice more or less halted among those who reported to me. But the chairman's proclivity for setting himself above the rules continued to pervade the corporate culture, behavior that flew in the face of the values I had been taught to regard as basic.

Meanwhile, I used talks, interviews, op-ed pieces in leading newspapers, and congressional testimony to fulfill my personal role as both a nag inside and an advocate outside the company. The world I described on the other side of the "windows out" was being shaped by the rapid globalization of the automobile industry; the increasing diversity of the many publics, or stakeholders, with which GM interacted; and the heightened expectations for corporate good citizenship. These developments demanded that GM find creative ways to integrate its business goals with political and social agendas. The competition from Japanese producers was just the beginning, I warned, as more and more developing nations—of which Korea was the first—were positioning themselves to join the competitive fray. And, finally, the success of the Japanese-owned "transplant" facilities in the United States should have hammered home the message that geography is not destiny, that it is management that bears the primary responsibility for competitive success.

One of my most important tasks as an advocate for GM—the "windows in" part—was testifying before congressional committees and subcommittees. Every detail of these hearings was designed to intimidate the witness, who sat at a wooden table, facing the committee members. These inquisitors were ranged along an elevated dais well above our level, forcing us to look up constantly as we read our scripts and reminding us, as if we needed reminding, where the power lay. The committee chairman gave each witness a strict time limit, often reinforced by a light that changed from green to yellow to red as the deadline approached. I learned not to take either one questioner's encouragement or another's withering hostility personally; what mattered was not me as an individual on the dock but the position or interest group I represented and how my questioner could best score his own points with the audience and, more important, the next day's newspaper accounts.

The subject on which I testified most often was the Corporate Average Fuel Economy (CAFE) standards, which required each manufacturer's fleet of vehicles to meet or exceed a specified average miles-per-gallon number. During the decade in which these requirements were being phased in, from 1975 to 1985, fuel prices were generally high or rising, pushing customers to want smaller vehicles, and the US manufacturers had no difficulty in meeting the steadily tightening mileage standards. The average mileage of passenger vehicles doubled, from 13.5 to 27.5 miles per gallon, and for light trucks it increased by more than 50 percent.[2]

But when gasoline prices fell, in the second half of the 1980s, customers once again favored larger and less fuel efficient vehicles. Then the standards began to bite hard on full-line producers like GM and Ford, which were torn between the mileage requirements and the desire to stem their decline in market share by selling more of the larger and more profitable vehicles customers wanted. Meanwhile, our Japanese competitors, whose production was naturally weighted toward the smaller vehicles suited to their crowded home country, faced no such difficulties and, in fact, had room under the standards to make their fleets *less* fuel-efficient by moving up-market to larger, more luxurious vehicles.

I testified in favor of loosening the CAFE standards more times than I care to remember, but the main points of my argument were always the same: that the standards failed all three relevant criteria, being neither effective, efficient, nor fair. Just about every economist who has looked at the issue agrees that specific "command-and-control" regulations like CAFE are the least desirable and costliest policies to use in pushing to maximize energy security and/or minimize production of the greenhouse gases that contribute to global warming. In fact, gasoline consumption per capita actually rose in the United States during the 1980s, as consumers more than offset increases in fuel efficiency by acquiring more cars per family and driving more miles in the course of a year.[3] A broad-based energy tax, I argued, would create the right signals to influence consumer behavior and would meet the triple test that CAFE failed.[4]

I got to play offense rather than just defense as an advocate for the US automakers when I was appointed by President Reagan to the private-sector advisory group to the US Trade Representative. I stressed that what American manufacturing industries needed from the US agency charged with trade issues was, above all, a reduction in uncertainty through stabilized rules, along with pressure on other countries to open their markets to US products and eliminate burdensome "performance requirements." These requirements, imposed mainly by developing countries, demanded that any foreign firm that wanted to produce and sell there had to meet a number of rigid conditions such as generating a specified volume of exports or employing nationals of the host country as a required share of its workforce.

My biggest impact on US trade negotiations, though, came in the task force formed to lay out objectives for the negotiations with Canada and Mexico that culminated in the North American Free Trade Agreement. My efforts were focused on ensuring that the provisions related to the automobile industry, which dominated US trade in manufactures with both Mexico and Canada and was treated as a special case in the agreement, met the demands of the Big Three American auto firms. These companies were ultimately successful in achieving provisions that treated them favorably in comparison with their Japanese competitors, while at the same time phasing out most of Mexico's rigid performance requirements.

I found myself playing an ambassadorial role within the company as well when I became secretary of the Public Policy Committee of GM's Board of Directors, the committee charged with monitoring GM's outlook and behavior on important issues of public policy. This seemed like an ideal assignment for someone with my interest and background in relationships between public issues and the private sector. But it was marred by the fact that my role as liaison quickly turned into that of mediator in an ongoing struggle.

The tension arose from Roger Smith's determination to keep GM's board under iron control, by making sure that it received only the information he wanted it to have and allowing virtually no time for discussion in board meetings. He also attended the meetings of those board committees he regarded as important, to ensure that no potentially troublesome discussions bubbled up from them. He didn't bother to attend meetings of the Public Policy Committee, which he regarded as the least relevant to the actual running of the business. In assigning the committee responsibilities of each outside director, he allocated to the Public Policy Committee not only people with a genuine interest and expertise in issues like safety, environmental impact, protection of employees, and relationships with plant communities but also those who he thought might be troublemakers on more important committees. Chief among the latter was Ross Perot.

The result of Roger's maneuvering was that the members of the Public Policy Committee decided that theirs was the only venue where directors could discuss an issue freely and thoroughly, without Roger's domineering presence. As a result, they were constantly demanding background information on, and a chance to ask tough questions about, matters that were not really issues of public policy at all but were at the core of GM's business decisions and their effect on the company's profitability and long-run viability. These included issues like the quality of the company's vehicles in comparison with its competitors' and the relationship between the firm and the dealers who were its direct link with consumers.

I tried to respond to the demands of the committee members that such issues be placed on its agenda, but their often critical comments and suggestions tended to be ignored by Smith and those executives who did his bidding. This only increased the committee's frustration and hostility toward management, while the background papers prepared by various GM staffs became increasingly defensive. And on subjects that were appropriately within the committee's purview, members sent numerous signals, through me, of their dissatisfaction with some of the company's policies. Don't undermine your credibility on CAFE, they warned, by overstating its negative aspects. Regarding safety, they asked, why didn't the other GM divisions follow Cadillac's lead in advertising safety, and why was the company so slow in introducing safety innovations into its products? I began to feel like a marriage counselor, trying to get each side to understand the other's position and prevent the tensions from erupting into open warfare.

The company's deteriorating situation in the second half of the 1980s cried out for innovations that would extend the reach of our public affairs mandate. The most urgent one, to my mind, came out of GM's announcement, toward the end of 1986, that it would be closing several plants in the near future. To soften the devastating effects that such closings were sure to have on the communities in which these plants were often the largest employer would require pulling together and coordinating all the relevant knowledge, expertise, and decision-making ability that was scattered throughout the company.

I did it by championing the creation of a Corporate Community Transition Team (CCTT), with representatives from various corporate staffs, as well as the major business units. This group had no role in deciding which plants would be closed or when, nor did we focus on layoff or relocation arrangements for GM employees, most of whom were covered by union contracts. Our concern was with alleviating the impacts on families and communities that Michael Moore had caricatured so devastatingly in *Roger and Me*.

One of the worst aspects of the situation was that the size of GM's contribution to the United Way charitable organization in each plant city was keyed to the number of people it employed there. If this rule had been applied to communities where plants were completely shuttered, GM's corporate contributions would have ended at exactly the time when laid-off employees' personal contributions were also plummeting, while the need for United Way services shot up. Instead, the CCTT persuaded the company to cushion the shock by phasing out its contributions over several years, a policy that has since been adopted by other large companies in communities where they shut down operations, including the pharmaceutical giant Pfizer when it closed its research facilities in my hometown of Ann Arbor.

The efforts of the CCTT couldn't dispel the bitterness created by plant closings. Although GM did win several lawsuits for "breach of contract" brought by affected communities, it became a poster child for many of the ills that befell communities heavily reliant on old-line manufacturing. One of the most emotionally wrenching encounters in my role as chairman of that committee was a meeting with the mayor of one of the cities strung northward from Detroit along the I-75 corridor—cities like Pontiac and Flint and Saginaw. In each of these cities, the GM plant was the biggest employer in town and, when the plants were built and expanded, they had attracted a large northward migration of African Americans from the rural South, drawn by the prospect of good wages for men with little formal education. Over the decades, the children and grandchildren of some of these original migrants rose to positions of responsibility in their communities; by 1986, several of the I-75 cities had elected black mayors, and these officials bore the brunt of coping with the social and economic repercussions of plant closings.

The unhappy mayor came to talk to me soon after the plant closings in his community were announced. The formality of his dress and manner matched the formality of my office, and he sat stiffly in one of its elegant chairs. He was unfailingly polite and soft spoken, but what he said made me sit bolt upright. That many of his constituents were angry and frustrated, and were venting their fury on him as a handy target, was no surprise. But, he added, many of them believed that the fact that their cities had been targeted for plant closings reflected GM's hostility toward African Americans and the cities where they were now leaders. That did shake me up.

I assured him that nothing could be further from the truth, that far from wishing its minority employees, suppliers, and dealers ill, GM had a variety of programs to encourage their participation in its business. But because so many of the workers in our Michigan plants were African American, this group was particularly vulnerable when shrinking plant capacity became essential to the company's survival. I recalled that when I first joined the company, one of the briefers plying me with facts about my new employer had told me, with evident pride, that GM accounted for some 98 percent of the manufacturing employment in Flint. "Good Lord," I thought to myself then, "that's a catastrophe waiting to happen."

But, deep down, I knew that the mayor I tried to explain all this to left without feeling he was taking with him a story that could dispel his constituents' suspicions, and I felt embarrassed and helpless.

I found myself in this painful position because I had moved up just as GM's fortunes plunged. When I was promoted to the Public Affairs job in 1985, the firm had appeared to be in great shape, having earned record profits and claimed 44 percent of all US car sales the previous year. In reality, though, it was perched at the edge of a cliff. In the words of two longtime observers of the industry at the *Wall Street Journal,* "On the three measures of success that mattered—quality, manufacturing efficiency, and new product design—GM by 1985 was dead last in the industry."[5] It didn't take these failings long to hit GM's bottom line: the very next year operating profits and cash reserves plunged, the company lost nearly five points of market share, and Ford outearned GM for the first time since the Great Depression.

As went the company's fortunes, so went the reputation of its chairman. Roger Smith had appeared on the cover of the *New York Times Magazine* with the title "The Innovator: The Creative Mind of Roger Smith" in 1985;[6] by 1987, he was seen as the "archvillain" of American industry. Eventually, I was able to give my own balanced evaluation of him as neither hero nor villain, and thereby did him a favor he never knew about. When Roger was about to retire, I received a call from a childhood friend who was then a dean at the University of Michigan and chairman of the committee that nominated its honorary degree recipients. The university wanted to award an honorary degree to Roger Smith, one of its most notable graduates and, it was hoped, a potentially generous donor. But the faculty and student members of the committee, with the image of *Roger and Me* fresh in their in their minds, were firmly opposed. Could I write a letter, the dean asked, that might turn the views of some of them around?

Finding words to describe Roger in the best possible light while remaining honest took careful thought. In the letter I wrote, I described him as a corporate visionary, admitting that "His vision is not perfect (he himself has discussed what he would do differently . . .), he has not always communicated it as broadly and effectively as he might, and the returns are not yet in." I tackled head-on the fact that the film *Roger and*

Me had, not surprisingly, engendered some lively discussion regarding his suitability to receive the University of Michigan's highest honor. "[He] has struggled with two major issues," I wrote. "One is how to respond to the dislocations that occur when Schumpeter's 'gales of creative destruction' blow through. The second is how GM can best balance its commitments to its multiple stakeholders . . . Each one of us, second-guessing Roger Smith's leadership in handling these overwhelming questions, would undoubtedly disagree with some aspect of his response or his balancing of claims. But one must recognize the magnitude and the seriousness of his effort."[7] That April, Roger Smith received an honorary degree from his alma mater.

I tried to put a brave face on the sudden shifts in GM's fortunes and reputation, telling a reporter, "I thought I was going to work for a big company in a stable industry, but it's been a real roller-coaster ride, and I wouldn't have missed it for the world."[8] As time passed, though, and the roller-coaster kept heading downward, I began to find the ride more emotionally wearing than exhilarating. Just how low GM had sunk, in reputation, competitive position, and financial results, became crystal clear to the eight hundred executives gathered for the company's triennial executive conference in 1986. These three-day gatherings of the company's elite were traditionally held at the luxurious Greenbrier resort in West Virginia, with participants' time divided between self-congratulatory presentations on the company's state of affairs and every possible form of outdoor recreation, led by golf and fishing. My chief memory of the first such event I attended, in 1979, was my red-faced embarrassment when I managed to crack my two front teeth with my own tennis racket, playing at the first GM Greenbrier event that included a woman.

The 1986 meeting couldn't have been more different. It was moved from the Greenbrier to the workaday environment of GM's Technical Center in Warren, Michigan, despite a huge expenditure in cancellation costs, when it became clear that meeting in the lap of luxury would infuriate our employees and shareholders alike. The tone of the "Techbrier," as it was instantly dubbed, was somber in the extreme, with one top executive after another outlining the various dimensions of our difficulties and the steepness of the hill we had to climb to return to profitability.

President Jim McDonald spoke words never before uttered in a GM executive conference when he told the group, "I don't really feel that I can say I'm proud of you, because we have not accomplished what we set out to do here." Executive vice president Alan Smith detailed the gloomy financial picture, telling the group, "From 1980 to 1985, GM spent $45 billion in capital investment, yet increased its worldwide market share by only 1 percentage point, to 22 percent . . . For the same amount of money, we could buy Toyota and Nissan outright, instantly increasing the market share to 40 percent."[9]

Once the direness of the situation was finally recognized, the company's top leadership concluded that we couldn't wait the full three years for another executive conference. So in June of 1988 another one was held, this time at a resort in Traverse City, Michigan, far less luxurious than the Greenbrier but still a pleasant contrast to our everyday environment. There was plenty of outdoor recreation available, but the meeting sessions were so long and intense that few participants had the time or energy for play. This conference, so dramatically different in both format and substance from its predecessors, was shaped by the intersection of two initiatives that had been developing during the time between the Techbrier and Traverse City meetings.

One was the creation of the Group of 18, the executive vice presidents and group executives, who had begun meeting to establish priorities and build a strategic plan for the company's turnaround. The process had begun informally, growing out of a suggestion of mine over the lunch table that we group executives might want to take a look at each other's group business plans and try to see where they interacted and how they might be fitted together. One of my colleagues supported the idea, saying, "Gosh, Marina, you may just be new enough around here and dumb enough not to know that you can't do that, and actually get it done." Here was my chance, I said to myself, to be a player in bringing about the cultural change GM so desperately needed.

Mike Naylor, who had been preaching the gospel of strategic planning at GM for two decades, became the facilitator for a series of meetings where the group executives began to flesh out an integrated planning process for the company, incorporating a long-range vision, critical priorities, and plans for effective interaction to create a whole greater than the sum of its parts. After we had made some progress, we invited

Bob Stempel and Alan Smith, both members of the Executive Committee, to lead our efforts, and they accepted.

The second initiative was a program called Leadership Now, a training program for executives designed to change not the structure but the culture of the company, stressing the importance of openness, mutual trust, and empowerment—a combination of sensitivity training and personal empowerment the likes of which GM had never seen before. The need for a program to root out the company's traditional culture had first been voiced by John Stewart, a tall, lean New Englander with a patrician bearing, a brilliant analytical mind, and a no-nonsense manner. One of the McKinsey consulting firm's most senior consultants, he had been trying for years to push GM in the directions it needed to go, including making a clear-eyed assessment of its deteriorating competitive position and drastically streamlining its decision-making processes.

The Leadership Now trainer assigned to work with GM couldn't have been more different from Stewart. Mark Sarkady was a casually dressed, boyish-looking man with an unruly mop of black hair whose excitable manner undoubtedly stemmed from his Hungarian background. Executives who went through his training program, reported one observer, "seemed to have undergone—for the short term, anyway—some sort of religious conversion."[10] Despite their sharply different styles, both men had the same goal—to bring about change at GM dramatic enough to ensure its long-term viability—and neither underestimated the difficulty of the task.

The Traverse City conference was shaped by a combination of the Group of 18's work and the Leadership Now training program. We, the group executives, took the lead in laying out the company's most urgent priorities. I had been arguing for some time that this list should embody a broader vision for GM, extending beyond the vehicles themselves to being a leader as a "total transportation organization," reviving the slogan that GM had showcased but never implemented twenty years earlier at Transpo '72. Saturn was already demonstrating the attractions of its unique no-haggle purchasing experience, and anecdotes abounded about why the quality and convenience of postpurchase relationships with the dealer were important to decisions about what car to buy. I also tried to arouse enthusiasm for experimenting with a fleet of city cars that could be rented by the hour and picked up and dropped off at convenient locations around town—another idea that had surfaced at Transpo '72. But I couldn't drum up support, and "great cars and trucks" remained the embodiment of GM's vision of how to attract and hold customers.

The traditional speeches from top management to a passive audience of executives sitting in straight rows of chairs were replaced with an interactive workshop format in which everybody present was involved in sharing ideas. At the end of the conference, Roger Smith wound things up by proclaiming, "A corporation, like any living thing, must change if it is to survive. You see, we—that's you and I—have the vision to point the way for change. And we—that's you and I—have the courage to change."[11] At that moment Smith, wearing a casual brown sweater rather than his usual suit and tie, appeared more human than he ever had before, and many of those who heard him dared to hope that we were experiencing the birth of a fundamental change in GM's culture.

My own reaction combined hope with caution: "We are all very conscious of the fact that we raised expectations at Traverse City. There was an immediate afterglow and there will be an immediate letdown, because the world is not going to change overnight. But even the letdown will leave us at a higher level than we were before."[12] But Roger Smith's conversion couldn't conquer his domineering style, and the dramatic changes the Group of 18 had hoped to initiate didn't happen. Once again, the GM culture of inertia prevailed over efforts to dislodge it.

When Roger Smith retired as CEO in mid-1990, the world both inside and outside GM breathed a collective sigh of relief. Both GM's reputation and its financial condition were at an all-time low, and Roger was seen as the man responsible. The board's choice as Roger's successor, Robert Stempel, offered many reasons for optimism. An automotive engineer who had risen through the ranks to become GM's president, he had a string of successes under his belt and was widely regarded as a shining example of engineering talent. Stempel broke the long-standing tradition of a finance man as CEO; now the guys who designed and built cars and trucks had one of their own at the top. A huge man with a booming voice, a firm handshake, and an inclusive manner as he took copious notes on what other people said in meetings and conversations, he would have won any companywide popularity contest for the top position.

The man Stempel designated as president, Lloyd Reuss, was another matter. He was also an engineer, but there the resemblance ended. A small, taut, wiry man with an aggressive manner and zero tolerance for bad news or dissenting opinions, Reuss had as many failures behind him in his GM career as Stempel had successes, but he had somehow managed to leave them behind as he was promoted to the next level. The board neither understood nor was comfortable with Stempel's choice, but it acquiesced to his stubborn insistence that Reuss was the man he wanted as president.

Stempel's timing couldn't have been worse. He became GM's chairman and CEO on August 1, 1990; on August 2, Iraq invaded Kuwait, creating a climate of uncertainty devastating to car and truck sales. Furthermore, Roger Smith had used creative (though legal) accounting methods to push the bow wave of disaster ahead of him, to ensure that it crashed over the head of his successor rather than his own. The result was that Stempel, a smart, decent man who might have become a successful chief executive in more "normal" times, was overwhelmed. His horror of confrontation and his belief in incremental rather than radical change rendered him unequal to a situation that cried out for both. By early 1992, GM was on the edge of bankruptcy.

Despite the fact that he had been welcomed as a breath of fresh air, Stempel carried with him into the job some of GM's most counterproductive behaviors. In 1990, he maintained the company's aversion to a UAW strike—and the resulting drop in sales and market share—by agreeing to the most generous labor contract ever, just at the time when a reduction in labor costs was key to GM's ability to compete. Beneath Stempel's hail-fellow-well-met exterior lay the institutional arrogance and imperious style characteristic of the company's senior executives. This was brought home to me when both he and I were flying to Europe for a meeting of the European Advisory Council. He was using one of the company planes, configured to seat ten to a dozen people, so I naturally assumed that I would fly with him. Not so; he insisted that I take a commercial flight, business class, presumably so that he and his wife, Pat, would have privacy on the overnight flight.

Lloyd Reuss's executive style exacerbated Stempel's difficulties. As the company's top operating officer, he made some major strategic mistakes. He insisted on the importance of keeping the plants working at capacity even though, under current competitive conditions, it meant building vehicles he knew we would have to sell at prices below the additional cost of making them. He also resisted investment to make GM a leader in fuel efficiency and safety features like air bags because he felt they weren't high on customers' priority lists. His first decision violated one of the most basic tenets of my economist's soul, while his second made me despair of GM ever recapturing its reputation as a forward-looking leader in its industry. But there was no arguing with him on these issues.

Meanwhile, the Group of 18 and many of the midlevel managers were plugging away at streamlining GM and reshaping its traditional culture. That group also took to heart the "black book" compiled by General Counsel Harry Pearce on the basis of more than thirty interviews with GM's top executives (other than the chairman and president) and intended as a set of recommendations for the new chief executive. Because the interviewees were assured of confidentiality, their evaluations of the existing GM organization were devastatingly candid and their proposals for reform sweepingly comprehensive. We were about to present the book to Bob Stempel, with our strong endorsement, when the executive in charge of the Buick-Oldsmobile-Cadillac Group invoked the authority of President Reuss to quash it—yet another example of the old boys' network's protectiveness and resistance to radical change.

After Howard Kehrl retired, Alan Smith became my boss again, and I saw as my major task working with him to implement the initiatives the Group of 18 had championed. Alan was also busy reshaping himself, from a hard-eyed finance man into the guru of the people he had championed at Traverse City. Some of the people who worked with Alan felt that he had indeed undergone a conversion, from a top-down management style to a more collegial and inclusive one. Although I now found his office door open to me once again, I wasn't persuaded.

When Jack McNulty retired as vice president of Public Relations, I began a search both inside and outside the company for a successor who engendered trust, could improve GM's communications, and would contribute to burnishing its tarnished reputation. This was a critical appointment at a time when the public perception of an uncaring, arrogant automaker needed desperately to be replaced with the image—and the reality—of a friendly, open, responsible one.[13]

With the help of a search firm, I compiled a list, interviewed candidates, and made a recommendation to Alan. But when his response came back, the name on it had not appeared on anyone's list. The chosen successor was Jim Fitzpatrick, a GM lifer who started out in Finance and was a member of long standing in Alan's old boys' network. I was infuriated by this total rejection of an orderly selection process in favor of blatant favoritism, and Jim and I started out on the wrong foot. Our tense relationship eventually burst out into open warfare, with Jim trying to exclude me from meetings he had called and me complaining about his behavior to Alan. Such goings-on were unheard of in a world where hostilities and backbiting were never allowed to break the surface of correct behavior, and both of us found our credibility undermined.

One of the follow-ups to the Leadership Now process had been an evaluation, or feedback report, from each participant's peers and subordinates. Everyone was judged on five criteria: vision, urgency, empowerment, trust, and responsibility. I had found myself from time to time questioning my effectiveness as a general executive, but I was unprepared for the devastating evaluations I received from the four vice presidents who reported to me and the five peers (other group executives) who turned in responses. With one exception—my subordinates scored me high on trust—I scored below the median of the GM executives who had gone through the Leadership Now program and, in some cases, far down in the percentile rankings.

After I recovered from the initial shock, I started to look for reasons why my peers and subordinates rated me so low in leadership qualities, despite my efforts to get people to work together. The most comfortable explanation, of course, would have been to attribute their responses to sexism, their refusal to recognize that a woman could perform well as a high-level executive. Certainly, the GM executive ranks still were basically a male preserve. My male colleagues didn't engage in overt harassment or put-downs, but it was quite clear that they saw me as a sort of "third sex," regarding me in an entirely different light than their wives and female social acquaintances. It was only when their daughters with

MBAs started to bring home tales of their own difficulties in the work-place that they began to understand what it meant to be both a woman and an executive in a male-dominated environment.

The most outrageous example of sexist behavior I learned of at GM surfaced when I enlisted the advice of the company's chief of security on how to deal with the persistent attentions of a man—a highly regarded mathematician and professor I had met briefly when I was in college twenty-five years before—who had been stalking me for several years, in person or by telephone when he had the chance, but most persistently through a constant stream of unanswered letters. The message was un-varying; he proclaimed his passionate love for me and insisted that we should abandon our families and run off together. I was unnerved, and my daughter was downright terrified.

The security chief I asked to come up to my office to give me his view of the situation looked as if he had been sent from central casting. A former FBI operative, he was tall and stolid, with a craggy face that could have been carved out of granite. When I told him my predicament, he asked to see some of the offending letters. I produced them with some embarrassment, commenting that he had probably never dealt with quite such a situation before. Suddenly, a smile appeared on his stern visage. "Well, Dr. Whitman," he drawled, "I've never dealt with an executive who received such letters. But I've had to handle executives who sent them."

The more I reviewed my own behavior, though, the more I realized that, even though the GM executive ranks still harbored conscious or unconscious sexism, a lot of the responsibility for my low evaluations rested with me. For one thing, I was a control freak, micromanaging people, looking over their shoulders, and even editing their work, which kept them from feeling empowered to use their best judgment in carry-ing out their tasks. And I hadn't mastered the art of making people take possession of ideas as their own, too often insisting on the superiority of my own particular way of stating an idea, rather than letting others modify and adapt it.

I had also failed, apparently, in my effort to act on a sage piece of advice from that wise old owl, the McKinsey consultant John Stew-art. Given the ambiguity of a group executive's role, John warned me,

I needed to seize on some particular issue or goal, make it my own, and become its corporate champion. I thought I had such a goal: to work on breaking down the organizational "silos" that stood in the way of effective communication and integration at GM, and to encourage greater candor and openness both within the company and in our interactions with the outside world. Whether because of the rigidity of the GM culture and the broad scope of my effort or because my personal style got in the way, I didn't manage to elevate that goal and become its successful champion. I could have used more lessons from my mother, an expert in using her charm to get people, men and women alike, to do what she wanted.

Finally, and most devastatingly, I didn't have the guts to follow through on suggestions for cutting costs by eliminating activities and streamlining the organizational structure of the Public Affairs staffs. When I asked for, and received, dozens of suggestions from members of the Public Relations staff along these lines, I responded to too many of them by explaining why the idea wouldn't work, rather than telling them to get to work on implementation. I never pushed the vice presidents of Government Relations and Public Relations hard enough to come up with ideas for combining some or all of their functions under a single vice president. And when the deputy head of Environmental Activities assembled a task force to come up with a plan for parceling out that staff, which was widely regarded as ineffective, to other parts of the company, I vetoed it as too risky.

I realized gradually, but too late, that if there's anything worse than failing to solicit suggestions from subordinates, it's asking for them and then not giving them serious consideration. How much of my clumsy response came from wanting to avoid confrontations with my vice presidents, how much from my own insecurity about giving up large pieces of my turf, and how much from genuine concern about risks to the company's reputation and/or compliance with regulations, I can't sort out. But I had definitely dropped the ball at a time when cost cutting and streamlining were becoming increasingly essential to the company's survival.

It hit me suddenly that many of the mistakes I was discovering in myself—the tendency to micromanage, the failure to look reality full in the face, to hear what people were really telling me, and to implement suggestions I had solicited—reflected the sins that had long afflicted the GM culture. Even as I fought so hard to change that culture, was I being co-opted by it, I asked myself?

My sense of self-worth shrank further as it dawned on me that the position of group executive in the corporate staffs arena offered little if any added value and was increasingly resented by other parts of the company as they struggled to downsize their own ranks. The evidence that the role was superfluous moved front and center when the other group executive who reported to Alan retired and was not replaced, so that his staffs now reported directly to Alan while mine still had me in between. It didn't take any time at all to see which staffs felt better positioned. As I did silent battle with Alan for a leadership role on the dual task of streamlining our staffs and shepherding the process of culture change, I gradually realized that he felt as insecure in his position as I did in mine and was trying just as hard as I was to be seen as a positive force for change. Being higher up in the organization than me, and with a much broader reach, he of course won that battle, but in the end he lost the war, a war that dominated my final months at GM and ended a few weeks after I left the company.

Dissatisfied with the way things were going, the GM Board of Directors, led by John Smale, whose leadership skills I'd grown to admire when he was CEO of Procter and Gamble and I was a member of that board, was conducting its own investigation and making its own decisions. The directors felt that change wasn't occurring nearly fast enough and that Stempel was not giving satisfactory answers to the increasingly tough questions they were putting to him.

The first blow of the ax fell at the April 1992 board meeting. Lloyd Reuss was replaced as president by Jack Smith, vice chairman for international operations, and, when Stempel refused to fire Lloyd outright, he was relegated to a marginal job. Bob O'Connell, the chief financial officer whose accounting talents had kept Roger Smith's ship afloat, was also demoted. Alan Smith kept his job but was forced to give up the seat on the Board of Directors that he had held for eleven years, a devastating signal of dissatisfaction from the outside directors. The final blow came six months later, in October, when under irresistible pressure from a public message of no confidence issued by the board, Bob Stempel resigned as chairman and CEO. Lloyd Reuss, Alan Smith, and Bob O'Connell, along with one or two other holdovers from Roger Smith's era, left the company with him. The senior rank of the old boys' club was gone, clearing the decks for new leadership that would, hopefully, create the kind of company that I, along with like-minded colleagues, had spent my years at GM advocating.

While this top-level drama was unfolding, I tried to push my gnawing loss of self-confidence to the back of my mind as I went about my daily business. I struggled to develop ways of prodding GM on the safety and environmental fronts, teaming up with the group executive for the Technical staffs to develop an integrated approach to these issues. I initiated a dialogue between GM and the Environmental Defense Fund, the first such interaction between an American auto company and an environmental organization.

These initiatives were part of my underlying goal as Public Affairs group executive: to incorporate social considerations into GM's operating decisions. Well before *corporate social responsibility* (CSR) became a buzzword and its promotion a cottage industry, I was trying to persuade my GM colleagues that the link between a company's social reputation and its business performance had indeed gone global. Another way of putting this to my colleagues and superiors was that the outside world's opinion of GM would change—the "windows in" would reveal a new view—only when what we *make* and *do* (our products and our policies) are congruent with what we *are* and *say* (our vision of the company and the claims we make for it). But, with Lloyd Reuss and his rose-colored glasses setting the course, my urgent insistence on a tight link among our product programs, capital allocations, business plans, public positions, and communications strategies didn't have a discernible impact.

My ongoing tensions with Alan Smith—I actually hurled the epithet "You turd" at him when he abandoned me in midsentence to answer a summons from the chairman while we were discussing my future at GM—and my increasing sense that I had become ineffective as an individual and redundant as a line on the organization chart, along with the endless discussions of GM's urgent need for reform but total lack of effective action, combined to throw me into a state of depression. I continued to go to work every day, attend meetings, write memos, and move endless piles of paper from the inbox to the outbox, but I was increasingly unable to concentrate or enjoy life. After this had gone on for some time, I was miserable enough to seek professional help. The psychiatrist I consulted, a frail-looking man with a wise expression, a sharply beaked nose, and a benign demeanor, wasn't convinced at first that I was clinically depressed. "You're so well-dressed and never cry in my office," he averred. But my description of my mind as "constantly whirring around like a squirrel in a cage, with no way of stopping to rest," persuaded him that I needed his help. The combination of a series of talk sessions and an antidepressant put me back on a more or less even keel and also helped me to recognize that it was high time I got out of GM.

In telling Bob Stempel that I intended to retire, I strongly recommended that he abolish not only my job but the entire group executive layer of management in the staff (as opposed to the line) areas of the organization. Bob's immediate response was to express his confidence in me and urge me to propose a more meaningful job for myself somewhere in the GM organization. I was grateful for his courtesy, but, however hard I tried, I lacked the imagination to design such a position, given my current high level in the organization and my nonautomotive background. Basically, I didn't want to. General Motors had become quicksand into which my sanity was rapidly sinking; only total separation, I felt, could save it.

I didn't look forward with any great enthusiasm to my formal retirement dinner at the Detroit Athletic Club or to the gift traditionally presented there to a retiring GM officer, a huge sterling silver tray engraved with the signatures of all my fellow corporate officers, which was called, in company parlance, a pickle dish. But GM's rigid commitment to long-standing rituals and its tendency to lay elaborate plans and then foul up somewhere in their execution combined to turn this particular evening into a nightmare. Jim Fitzpatrick was slated to retire at about the same time as me, a decision arrived at reluctantly by Alan Smith when he discovered, as I had warned him, that Jim was not trusted by the group executives who headed the operating units. The result was that our retirement dinners were combined—a practical, cost-conscious decision. But the news that I would have a man who had become my nemesis as cohonoree made my spirits sink even further.

Following tradition, the full complement of GM officers was seated along one huge table in strict order of rank and seniority. Our progress through numerous dinner courses was punctuated by speeches praising the retiring honorees and videos that memorialized high points in each of our lives. Jim Fitzpatrick's video was first (because I was the more senior of the two, my recognition was scheduled as the evening's windup) and went off without a hitch. Just as mine started, the video machine broke down and resisted all efforts to repair it. Bob Stempel had to extemporize as best he could, but he was fuzzy on the details, and most of the point was lost. When I finally saw the tape, I was touched by the effort that had gone into it and flattered by the comments of people I'd worked with, in government as well as in GM. But the letdown of the evening itself symbolized my frustration and disenchantment as I left the company I had joined with such high expectations for what I might be able to accomplish in a totally new arena.

Bob Stempel and Lloyd Reuss both forged new careers for themselves after leaving GM. Stempel became CEO of Energy Conversion Devices, a Michigan firm known for pioneering work in the development of non-polluting alternative energy sources to power cars and trucks. Reuss, a committed Christian, became the much-admired volunteer executive dean of the Center for Advanced Technologies at Focus: Hope, a non-profit organization that provides technical training in a variety of fields for inner-city Detroit youths. But for the company they left under duress there has been no such vibrant second life, but rather a humiliating decline into dependency and dismemberment—a fate not even I, GM's resident Cassandra, could have foreseen. That fate has included bankruptcy, a rescue that put the US government in the driver's seat, the forced departure of two CEOs in the space of a year, the sale or abandonment of four of GM's eight vehicle lines, the replacement of most of the Board of Directors, and a management shakeup that promoted a new generation of executives (including Lloyd Reuss's son, Mark) to top positions. Both the company and the new vehicles it is introducing are today commanding new respect. Perhaps, just perhaps, the GM culture against which I did battle in vain has at last been uprooted.

· 11 ·

*H*aving It All

"Well, Marina, you're reaching the crone stage," opined Margaret Molinari, the expert from Human Resources who had been my in-house consultant on personnel issues, as we chatted about what life after GM might hold for me. Instantly conjuring up a sharp-chinned old witch, I said, "Thanks, Margaret, with a friend like you . . ." Margaret, a PhD in anthropology, explained that in the anthropological world a crone is not an ugly old woman at all, but rather one whose wisdom and experience made others seek her out for advice and guidance. It took me some time, and some false starts, to find out how right she was.

The career-guidance firm (often called, more bluntly, an outplacement firm) that GM had agreed to pay for when we worked out the conditions of my early retirement, suggested that I explore possibilities for college presidencies, for which my combination of academic and executive experience seemed to make me a natural. But I had been down that road too many times before. Over the space of some twenty years, I had been a finalist for college presidencies several times, in each case backing off at the last minute. After the fourth such episode, my children put the question to me, asking, "Are you sure, Mom, that you really *want* to be a college president?" Thus starkly confronted, I finally decided that the answer was no. The career-guidance firm did perform a valuable service, though. The consultant there told me that, to turn my resume into a marketing pitch, I should set down in bullet points my major accomplishments at General Motors. Seeing these laid out in succinct black and white made me feel less despairing about what I had actually achieved there, putting closure on that chapter and allowing me to look forward to the next one.

Even during the hectic years at GM, I had at least twice been deeply involved in academic projects focused on broad issues far removed from Detroit and its daily concerns. One was a panel assembled at Notre Dame University at the request of the five Roman Catholic bishops who, after more than five years of study, were composing a pastoral letter on American capitalism, to be presented at the annual meeting of the National Conference of Catholic Bishops.

When I was asked to lay out my own views for the bishops, I told them that, as a non-Catholic, I wasn't used to making confessions even privately, never mind in public. But I overcame my reticence, apparently to good effect, according to *Time* magazine: "Their [the invited experts] testimony sometimes strongly influenced the letter. For example, committee members had been leaning toward a call for strong government economic planning, before hearing that approach sharply criticized by Marina von Neumann Whitman, chief economist for General Motors. After Whitman spoke, one panelist said, 'Well, there goes the emphasis on central planning.'"[1] I disagreed with some of the bishops' policy recommendations, but I felt privileged to have been invited to engage in a dialogue with them, particularly since my arguments seemed to have had some impact on a letter that ran to more than a hundred pages.

An even more challenging assignment started with a call in 1998 from Frank Press, a leading physicist who was president of the National Academy of Sciences (NAS) in Washington, asking me if I would lead a delegation of ten professors and businessmen to Moscow for a seminar with Soviet academicians and heads of state economic institutions entitled "Economic Growth in Modern Industrial Societies: USSR and USA." I jumped at the opportunity; we didn't expect to learn much about economic policy or business management from the Russians, but we were curious about their views on economic issues and eager to introduce their leaders to the way a market economy works.

The seminar would have been hard to manage under any circumstances, partly because it was cochaired on the Russian side by academicians from two competing institutions who clearly hated each other and also because the American and Soviet approaches to analyzing economic problems were so different as to make the two groups' papers mutually unintelligible. What really complicated things for me, though, was that on the second day of the seminar, which was supposed to be led by the Soviet side, all the high-level Russians simply vanished. That left me to try to bring order among presenters whose names I didn't even know how to pronounce and to promote meaningful dialogue between two groups that had in common neither language nor experiences nor modes of thought.

Only later did I learn that the reason for my counterparts' disappearance was a suddenly called special meeting of the Supreme Soviet. Its purpose was to adopt a constitutional amendment implementing General Secretary (later president) Mikhail Gorbachev's plans for political reform, including the democratization of the electoral system, which led to a genuinely democratic election of the Congress of People's Deputies in March of the following year. I reported to Frank Press, "Clearly, this is a unique moment in the Soviet Union, and we may be seeing an important new chapter in their history in the making."[2] But neither our delegation nor Gorbachev himself had an inkling that the first step toward the demise of Soviet communism and the dissolution of the Soviet Union had just been taken in a building close to where we sat.

Now, having closed the book on the GM chapter, I felt the pull to focus once again on the big picture of international issues in the more sustained way that was only possible in an academic setting. Because I wasn't certain how well I would fit back into that world, I decided to test the waters by taking a half-time visiting professorship, divided between the School of Business and the School of Public Policy at the University of Michigan. Gradually, without my actually noticing it, the university began to look less and less like a way station and more and more like a permanent home.

As I settled back into the life of a professor, I taught courses on international trade and investment, combining information and analysis with war stories from the GM trenches to hold the attention of students who were far more demanding than the ones I had taught at the University of Pittsburgh fifteen years before. I also wrote a book that built on my GM experience to analyze the developments that transformed the dominant, paternalistic multinational corporations of the mid–twentieth century into the lean, mean, global competitors they had become by its end.[3] In his review for the *New York Times Book Review,* Louis Uchitelle complained, "[S]he shares with her readers almost none of what she witnessed at GM or felt in those stressful years . . . Absent are the anecdotes, the feelings, the judgments from her own experience."[4] Well, Mr. Uchitelle, you have had to wait more than a decade, but here in this memoir is my account of how things looked from the inside.

Most of what I do at the University of Michigan, though, cannot be described in a resume. Having learned as much from my failures in leadership as from my successes as an individual, I try to share the wisdom I've acquired as widely as I can. Now that I no longer have to worry about career building in my specialty, I've been drawn onto advisory committees across the university. More influential, though, than my role in any organized group is the advising and networking I provide informally, one-on-one. I counsel graduate students about their careers and provide my colleagues with from-the-trenches observations on their research. I've worked closely with two successive deans of the Public Policy School, using my broad network of contacts in business and government to help with fund-raising and outreach, as well as serving those same deans as a sounding board on difficult issues.

I sense that I hold more power now, as a part-time, nontenured faculty member—although it is a very soft power indeed—than I did when I was a public figure, high on the organization chart of the U.S. government or the General Motors Corporation. All kinds of people seek my opinion, take it seriously, and even act on it. My credibility comes partly from the wisdom of experience but, even more, from the fact that people know I am not acting for personal gain; I'm not looking for a promotion, a better job, or a big salary increase. Once again, I have a useful double vision; I know the organization as only an insider can, but I have the outsider's disinterestedness and ability to make external comparisons.

Because I am known as a woman who has been there and done that, women and girls at all stages of their lives ask me how I got where I did, what it was like, and how I juggled all the pressures and obligations I felt. The combination of factors that shaped my life included parental expectations, a steadfastly supportive spouse well ahead of his time, a high energy level, and, most critical of all, good luck. A serious illness in the family or a child with special needs could have brought the whole fragile structure crashing down on me. Timing was also critical; I came of age just as new opportunities were beginning to open up for women, and there were not many women as fully prepared to take advantage of them as I was, thanks to my family environment and the path it set me on early in life.

Timing was critical in another sense as well. I had turned down several promising job opportunities when the children were young, but by the time the GM offer came along, they were grown and more or less independent; I had the career-family conflicts behind me not ahead of me. I tell young women today what I first said twenty-five years ago, that "the myth of the superwoman is dying a well-deserved death. One can't do and be everything at once—the choices and the trade-offs are very real. But there is not just one choice; we have some leeway regarding what we give up at various points in our lives."[5] As I pass on these reflections to others, I see that Margaret Molinari was right about the meaning of the "crone stage" after all.

My year of moving on from GM, 1992, was highlighted by two far more personal milestones: Laura's wedding to David Downie in June and my mother's death in December. The wedding was one of those perfect occasions that I would have liked to preserve intact forever but had to settle instead for joyous memories and glorious photographs. Laura's beauty as a bride brought tears to her parents' eyes; David was a beaming, handsome groom, having even cut his unruly curls for the occasion. They were married at St. Andrews, the Episcopal Church whose gray stone grandeur marks it as one of the oldest churches in Ann Arbor. The bride and groom wrote large parts of their own marriage service, which was designed to allow a number of their closest friends, whether Christian, Jewish, or agnostic, to participate in the ceremony without being made to feel uncomfortable.

On that glorious June day, the guests at the reception had a panoramic view of the entire city from the four-sided terrace that encircles the top floor of the university's magnificent, art deco Rackham Building. A trio of violin, harp, and flute played classical music softly before and through dinner, but afterward the bridal pair and their friends, who had gathered from all over the world, danced to the earsplitting beat of a steel drum band. It was a fabulous send-off.

For my mother, that occasion represented the fulfillment of a long-delayed dream. My own wedding had been a small, low-key affair, out of respect for my father's terminal illness. Now she could help plan and be part of the sort of elegant, formal event that she had to forego thirty-five years earlier. But her granddaughter's wedding marked one of the few happy days my mother spent during her brief life in Ann Arbor. Physically frail and beset by depression, she was no longer able to deal with her husband's dementia. These developments forced me to recognize, painfully, that my mother, the awesome figure who had been both my role model and the primary source of my lifelong feelings of insecurity, was now old and vulnerable and desperately in need of support from her children. My brother George and I felt that the only solution was to move her and Desmond from their Long Island home of more than forty years to a retirement residence in Ann Arbor.

We had made this decision with the best of intentions, but our plan misfired badly, leaving George and me with a sense of guilt that haunts us to this day. My mother, torn from her home and her circle of friends and too embarrassed by her husband's mental state to make new ones, was thoroughly miserable, ate almost nothing, and dwindled down to eighty-five pounds. This was one case where superwoman fell badly down on the job. Distracted and exhausted by my battles at GM, I failed to notice how desperately she craved my support. While George and I were away with our families for Thanksgiving—a desertion for which she never forgave us, even though we had invited her to come along with us to our vacation cottage—she had a bad fall.

Although her injury, a hyperextended neck that damaged several vertebrae, would not have been life threatening to a person in good health, it did mean a difficult surgery and an extended, uncomfortable recovery. Confronted with this prospect, my mother developed a variety of complications that led ultimately to her death. Her physical frailty may have made this outcome inevitable, but I couldn't help but be reminded of her own mother who, when her quality of life fell below her minimum standard, simply willed herself to die. In my heart, I wondered if my mother, a proud and stubborn woman, hadn't come to the same decision.

In death, my mother went home to the church she had attended for more than forty years, the one where Bob and I had been married, and to a grave in its churchyard. The occasion was marked by the worst storm Long Island had seen in many years. The car in which Malcolm, Laura, and David drove to the funeral was the last one allowed across the Throgs Neck Bridge from Connecticut, trucks floated on the roads running along Long Island Sound, and the basement of our hotel was flooded, cutting off all electrical power. The funeral service was conducted by candlelight and without the electric organ; a fire truck stood by outside, lest the sparks shooting out of a short-circuited transformer close to the church should start a fire. The rain pelted down on us as we stood at the graveside; it seemed a fitting farewell to a woman as tempestuous as my mother. We privately dubbed the storm "Hurricane Mariette."

A reporter who interviewed me when my promotion at GM first brought us to Ann Arbor in 1985 wrote, "For Whitman, 'having it all' was not so much an aim as a confident expectation. 'I always assumed I would marry, have children, and work,' she explains, 'like my mother.'"[6] Yes, by this definition I have indeed had it all, but the truth isn't nearly as simple as this crisp sentence suggests.

Having it all is a many-splendored thing. It means a marriage that has only grown closer with the passage of more than half a century and a husband who insists that I'm still the girl he first fell in love with, as if fifty years and nearly as many pounds has made no difference. It includes children who grew into adults we not only love but enjoy, respect, and profoundly admire. Both have chosen biomedical careers. Malcolm, a cell and developmental biologist on the Harvard medical faculty, conducts basic research on fundamental chemical processes in living and growing organisms, research essential to explaining how things go awry in the human body as a first step toward repairing them. Laura, a physician specializing in internal medicine, is on the faculty of the Yale Medical School, where she supervises the training of medical residents in her field and is an attending physician in a clinic that serves mainly the poor and the uninsured of New Haven. If John von Neumann were around today, he might have mixed feelings about the way his electronic offspring, the modern stored-program computer, has developed and the uses to which it has been put. But he would feel only satisfaction, I know, at the way in which the children of his biological offspring have fulfilled his mandate to use their intellectual gifts to the fullest.

To top it off, Laura and her political scientist husband, David Downie, have produced two bright, thoughtful, caring children of their own. When William sends us a poem entitled "Redemption," reflecting on his feelings about getting in trouble in school, and Lindsey chooses as her display on the fifth grade's "special persons day" a photograph of her grandfather as an impossibly handsome nineteen-year-old lieutenant in the Army Air Corps sitting on the tail of his B-29 during World War II, I wonder what I have done to deserve such joy.

On the professional side, I have enjoyed the challenge and satisfaction of recognition in three different careers, each of which complemented and enriched the others, and of blazing a trail in two of them. Mine were transitional victories; other women have since risen higher and had a broader impact than I did, in both government and business. Laura Tyson, Janet Yellin, and Christina Romer have chaired the Council of Economic Advisers; Madeleine Albright, Condoleezza Rice, and now Hillary Clinton have served the nation as secretary of state. In the auto industry, women have been appointed to powerful operating, as opposed to staff, positions: Mary Barra is GM's senior vice president for global product development; and Ann Stevens was executive vice president of Ford and chief operating officer of its Americas Division, which includes the United States, until she left to become chairman and CEO of a technology company. But I led the way, and I hope I cleared away some of the underbrush for those who came later.

Despite having had it all, as I look back, I realize that I haven't completely fulfilled the high expectations I set for myself as a young woman. I take pride in the gap I've filled as a role model, a symbol of what a woman can achieve in different arenas. But in terms of substantively making a difference, nudging the world, or at least some part of it, in the direction I wanted it to move, I'm not completely satisfied. Many of the barriers were external, set up by a society that was beginning to open new doors to women but wasn't yet ready to accord full weight to their ideas or make the changes they were trying to effect. Some of the barriers were inside me—the desire to be liked, to avoid confrontation, to push from inside the golden circle rather than from outside. But if one of the requirements for breaking new ground is to set goals that, like the Holy Grail, will always be just out of to reach, then I have no regrets.

Today, I am more than making up for the things I gave up during the years when I was building my career. I remain engaged in the world of ideas but on my own terms, working only as much as I want and on what interests me. Bob and I travel extensively, aiming, as I once told a US border guard peering suspiciously at some of the more exotic stamps in my passport, to see as much of the world as we can while our legs and wits hold out. We treat our children and grandchildren to three-generation trips, to destinations as varied as the Galapagos, Provence, Namibia, and heli-hiking in the Canadian Rockies, one of the benefits of the affluence my career has afforded us. Another is that we are now able to give back to a society that has given so much to us by donating time, effort, and money to cultural and charitable activities.

All this is possible only because we are blessed with reasonably good health at a time of life when it can no longer be taken for granted. Bob, ten years older than I, is coping with serious vision problems but manages to lead a busy, active life despite the limitations he has had to surmount, including a role reversal in which I have become the driver and he the not so silently suffering passenger. Like so many women my age, I have had to deal with a diagnosis of breast cancer, but now that ten years have passed, I allow myself to look back on it as an unpleasant but surprisingly untraumatic episode—in part because my medically sophisticated children took the news so calmly. Bob and I are acutely aware that these golden years are fragile, that they cannot last forever, but we savor every moment of them.

Looking back from my current vantage point is, of course, very different from the view that lay before me when I was starting out. I knew I wanted a fulfilling career, but I had no idea doing what. I was filled with doubt, uncertainty, fears that I wouldn't be able to handle a family and a demanding job without slighting one or the other, or perhaps both. The fact that I was generally regarded as a freak rather than the role model I later became increased the tension, and I had moments of believing that the conventional judgment might be right. There were nights when I cried silently into my pillow—hoping Bob wouldn't notice—either from a sense of failure on my own part or because I had turned down a tantalizing offer that wasn't feasible at the current stage of our family's life. At one point, as I've recounted, job pressures brought me perilously close to emotional collapse. The ambitious but apprehensive young girl still lives deep inside the woman who now presents a confident and sometimes intimidating face to the world.

The world that confronts women starting out today is different in many ways from the one that greeted me. The overt, explicit barriers I faced have largely been abolished, only to be replaced sometimes by more subtle, unspoken ones that can be even more damaging psychologically. A successful career path requires constant, unabashed self-marketing by both women and men, an exercise I recoiled from and still regard with amazement. Staying on top of things requires becoming comfortable with new technologies at a faster pace than my generation ever anticipated. This is yet another legacy of my father's pathbreaking advances in the tools for collecting and analyzing data and, more recently, for the extensions of human interaction through the Internet and the offspring it has spawned. I warily circle the margins of the world of texting, Facebook, and Twitter in which my grandchildren dwell so comfortably. If I were around to encounter the next generation down, I fear that meaningful communication would be well-nigh impossible.

Whereas members of my generation saw their options as a stark choice between homemaking and professional advancement, the women of today move more freely from one point on that continuum to another at different stages of their lives. My own daughter has so far chosen a work-life balance different from mine. She has opted to work part-time—or at least, to receive part-time pay for what looks to me like a full-time commitment—in order to have more freedom for involvement in her children's activities. She once said to me, "Thank you, Mom, for being a pioneer, which has given me the freedom to make different choices." Whereas my approach to motherhood was low key and somewhat hands-off, Laura's children are experiencing both the security and the limitations of her fierce protectiveness.

Through all the changes in my life and in the world that surrounds it, my father's presence has never been far away. Today I am a trustee of the Institute for Advanced Study in Princeton, where he came as one of the first members in 1933. As they did in his day, leading scholars from all over the world make up a small permanent faculty, free of all teaching duties to focus on research, writing, and mentoring the larger number of younger members, who spend anywhere from a term to several years there. The institute's board is probably the most intellectually exclusive collection of trustees in the world. Some of its members are billionaires, others are professors, but all of them have been chosen for their ability to oversee and nurture the institute as a place where some of the world's greatest minds can operate in a serene, comfortable environment unhindered by distractions.

The tie that binds is in my mind whenever I sit with my fellow trustees in the glass-walled boardroom, which looks out on a picture-book pond and the woods beyond, around which several generations of geniuses have strolled. I find myself conjuring up my father's astonished ghost, seeing his daughter sitting on the governing body of the institution he helped found, the place where he spent most of his adult life and built his own prototype of the modern computer. While I'm summoning this ghost, my husband is tending his grave in the Princeton cemetery, clipping, weeding, raking, and occasionally replacing a dead plant with a new one—a task he performs faithfully twice a year. The son-in-law John von Neumann feared would fatally cramp his daughter's future is doing his part to make sure the father's memory is not neglected.

My father's presence was closest in 2003, when Hungary staged a national celebration commemorating the hundredth anniversary of his birth. I was invited to participate as an honored guest, an honor that carried with it one of the most hectic schedules I've ever encountered. A couple of weeks after finishing treatment for breast cancer, I found myself not only giving talks about my father at internationally attended meetings of the Hungarian Mathematical and Computer Science societies in Budapest but also giving informal talks about him, in English, to students in schools all over Hungary.

Thank goodness it's a small country; Bob and I were transported to every corner of it in the cramped elderly vehicle belonging to one of my father's self-appointed promoters, who enthusiastically acted as our chauffeur. Some of the schools were actually named after John von Neumann, but in all of them students knew who he was and what he had accomplished and had created various exhibitions to honor him. I tried to imagine American high-school students according a long-dead mathematician the sort of veneration reserved here for sports and entertainment celebrities!

That week of talking about John von Neumann's life and accomplishments in the land of his birth brought closure for me, a recognition that what I'd feared were the conflicting expectations—my father's, my mother's, society's, and my own—that had shaped my life had finally converged. I had fulfilled my father's moral imperative that I make full use whatever intellectual gifts I had; my mother's ugly duckling had developed a swan's poise and self-confidence. A society where women head Fortune 500 corporations, where half the Ivy League universities, and several of the leading public ones as well, are headed by women, and where a female has been a serious contender for the nation's highest office now allows the most daring and talented women expectations that far exceed mine. By their own lives, my husband and our children have given the lie to the fears of Bob's mother that all three would pay dearly for my career ambitions; my expectations of a close and loving family life have extended to encompass a third generation. My father's shadow has lifted at last; if we meet again, it will be in sunlight.

Notes

Note: All the materials cited in this book that are currently in my personal collection will ultimately be deposited either with the rest of the John von Neumann papers in the Library of Congress (JvN's letters in Hungarian to Klari and Klari's unpublished autobiography) or in the Schlesinger Library of the Radcliffe Institute for Advanced Study at Harvard University (my own unpublished writings and correspondence between JvN and me).

CHAPTER I

1. Freeman Dyson, "A Walk through Johnny von Neumann's Garden," talk given at Brown University, May 4, 2010.

2. "Nomination of John von Neumann to be a Member of the United States Atomic Energy Commission," March 8, 1955, JvN Papers, Library of Congress, quoted in Giorgio Israel and Ana Millán Gasca, *The World as a Mathematical Game: John von Neumann and Twentieth Century Science*, Science Networks Historical Studies, no. 38 (Basel, Boston, and Berlin: Birkhauser Verlag, 2009).

3. Norman Macrae, *John von Neumann: The Scientific Genius Who Pioneered the Modern Computer, Game Theory, Nuclear Deterrence, and Much More* (New York: Pantheon Books, 1992), 145.

4. Kati Marton, *Enemies of the People* (New York, Simon and Schuster, 2009), 12–13.

5. Macrae, *John von Neumann*, 139.

6. Ibid., 169.

7. Ibid., 171.

8. John von Neumann to Rudolf Ortvay, Princeton, March 17, 1938, in *John*

von Neumann: Selected Letters, History of Mathematics, vol. 27, ed. Miklos Redei (American Mathematical Society and London Mathematical Society, 2005), 194–96.

9. Ibid., 195.

10. John von Neumann to Rudolf Ortvay, Princeton, February 26, 1939, in *John von Neumann: Selected Letters: History of Mathematics,* vol. 27, ed. Miklos Redei (American Mathematical Society and London Mathematical Society, 2005), 199.

11. Clay Blair, "Passing of a Great Mind," *Life,* February 25, 1957, 96 (citing an earlier interview).

12. Dyson, "A Walk through Johnny von Neumann's Garden."

13. Tibor Frank, "Double Divorce: The Case of Mariette and John von Neumann," *Nevada Historical Society Quarterly* 34, no. 2 (summer 1991): 361. Mariette's letters are translated from the Hungarian by the article's author. I have left his syntax, spelling, and punctuation unchanged.

14. Klara von Neumann, *A Grasshopper in Very Tall Grass,* undated and unpublished manuscript. Marina v.N. Whitman Personal Collection.

15. Ibid.

16. John von Neumann to Stan Ulam, Princeton, October 4, 1937, in *John von Neumann: Selected Letters, History of Mathematics,* vol. 27, ed. Miklos Redei (American Mathematical Society and London Mathematical Society, 2005), 251.

17. JvN letter to Klari, August 27, 1938. All the unpublished letters cited in this chapter were translated from the Hungarian by Gabriella Bollobas and are in my personal collection.

18. JvN letter to Klari, August 28, 1938.

19. JvN letter to Klari, October 23, 1938.

20. Robert Leonard, *Von Neumann, Morgenstern, and the Creation of Game Theory* (Cambridge: Cambridge University Press, 2010), 244.

21. John von Neumann, "Can We Survive Technology?," in *The Fabulous Future: America in 1980,* ed. *Fortune* magazine (New York: E. P. Dutton, 1956), 34.

22. JvN letter to Klari, October 4, 1946.

23. Von Neumann, "Can We Survive Technology?"

24. Quoted in Israel and Gasca, *The World as a Mathematical Game,* 17.

25. Ibid., 83.

CHAPTER 2

1. Robert P. Crease, *Making Physics* (Chicago: University of Chicago Press, 1999), 20. The participant cited was William Higinbotham, a physicist at Los Alamos and, later, at Brookhaven National Laboratory.

2. Klara von Neumann, *A Grasshopper in Very Tall Grass,* undated and unpublished manuscript. Marina v.N. Whitman Personal Collection.

3. JvN letter to Klari, July 13, 1952.

4. JvN letter to Klari, September 17, 1952.

5. JvN letter to Klari, October 15, 1955.

6. Crease, *Making Physics,* 17–18.

7. Ibid., 32.

8. Mariette K. Kuper, transcript of "Living with the Atom," radio talk on station WHLI, June 1, 1948

9. Ibid.

10. Mariette K. Kuper, typescript of graduation speech delivered at Medford High School, Medford, New York, June 1948.

11. George Gamow, *One, Two, Three, Infinity* (New York: Viking Press, 1947).

12. JvN letter to Klari, August 28, 1938.

13. September 2, 1938. All the letters to Klari cited in this chapter were translated from the Hungarian by Gabriella Bollobas.

14. JvN letter to Marina, December 16, 1946.

15. Ibid.

16. Letter from Marina to JvN, December 5, 1945.

17. Letter from Klari and Marina to JvN, undated.

18. Letter from Marina to Klari, August 28, 1945.

CHAPTER 3

1. Kati Marton, *The Great Escape* (New York: Simon and Schuster, 2006), 152.

2. Klara von Neumann, *A Grasshopper in Very Tall Grass,* undated and unpublished manuscript. Marina v.N. Whitman Personal Collection.

3. Silvan S. Schweber, *Einstein and Oppenheimer: The Meaning of Genius* (Cambridge, MA, and London: Harvard University Press, 2008), 16.

CHAPTER 4

1. John von Neumann to Marina von Neumann, May 23, 1953, Marina v.N. Whitman Personal Collection.

2. Marina von Neumann to Robert Whitman, June 13, 1953, Marina v.N. Whitman Personal Collection.

3. Ibid.

4. Marina von Neumann to Robert Whitman, September 3, 1953, Marina v.N. Whitman Personal Collection.

5. Priscilla J. McMillan, *The Ruin of J. Robert Oppenheimer* (New York, Viking Penguin, 2005), 2–3.

6. United States Atomic Energy Commission, *In the Matter of J. Robert Oppenheimer: Transcript of Hearing before Personnel Security Board and Texts of Principal Documents and Letters* (Cambridge, MA: MIT Press, 1971), 726.

7. Ibid., 649–50, 656.

8. John von Neumann to Marina von Neumann, October 28, 1954, Marina v.N. Whitman Personal Collection.

9. John von Neumann to Marina von Neumann, April 19, 1955, Marina v.N. Whitman Personal Collection.

10. John von Neumann to Marina von Neumann, May 13, 1955, Marina v.N. Whitman Personal Collection.

11. John von Neumann to Marina von Neumann, October 9, 1955, Marina v.N. Whitman Personal Collection.

12. Ibid.

CHAPTER 5

1. Norman Macrae, *John von Neumann* (New York: Pantheon Books, 1992), 377.

2. John von Neumann, *The Computer and the Brain* (New Haven: Yale University Press, 1958), xi.

3. Father Anselm Strittmatter, "Allocution Pronounced at the Obsequies of Professor John von Neumann," Chapel of Walter Reed Hospital, Washington, DC, February 11, 1957, Marina v.N. Whitman Personal Collection.

4. Interview with Jean O. Rainey for "A Few Good Women Oral History Collection" (Penn State University Archives), September 30, 2004.

5. Pittsburgh Regional Planning Association, *Region with a Future: Economic Study of the Pittsburgh Region,* vol. 3 (Pittsburgh: University of Pittsburgh Press, 1963).

6. Office of the Coroner, County of San Diego, California, "Investigative Report CC# 1772-63," November 10, 1963.

7. Klara von Neumann Eckart, *A Grasshopper in Very Tall Grass,* undated and unpublished manuscript. Marina v.N. Whitman Personal Collection.

8. "Dementia in the Second City," *Time,* September 6, 1968.

CHAPTER 6

1. *Nixon: A Presidency Revealed,* History Channel documentary, directed by David C. Taylor (first airing February 15, 2007), DVD.

2. U.S. Department of State, *Foreign Relations, 1969–1976,* vol. III (summary), Foreign Economic Policy, 1969–72; *International Monetary Policy,* 1969–72, 1.

3. Marina Whitman to Paul McCracken, memorandum, May 4, 1971, Marina v.N. Whitman Personal Collection.

4. *Economic Report of the President,* January 1972 (Washington: U.S. Government Printing Office, 1972), 165–66.

5. Paul Volcker and Toyoo Gyohten, *Changing Fortunes: The World's Money and the Threat to American Leadership* (New York: Times Publishers, 1992), 73.

6. Ibid., 73.

7. Marina Whitman to Paul McCracken, memorandum, August 27, 1971, Marina v.N. Whitman Personal Collection.

8. C. Jackson Grayson Jr, with Louis Neeb, *Confessions of a Price Controller* (Homewood, IL: Dow Jones-Irwin, 1974), 64.

9. "The Economy: A Blurry Banner for Phase II," *Time,* October 18, 1971, 15.

10. Richard M. Nixon, "The Continuing Fight against Inflation," radio and television address, October 7, 1971.

11. Richard Nixon recorded conversation with H. R. Haldeman, January 24, 1972, Conv. No. 654-1, tape subject log, Richard Nixon Presidential Library and Museum, National Archives and Records.

12. Ibid.; Richard Nixon recorded conversation with H. R. Haldeman, January 28, 1972, Conv. No. 659-1.

13. Richard Nixon recorded conversation with H. R. Haldeman, Conv. No. 654-1; Richard Nixon recorded conversation with H. R. Haldeman, Conv. No. 659-1; Richard Nixon recorded conversation with H. R. Haldeman, January 29, 1972, Conv. No. 660-8.

14. Richard Nixon recorded conversation with H. R. Haldeman, Conv. No. 654-1; Richard Nixon recorded conversation with H. R. Haldeman, Conv. No. 660-8.

15. Richard Nixon recorded conversation with H. R. Haldeman, Conv. No. 654-1.

16. Ibid.

17. Richard Nixon recorded conversation with H. R. Haldeman, Conv. No. 659-1; Richard Nixon recorded conversation with H. R. Haldeman, Conv. No. 660-8.

18. Richard Nixon recorded conversation with H. R. Haldeman, Conv. No. 659-1.

19. Richard Nixon recorded conversation with H. R. Haldeman, Conv. No. 660-8.

20. *Boston Sunday Globe,* January 30, 1972.

21. *Detroit News,* February 1, 1972.

22. Richard F. Janssen, "Woman Nominated for First Time to Serve on President's Economic Advisers Council," *Wall Street Journal,* January 31, 1972.

23. Ibid.

24. *Life,* February 25, 1972.

25. Michael C. Jensen, "Mrs. Whitman; Council Appointee Sees Self as Solver of Problems," *New York Times,* February 6, 1972.

26. Senate Committee on Banking, Housing and Urban Affairs, *Hearing before the Committee on Banking, Housing and Urban Affairs,* United States Senate, 92nd Cong., 2nd sess., 1972, 7–17.

27. Joint Economic Committee, *Review of Phase II of the New Economic Program: Hearings before the Joint Economic Committee on April 14, 1972*, 92nd Cong., 2nd sess., 1972, 4.

28. "Two Top Economists Optimistic for 1972: Dr. Whitman and Dr. Heller Predict a Vigorous Recovery," *New York Times,* May 18, 1972.

29. *Economic Report of the President,* 1972, 154.

30. Marina v.N. Whitman, "Some Reflections on International Monetary Reform," Remarks Before the International Fiscal Association, New York, October 27, 1972.

31. Ibid.

32. Joint Economic Committee, *The 1973 Economic Report of the President: Hearings before the Joint Economic Committee on February 6, 1973*, 93rd Cong., 1st sess., 1973, 8–9.

33. Ibid., 89.

34. William Chapman, "Women: Putting Bread on the Table," *Washington Post,* February 3, 1973.

35. *Time,* October 23, 1972.

36. *Business Week,* July 8, 1972.

37. Nicholas von Hoffman, "Washington's Rats on the Move," *Washington Post,* October 25, 1972.

38. *Parade,* December 31, 1972.

39. Laura Whitman, interview by Greta Walker, *Good Housekeeping,* August 1972.

40. Marion Bell Wilhelm, "Economist Whitman Goes to Washington," *Christian Science Monitor,* March 20, 1972.

41. *Life,* February 25, 1972.

42. *Time,* February 12, 1973.

43. *Philadelphia Evening Bulletin,* May 21, 1973.

44. Herbert Stein, "The Nixon I Knew," *Slate,* January 2, 1998.

45. *Wall Street Journal,* August 6, 1973.

46. *Money,* May 1973.

47. Herbert Stein, "Memorandum for the President, Observations on Japan," March 31, 1973. Marina v.N. Whitman Personal Collection.

CHAPTER 7

1. Marina Whitman to the President's Files, memorandum, March 27, 1973, Marina v.N. Whitman Personal Collection.

2. *Washington Post,* June 3, 1973.

3. Marina Whitman to President Nixon, June 14, 1973, Richard Nixon Presidential Library and Museum, National Archives and Records Administration, College Park, MD.

4. President Richard Nixon to Marina Whitman, June 27, 1973, Richard Nixon Presidential Library and Museum, National Archives and Records Administration, College Park, MD.

5. Statement of Representative Henry Reuss, Joint Economic Committee, *The 1973 Midyear Review of the Economy: Hearings before the Joint Economic Committee on August 1, 1973*, 93rd Cong., 1st sess., 1973, 146.

6. Statement of Senator Jacob Javits, Joint Economic Committee, *The 1973 Midyear Review of the Economy: Hearings before the Joint Economic Committee on August 1, 1973*, 93rd Cong., 1st sess., 1973, 146.

7. Statement of Senator Sparkman of Alabama, Joint Economic Committee, *The 1973 Midyear Review of the Economy: Hearings before the Joint Economic Committee on August 1, 1973*, 93rd Cong., 1st sess., 1973, 146.

8. Statement of Senator Proxmire, Joint Economic Committee, *The 1973 Midyear Review of the Economy: Hearings before the Joint Economic Committee on August 1, 1973*, 93rd Cong., 1st sess., 1973, 147.

9. Both these ideas had been suggested by John Maynard Keynes, who represented Great Britain at the Bretton Woods negotiations in 1944 but had been overridden by the objections of the US representative to the conference, Harry Dexter White.

10. *American Survey, The Economist,* October 6, 1973.

11. Bob Arnold, "Marina Whitman's Back in Town," *Renaissance Pittsburgh*, vol. 5, no. 2 (February 1974): 26.

12. Marylin Bender, "Women Take Transfers Companies, Pressured, Offer," *New York Times,* July 23, 1974.

13. *Pittsburgh Press,* December 5, 1976.

14. Leonard Silk, "Peers Give Nixon's Advisers Bad Reviews," *New York Times,* October 17, 1973.

15. *University Times* (Pittsburgh), October 4, 1973, 8.

16. Marina Whitman, "The 'Dismal Science' Comes of Age: Economics in America's Third Century," *Sloan Management Review (SMR Forum),* vol. 17, no. 3 (spring 1976), 89.

17. Office of the White House Press Secretary, "Remarks of the President at the Opening of the Conference on Inflation," September 5, 1974, Gerald R. Ford Library and Museum, National Archives and Records Administration, Ann Arbor, Michigan.

18. Arthur Okun, "Summary of September 5 Economists' Conference on Inflation," meeting, Washington, DC, September 5, 1974, Gerald R. Ford Library and Museum, National Archives and Records Administration, Ann Arbor, Michigan.

19. "Summary of September 23, 1974, Meeting of Economists," meeting, New York City, September 23, 1974, Gerald R. Ford Library and Museum, National Archives and Records Administration, Ann Arbor, Michigan.

20. Soma Golden, "Self-Interest Stymies Inflation Fight," *New York Times,* September 22, 1974.

21. Edwin L. Dale Jr, "Carter Sees Permanency in Floating Money Rates," *New York Times,* August 19, 1976; Edwin L. Dale Jr, "Carter's Foreign Economic Plan," *New York Times,* August 24, 1976.

22. Dale, "Carter's Foreign Economic Plan."

23. The one exception was the Railroad Revitalization and Regulatory Reform Act of 1976, which was passed close to the end of President Ford's term and implemented under President Carter.

CHAPTER 8

1. Pam Proctor, "New Voices in Business: Ladies of the Boardroom," *Parade,* July 28, 1974.

2. *The Economist,* September 22, 2007, 86.

3. Vijay Vaitheeswaran, "Something New under the Sun: A Special Report," *The Economist,* October 13–19, 2007, 12.

4. CDA-Collaborative Learning Projects, "Yadana Gas Transportation Project, Fourth Field Visit Report," April 17–May 6, 2005, http://cdainc.com/publica tions/cep/fieldvisits/cepVisit16MyanmarBurma4.pdf.

5. "Agreement between the President and Fellows of Harvard College and the President of Radcliffe," Cambridge, MA, 1977, http://pds.lib.harvard.edu/pds/view/2573641?n=700&s=4&print.

6. *Governance of the University,* The Harvard Guide, http://www.hno.har vard.edu/guide/underst/index.html.

7. "Governance Review Culminates in Changes to Harvard Corporation," *Harvard Gazette,* December 6, 2010. One of these changes was expansion of the corporation's membership to thirteen.

8. "Overseers and Associated Harvard Alumni Directors: A Guideline on Qualifications," http:news.harvard.edu/gazette/2000/03.02/report.htm).

9. "Meeting of the Committee of the Board of Overseers to Visit the Department of Economics," Harvard University, Cambridge, MA, February 13–14, 1976. Marina v.N. Whitman Personal Collection.

CHAPTER 9

1. Emma Rothschild, *Paradise Lost: The Decline of the Auto-Industrial Age* (New York: Random House, 1973).

2. "The Squeeze on Oil," *Time,* February 5, 1979.

3. Charles Belle, "Business in the Black," *San Francisco County Sun-Reporter,* April 1981.

4. *Fortune,* August 20, 1984, 31.

5. Marina Whitman, "Economics from Three Perspectives," *Business Economics,* January 1983, 20–24.

6. *The Dartmouth,* February 25, 1982.

7. Giorgio Israel and Ana Millán Gasca, *The World as a Mathematical Game: John von Neumann and Twentieth Century Science,* Science Networks Historical Studies, no. 38 (Basel, Boston, and Berlin: Birkhauser Verlag, 2009), xi.

8. Ibid., 51.

9. Maryann Keller, *Rude Awakening: The Rise, Fall, and Struggle for Recovery of General Motors* (New York: William Morrow, 1989).

10. Marina Whitman, "Economic Scene: Auto Industry's New Challenges," op-ed, *New York Times,* September 3, 1980.

11. Marina Whitman, "Economic Scene: Shape of Power in Next Decade," op-ed, *New York Times,* September 5, 1980.

12. See, for example, Neil Sheehan, *A Fiery Peace in a Cold War: Bernard Schriever and the Ultimate Weapon* (New York: Random House, 2009).

13. Marina Whitman, interview with Maryann Keller, transcript, 1991.

14. "Healing the Auto Industry," GM Economics Staff and Financial Staff to the GM Executives, memorandum, September 3, 1982.

15. Ibid., 2.

16. "Trends," *Forbes,* August 3, 1981.

17. *Forbes,* August 31, 1981, 10.

18. Henry Ford II to Ford CEO Philip Caldwell, memorandum, May 17, 1981.

19. *Washington Post,* April 2, 1981.

20. "Import Restrictions Revisited," Marina Whitman to Chairman Roger Smith, Vice Chairman Howard Kehrl, and Executive Vice President Alan Smith, memorandum, January 12, 1981.

21. Roger Smith, "Its Time to End the Auto Quotas," op-ed, *Washington Post,* January 30, 1985.

22. Oscar Frenette, "Automotive Report," WJR-Detroit, January 6, 1986.

23. Ibid.

24. Ibid.

25. Statement of Marina Whitman, *The Future of the Automobile Industry: Hearings before the Subcommittee on Commerce, Transportation, and Tourism of the House Committee on Energy and Commerce* (February 8, 1984), 98th Cong., 2nd session, 1984, pp. 237–44.

26. *Wall Street Journal,* June 10, 1987.

27. Ibid.

28. *Business Week,* September 6, 1986.

CHAPTER 10

1. General Motors Annual Report, *America's Corporate Foundation,* 1985; General Motors Annual Report, *America's Corporate Foundation,* 1990; General Mo-

tors Annual Report, *America's Corporate Foundation,* 1992; General Motors Annual Report, *America's Corporate Foundation,* 2005.

2. Pew Environment Group, "History of Fuel Economy: One Decade of Innovation, Two Decades of Inaction," The Pew Charitable Trusts, http://www.pew fuelefficiency.org/docs/cafe_history.pdf.

3. *Wall Street Journal,* April 23, 2008; US Department of Transportation, Federal Highway Administration, Office of Highway Policy Information; US Census Bureau.

4. Marina v.N. Whitman, Global Warming and CAFE Standards, Hearings before the General Motors Corporation submitted to the Senate Consumer Subcommittee of the Committee on Commerce, Science, and Transportation, 101st Cong., 1st Sess., May 2, 1989, pp. 130–47.

5. Paul Ingrassia and Joseph B. White, *The Fall and Rise of the American Automobile Industry* (New York: Simon and Schuster, 1994), 93.

6. "The Innovator: The Creative Mind of Roger Smith," *New York Times Magazine,* April 21, 1985.

7. Letter from Marina Whitman to John H. D'Arms, February 7, 1990, in my personal collection.

8. Nick Poulos, "Economist's Ride with GM Exhilarating," *Atlanta Journal and Atlanta Constitution,* February 16, 1986.

9. Maryann Keller, *Rude Awakening: The Rise, Fall, and Struggle for Recovery of General Motors* (New York: William Morrow, 1989), 196.

10. Ibid., 139.

11. Ibid., 243.

12. Ibid.

13. *Automotive News,* March 12, 1990.

CHAPTER 11

1. *Time,* November 26, 1984.

2. Marina Whitman to Frank Press, December 5, 1988, in my personal collection.

3. Marina von Neumann Whitman, *New World, New Rules: The Changing Role of the American Corporation* (Cambridge, MA: Harvard Business School Press, 1999).

4. Louis Uchitelle, "Company Woman," *New York Times,* June 27, 1999.

5. Marina Whitman, "Women Who Take the Corporate Climb" (letter to editor), *Business Week,* July 31, 1987.

6. Annette Churchill, "GM Vice President Marina Whitman: An Academic Makes It to the Fourteenth Floor," *Ann Arbor Observer,* March 1986.

Index